OPEN CITY

CITY

True Story of the KC Crime Family

1900-1950

D1547065

OPEN CITY

True Story of the KC Crime Family

1900-1950

by William Ouseley

ISBN 978-1-58597-480-1
Library of Congress Control Number: 2008928638

4500 College Boulevard
Overland Park, Kansas 66211
888-888-7696
www.leatherspublishing.com

To my loving wife Jo, without whose support this book would never have been completed; and to our children, John and his Barbara, and Elizabeth and her Nathan.

My tradition - the traditions of my fathers - allowed a small Group of men operating in secret, often against the law and convention, not only to survive but also to thrive. The Mafia for a long time was part of the power structure of the country itself. No history of the United States from 1930 on that doesn't take that into account will be a false history.

Bill Bonano
Bonano Crime "Family"

TABLE OF CONTENTS

Chapter I

A City Is Born

I N THE BEGINNING there was only wilderness, native Indians, and the river, the mighty Missouri. In the early 1800s French fur trappers found a haven at the confluence of the Missouri and Kaw rivers where a natural rock outcropping formed a levee. It was not only an accommodating landing site, but also one of the western most places where steamboats coming from the east could navigate. The settlement there was called Kawsmouth and although small, 25 or so, the trading business was brisk. The French fur trader Francois Chouteau built a warehouse on the river to the east of this point in 1821 to service traders, settlers and the like, as the push for westward expansion was on the up take.

At an 1838 land auction, 14 men, having formed an association, made a winning bid of $4220 on 271 acres of land situated at the natural rock-landing site. The owner of this parcel of land, a French trader, had been killed some years prior in a bar brawl leaving a pregnant wife, six children, and the 271 acres. The new owners considered a number of possibilities before deciding on a name for their settlement, The Town of Kansas. By 1842 the town had not prospered greatly, its population less than 50 residents. Meanwhile, Independence, Missouri to the east was populated by some 2000 to 3000, and was the favored outfitting post for pioneers pushing westward. Also better known was the Indian trading store at Westport, a few miles to the west. This was a lodging and trading post settlement and a transportation and distribution hub for goods.

Growth would come to The Town of Kansas thanks to a series of historical events including the 1848 California gold rush, reconstruction following the civil war, and a decision by the Hannibal & St. Joe railroad to lay tracks over the Missouri River at the Town of Kansas rather than St Joseph, Missouri. The completion of the Hannibal Bridge in 1869 transformed the town into a transportation hub. In June 1850 The Town of Kansas became a municipality gaining a charter from the county court. It wasn't until 1889, upon the adoption of a new city charter, that the official name became Kansas City.

America was yet a young nation in the 1800s, however the population of its cities would grow rapidly with the influx of immigrants. They started coming to this place, one day to be named Kansas City, in the mid 1800s and continued coming into the early 1900s. An 1850 census showed the beginning of an immigrant population, mostly German. The first to come in numbers were the Irish.

As the result of poor living conditions, religious persecution, and potato crop failures the Irish fled their homeland, and between 1820 and 1840 more than 700,000 set sail for New York City and Boston. By

1840, every other immigrant arriving in America was Irish. Between 1840 and 1860 another 1.7 million Irish immigrated to America.

Enduring a horrendous ocean crossing in overcrowded barely seaworthy vessels, arriving poor and bewildered, most settled together in Irish conclaves in east coast cities. Many would later move on to other cities, Pittsburgh, Chicago, St. Louis and The Town of Kansas. As was the case for most immigrant groups the Irish were forced to accept whatever work they could find, hoping to save enough money to send for other family members. For many Kansas City was simply a stop over on the way west to the 1849 gold rush, but enough remained so that by the mid 1870s 9% of Kansas City's population was Irish.

In 1854 the U.S. Government opened up the Kansas territory to settlers. Soon the Town of Kansas was overrun with travelers on the way west. Between 1853 and 1860 as many as 200 passengers every day got off steamboats and then pushed on to the west.

The Irish immigrants settled together in the west bottoms below the bluffs rising 130 feet from the intersection of the Missouri and Kaw rivers. They lived in ramshackle frame structures in disease ridden, unsanitary conditions. Most were uneducated, lacking any skills and all they had to offer was brawn and muscle. Hard labor was their main source of employment, cutting streets through the river bluffs in the late 1860s and early 1870 and other city works projects, along with jobs in the west bottoms stockyards, opening in 1871. They had to endure hardships, discrimination, exploitation and incivility.

Grow as it might the town was still a frontier community characterized as "a wild place filled with cowboys, gamblers and desperate characters", where violence and vulgarity seemed natural. It was indeed the wild west, rugged territory populated by fearless gun toting adventurers, prostitutes selling sex, thugs, thieves, cut-throats, con men train robbers, civil war soldiers and freed slaves displaced by the civil war, renegade Indians, and gangs, probably the most famous being the Jesse James gang. And speaking of the famous Jesse James he could well be considered the prototype for so many of the ner'-do-wells of the day inhabiting and visiting the city A former St. Joseph newspaperman and researcher of the James legend described James as having learned to kill in the civil war and too lazy to farm the land.

The 1878 city directory listed 80 saloons in the city many times the number of schools, churches, libraries and hospitals. The majority of them were clustered near Main Street in the vicinity of the city market, then known as Kansas Market Square. It was a popular location for some of the wild west's most celebrated characters during the 1870s, including Wyatt Earp, "Wild Bill" Hickok, Bat Masterson, and the aforementioned Jesse James, all known to frequent the gambling halls and patronize the local hotels. Jesse's brother Frank James was employed as bouncer in one of the joints. The Main Street side of Market Square came to be known as "Battle Row" in recognition of the constant fights and assorted violence associated with the over-abundance of establishments jammed into the area. Another popular feature of the Market Square area were its houses of prostitution, some 40 of them employing 250 or so women.

In contrast, the city had its cultural side gaining a reputation as a theatre town as documented in a book by Felicia Londre, "The Enchanted Years of the Stage." The city benefited from its status as a railroad hub allowing easy access for touring theatre companies, and they visited often. All the major stars of the day played the city. The Coats Opera House opened in 1870, the Crystal Palace, with its 80,000 square feet of glass, opened in 1887 at the Fairground located where the Benton curve is today. In 1887 Edwin Booth, considered one of theatre's greatest actors, and brother of the assassin John Wilks Booth who murdered President Lincoln, played the city on three occasions. As an historical aside, from 1868 to 1900 there were 42 engagements of Hamlet, while from 1979 to 2007 there have been but two.

By 1872 political activity became an important part of the Irish community marking the beginning of a powerful political base that would have a profound impact on Kansas City for the next quarter century making the name Pendergast famous.

Irish politicians gained increasing power in the 1880s and 1890s. Illustrative of their political influence they were able to make the fire department an Irish fraternity after city fathers created the first full time 35 member department in which three of five firemen in 1880 were Irish. It was an Irishman who helped establish a 25-member Police Department in 1867, and by the late 1880s and early 1900s the ranks were dominated by Irishmen.

An 1890 census report showed 13,700 black citizens residing in the city. That figure had by 1910 increased by 10,000, and by 1940 the number stood at 38,574. Blacks settled in political wards controlled by Irish democratic faction leader Casmire Welch, a prominent figure in Kansas City's early history. The area encompassed Charlotte Street east to Cleveland Street, and 10th Street south to 29th Street. In all Welch controlled thirty-six predominately black precincts, mainly in the notably poor second ward. In these early times no black held any public office of note and had little influence, except when it came to gambling and crime. Black vice bosses had their own special relationship with the police and the political machine, a common dynamic in the poor and ethnic neighborhoods. As an added burden for the black population, segregation was the rule of the day.

The city's population was approximately 130,000 in 1890 and the tide of immigrants coming from Ireland had been reduced to a trickle. However, the earlier throngs of Irish settlers produced huge numbers of first and second generation Irish-Americans allowing the

Irish to maintain a firm hand in city affairs. The immigration cycle was changing, and in the early 1900s those immigrating here were mainly Germans, Italians, Poles, Croats and Slavs fleeing deteriorating conditions in Europe.

In the following eighteen years the city's population grew to approximately 300,000 with an estimated 70,000 foreign born inhabitants scattered around the city in various ethnic neighborhoods. For the most part, these were individuals who did not speak English and remained wedded to the customs and culture of their country of origin.

The "Patch", a one block square area located between State Line and the Kaw River immediately north of Armour's packing plant, and blocks emanating out, was home to some 1000 Croations, the ratio of men to women was 10 to 1. They lived in shacks constructed of driftwood, old boards and scraps of lumber, under the crudest of sanitary conditions.

There were said to be 4000 Slavic residents of the city, one portion of this number a small conclave of Bohemians residing in the Armourdale and West Bottoms section, while some 1400 Slavocs, another class of Slavs, resided in the same area.

Some 7000 foreign-born Jews had settled in the city many living east of Main Street and North of Seventh Street. Scandinavians in the city settled largely west of Main Street and south of Eighteenth Street. Other nationalities dotting the city included a Greek conclave, approximately 400 Syrians, primarily employed as "peddlers, and a smaller group of Armenians.

After the flood of Irish dwindled the largest number of foreign born immigrating to America were the Italians. In 1908 the number of Italians residing in the north end was set at 4500, a number that would grow to 6000-8000 by 1919, and 10 years later stand at some 31,000

The Italian Influx

Immigrating primarily from southern Italy and Sicily to escape poverty, semi-slavery, oppressive landlords and high taxes more than one and a quarter million Italians left their homeland for the United States between 1900 and 1910. The main influx of Italians into Kansas City came in the late 1800s continuing on to the 1920s. Primarily these were poor farmers with little education or skills, seeking a better life for them and their families, lured by stories of great opportunity and fortunes to be made in America.

Many of those settling in Kansas City came by way of the so-called "New Orleans connection." Initially traveling from the homeland, via a connection in New York City, directly to New Orleans where laborers were needed for the sugar plantations. Enticed by word of work opportunities in packing houses and rail yards many moved north to Kansas City. Others came from east coast cities working the railroad as it extended westward.

They settled together in the North End, an area bounded by the Missouri River on the north, Admiral Boulevard on the south, Highland Ave on the East and Grand Ave. on the west, and abutting the industrial west bottoms, the Irish domain. Following a well established pattern, the Italians recreated in the north end an environment similar to that they knew in the old country. They had their own shops, restaurants, groceries, church, saloons and pool halls. Many of the residents did not speak English, and to some extent it hindered assimilation. Others resisted assimilation as evidenced by a 1908 report revealing that some north side women, after twenty years of living in the area, had never ventured as far south as Eight Street.

The Italian community was characterized in a 1915 Board of Public Welfare report as made up of proud, hard working, deeply religious, family oriented and frugal people. The majority had been farmers in the old country, a way of life not available to them in Kansas City due to a lack of money. They had a high standard of morality along with strong religious beliefs resulting in few divorces, separations or family desertions. The report labeled the retention of old world ways, customs, culture and language as a by-product of life in "Little Italy."

It was recognized these newcomers faced a cultural change from peaceful country life to that of a congested city that was prejudiced against them. Signs reading "Italians Not Allowed", or "Italians Need Not Apply" were common. They were faced with a workplace where employers were prone to pay them less than their American counterparts. They were criticized for the unhealthy, substandard living conditions of the North End, and the practice of allowing their children to skip school in order to earn money to assist the family.

A misleading part of the report cited a lack of parasites among the Italians. In fact among them, a minority to be sure, were those who were criminally inclined, and those previously affiliated with criminal societies in the old country, including the Sicilian Mafia, and the Neapolitan Camorra. To make matters worse, each time the Italian government cracked down on banditry or the Mafia, as it did in the 1890s and again under the dictator Mussolini, and on the Camorra in 1910, criminal types fled to the United States. These newcomers, many illegals, represented new recruits swelling the numbers within criminal associations that were forming. This minority would victimize their countrymen, extorting and terrorizing them, unfairly staining their good name and reputation.

False Hope and Urban Gangs

The immigrant population coming to 19th Century America arrived at a time when the nation was expanding in every direction;

conditions were chaotic, violent and often aimless. In the beginning this was also true in the world of crime.

The character of a society, government, and its leaders is dictated by the establishment, those at the top. The period between the end of the civil war and World War I has been described as the age of the robber baron. An age that could be best described as having as its primary goal the accumulation of wealth and power by any means whatsoever. From the highest levels of the Federal Government on down to the local precinct politico they all became rich selling inside information, trading favors, and becoming servants to their corruptors. In the quest to retain office, power and influence there was no tactic or strategy beneath them. By means of corruption, force, vote fraud, alliances with criminal gangs, wheeling and dealing, they perpetuated their power and position. Money talked and there was practically nothing that wasn't for sale, even respectability. There seemed little concern for the public good. The Vanderbilts, Harrimans, Carnegies, Rockerfellers, and so many other titans of industry, bought and sold politicians and ordinary people as if they were sacks of flour.

There can be little question that the predatory and corrupt climate established by this earlier generation had a profound impact on those who followed.

It was the immigrant hoards that followed, and they soon discovered the tales of untold riches and opportunity was but a myth. The poor from the old country became the poor and downtrodden of America. Outwardly America stood for the puritan ethic, preaching honesty and virtue, and against gambling, liquor, loose women and other sensual pleasures. They were sold a bill of goods that if they followed this ethic, worked hard, and saved money success was assured. In fact, it was a double standard as only the new poor were expected to follow these moral and ethical standards. It certainly did not apply to those who had already made it, or those well on the way to making it.

There were few within the establishment looking out for the interests of these newcomers to America. The politicians and police brazenly wallowed in corruption, immigration laws were easily evaded, and there was no national police establishment. The system protected the favored rich while for the poor there was nothing. The foreign born were destined to face only despair, afforded no real opportunity to progress and many simply could not cope with this reality. However, their American born children were far more capable of adapting, as were those already criminally bent.

The criminally inclined recognized the situation for what it was. If violence, corruption and the like was the route embarked on by those at the top for personal benefit, power, wealth and to perpetuate their position, then violence it would be. If those at the top need not adhere to any standards, code of morality or ethical behavior, then so be it. Their methods would have to be the way out of poverty and repression.

Not unlike the Sicilian experience, the prevailing hostile, oppressive, discriminatory climate of the era resulted in a backlash. It fostered an infestation of gangs in cities across the nation as frontier type settlements turned to metropolitan centers. Among the throngs of immigrants were criminal types and they settled together in urban ethnic ghettos where gangs sprang up and grew as the children of the immigrants joined up. For the most part they were composed of the young, violent, and undisciplined, but in time they discovered that in numbers and unity came power. Often formed for reasons of protection the gangs degenerated, becoming savage predators, completely unchecked, robbing, terrorizing, assaulting, mugging, and looting in their neighborhood domain.

In the eyes of the establishment immigrant crime was loathsome and contemptible, and their primary aim was to contain the problem by restricting these miscreants to their own particular turf with no further action required. Protection of the community's residents apparently was of no import. After all, the victims were the poor, the immigrant, the powerless, and so as long these crimes remained localized, contained within their own squalid neighborhood, no one had to be overly concerned.

Chapter II

The Black Hand

I N THIS RAUCOUS early era the majority of gangs were localized forming up on a neighborhood basis, ethnic basis, or on similarity of origin, for instance those coming from the same town, village or county in their country of origin banding together. Their crimes were local as well, normally crimes of opportunity and indiscriminate, what might be characterized as hooliganism and thuggery. Nothing too sophisticated. There was no intermixing as each considered the others strangers and dangerous, with frequent deadly battles raging between the gangs.

However there were those who came to our shores bringing with them criminal societies not native to America. It would be the Southern Italians and Sicilians who introduced a criminal society unlike any other.

In Italian neighborhoods in cities around the nation the crimes committed were the traditional crimes of the worst bands of the Mafiosi of Sicily, the Camorra of Naples, and the Calabrian organization known as the 'Ndranghita, all secret societies born in the old country.

Roots of Evil - The Sicilian Mafia

If one is to grasp what transpired in America it is essential one have some understanding of the history of Italy's criminal societies. And society is the proper term for it denotes the complex nature of these clans elevating them to a level far beyond the ordinary criminal gang. Further evidenced by the fact in America the Italian/Sicilian organization is described as made up of crime "families" indicative of the societal aspects in play. For present purposes a study of the Sicilian Mafia, its traditions, characteristics, attitudes, philosophy, and protocols will suffice, as they are essentially the same for all three of the most recognizable groups - Mafia, Camorra and "Ndranghita,

It is only natural those immigrating from Southern Italy and Sicily carried with them the history, traditions, culture, and outlook on life of their native land, to include their intimate familiarity with the criminal clans that came to dominate their life. In a similar fashion, the antisocial behavior of the criminal element mirrored that of the old country, putting into practice the ways and means of Southern Italian and Sicilian criminal clans.

Despite the obvious presence of such an organization, generations of scholars, historians, writers, etc., insisted the Mafia did not exist. The same was true in the United States. They could not get past the absence of tangible proof. Even the criminal clans didn't call themselves Mafia. Where was the smoking gun? The situation should have surprised no one, as the Mafia is secret, puts nothing in writing, its members sworn to deny its existence, its fellow travelers perpetuate the myth, and the populace too frightened to talk of it. This also was true in the United States.

At the outset in Sicily the word Mafia described a mind-set, an attitude, a lifestyle peculiarly Sicilian. The term Mafioso applied to the individual rather than an organization. Although a member of a criminal clan came to be known as a Mafioso, a noun, that person might not possess those qualities defined as Mafioso, the adjective. For instance, a man or woman having no affiliation with a criminal organization can be "Mafioso" by reason of their individual character traits. An elegant woman, a handsome, well-dressed man, is defined as Mafioso. Even a stately horse, a fine meal, a luxury automobile are described as Mafioso, meaning the person or thing display excellence, beauty, and grace.

As the word evolved it also came to describe a long established Sicilian concept of the individual, who beyond physical beauty, style and grace is capable of defending his person and property independent of any legal establishment or authority, from which he expects nothing and gives nothing. Such a man relied only on himself and his family, and is a person strong enough to avenge any insult whether to himself, his family or his interests, and doing so courageously without bravado or arrogance. He is one who displays absolute autonomy, and thereby a refusal to be dominated by others. For an individual or a clan member this is to be Mafioso.

Over time the term Mafia and Mafioso came to describe a criminal society, and its members were expected to display those long admired cultural traits. It was a society that stemmed from an intricate history characterized by foreign domination, injustice, bad government and social ills. The exact development of the Mafia is an elusive mix of fact, fantasy, legend, rumor and speculation. Generalizing, the Mafia evolved from various secret groupings formed to resist foreign domination, lend assistance to a downtrodden populace and to negate to the greatest extent possible abusive governments.

• By the time of unification in 1860, when Sicily became part of the new Italy, it had experienced 2000 years of foreign rule. Phoenician, Greeks, Romans, Vandals, Ostrogoths, Byzantines, Arabs, Normans, Germans, Spaniards, Bourbons, colonists all, and generally repressive in their rule. Governed by Popes Emperors and Kings, these invaders regarded the island as but a colony, displaying an indifference to the needs and welfare of its subjects. The ruling class of governors, viceroys and the like, centered themselves in the big coastal areas regarding the interior as a place only to be exploited for its land resources, extracting as much wealth as possible. The Sicilian populace was subjected to pillage, rape, robbery and exploitation conducted under the protection of the duly constituted government. Their land taken away, the countryside scarred, the living conditions horrendous.

Sicilians were forced to adjust to the successive conquerors and somehow get along with them. Since they were unable to throw them out, resistance took the form of secret sects, clans and other groupings. Some were protectors some were patriots, and some bandits. They resisted by means of subterfuge, conciliation and conspiracy. Retaliation took the form of cattle rustling, crop burning, kidnappings of wealthy noblemen, and vandalizing property.

The invaders were never able to subdue or domesticate the people who instead became the natural enemies of foreign rule, and eventually of any rule at all. Disrespect for the law, hatred of authority, and contempt for those who would deal with the authorities, characterized the Sicilian attitude. In this impersonal and hostile environment trust was reserved for the immediate family while outsiders, until their loyalty was proven, were looked on with suspicion and caution.

Starting with the Romans in 200 BC Sicily was looked on as one extensive granary to feed the people of the conqueror's homeland. The island then freshly deforested was turned into endless crop producing estates known as the latifundia.

As absentee landlords the Romans had to take steps to insure the required work on their estates was done, and the land, buildings and the livestock were protected. As much they feared roving bandit gangs, especially in the absence of any legal establishment in the interior, they were more concerned with the potential spread of peasant reform movements. To meet their needs they hired estate managers to run things. These were strong men having local power and influence, and many were leaders of secret sects, displaying no reluctance to commit murder or respect for authority. They were called Gabelloto, and served as go betweens for the landlords and the workers.

Under the authority of the estate managers, and their associates, the peasants were protected from the very worst landlord abuses while at the same time any effort on their part to overthrow the system, better their lot, or even occupy uncultivated land was brutally suppressed. Unlike the peasants working the estates whose existence was only slightly above that of a slave, the managers were well rewarded. Over the following two millennia, under each successive foreign rule, the estate managers and their armed guards assumed limitless powers and put it to their own use. The total lack of public authority, combined with the power delegated from the landlords, proved a formula for strengthening existing criminal associations and establishing them where none had existed. The Mafia was developing.

The year 1812 witnessed the abolishment of feudal privileges and serfdom, and the creation in Sicily's interior of public institutions and local governments. To the detriment of the peasants, nothing changed, and to the betterment of the Gabellotto and the Mafiosi the new public institutions established in the interior were inefficient, unable to cope, and thus incapable of guaranteeing the status quo for the landed class. As a result the Gabellotto was relied on, to an even greater extent, to maintain order and protect the landholders. In turn every step necessary was taken to buffer the estate managers from the legal establishment. A system of justice evolved administered by Mafiosi and based on extortion, force and fear, while the Mafiosi accumulated land, livestock, money and respect.

The common people were left to view all officialdom and gentry as villains seeking to impoverish them, and sought out a benefactor to look out for their interests in time of need. Such a person became a patron of a sizeable number of people, representing for him a considerable source of influence. Thus the Mafia from its inception was parasitic, inserting itself between the establishment and a populace beaten down by centuries of exploitation and poverty. The Mafia has been described as outlaw but tolerated, secret but recognizable, criminal but upholding of order. It ripped off everyone as it protected everyone. It was strong in proportion to the weakness of the State.

The early Mafia clans were independent, largely rural concentrated in the western portion of the island in the provinces of Palermo, Agrigento, Trapani and Caltanisseta, operating wherever there was economic production. Each town or district had its clan, not highly formalized. There were some working relationships between the clans but there were also hostilities between them, and at times even a lack of recognition. They were referred to as Cosca, never Mafia.

Any area of crime where money could be made was vulnerable, their activities running the gambit from cornering the market on cemetery plots, to kidnappings for ransom, cattle rustling, food smuggling, illegal control of water sources, control of mining operation, to fees extorted for use of the roads to the markets. As the Sicilian economy developed the Cosca altered their tactics to take advantage of new opportunities, displaying an ability to adjust and capitalize on changing times and conditions that has been an earmark of American crime "families" as well.

The word Cosca refers to any plant, such as an artichoke or thistle, having spiny closed-folded leaves, a symbol of the tight-knit resistant nature of a Mafia clan.

Initially the liberator Garibaldi viewed the Mafia, having joined the rebellion against Bourbon rule, as useful to his aims. By the time Garibaldi pushed the Bourbons out, achieving unification in 1860, the entrenched Mafia found it all too easy to subvert the liberal institutions he established. Schooled in conspiracy and subterfuge, and employing Mafia tactics of resistance rather than revolt, they successfully infiltrated the local establishment and the ranks of the new government. If anything, the Mafia had always known how to make itself needed, and how to cozy up to those in power.

The Bourbons were gone but in the eyes of the Sicilian people foreign domination continued under an even more oppressive and exploitive government in Rome controlled by northern Italians. Hostility toward the Italian government grew amongst the higher strata of churchmen, aristocrats, lawyers, and professionals, with many joining the Mafia ranks. More than ever the good offices of the Mafia were sought out.

Only when open defiance of the new government reached an unacceptable level were crackdowns instituted against the clans. With each periodic push more Mafioso fled to North and South America, and those fleeing the island were guaranteed assistance and a place within the germinating Italian criminal clans abroad

Although every form of Mafia activity, protocol, and custom existed long before 1860 some historians believe a more formalize version with rules, initiation rites and the like developed after that date, the glory days coming after 1890. In any event, a code of conduct was formalized, initiation rites established, as were protocols for selecting and carrying out racket activities, and the manner in which changes in leadership were to be effected. Even murder was ritualized, the favored weapon a sawed off shotgun called a lupara, also the weapon of choice for Italian gangs in America. Members used passwords, and talked, dressed and carried themselves in a characteristic way. All of which can been seen in the makeup of American Cosa Nostra "families."

Loyalty to the clan was foremost. To betray the secrets of the family, admit its existence or identify its members carried a death penalty. To collaborate with the law or turn to the courts for justice was considered disgraceful conduct, an "infame". This was the code of Omerta, literally meaning to be a man, remaining silent, and it carried over to America.

In 1886 the Commissioner of Police at Palermo wrote of the initiation ceremony for new members of the Mafia to include the drawing and melding of blood, the burning of a religious card as the an oath of induction was repeated by the candidate. The very same ceremony has been employed by most American Cosa Nostra "families."

The old world Mafia Don, belying his true nature, was normally modest in his demeanor, speaking and listening with an air of humility. His true power cloaked, he held himself out as but an ordinary man, yet one who spoke for everyone. He dressed with care, but modestly, was generous, a family man who would never consider divorce, cherished respect and honor, and was a patriot, outwardly supportive of a government he inwardly despised. Behind the cloak he was proud, suspicious, sly, conspiratorial and deceptive as only those who have long been conquered but never defeated could be.

To maintain his position the Don had to be seen as a prudent, levelheaded, cunning leader. Outside the clan he took on the role of authority/father figure, a friend to all, protector, mediator and advisor. He regulated social conflicts, maintained a semblance of order, generally overseeing matters normally within the purview of the establishment. As a preserver of social order he was recognized locally and by the State itself as guardian of the people. He granted favors willingly, understanding the more people witnessing his ability to help and get things done the greater his prestige. The Don saw himself as that person every society needs, able to put things right when they were out of kilter.

Within limits the Don alone imposed, he allowed everyday crime and wrongdoing thereby controlling all illegal activities and protecting himself from those with ambitions to topple him.

Since there was little in the way of official protection of one's property, wealth, or person, the Mafia Don stepped into the void. Where the legal system did not guarantee justice, the Mafia did, effectively and promptly. Those who refused to pay for the Don's protection, or come to some agreement with the clan, found their property stolen, damaged, vandalized or destroyed. Should resistance continue then the victim's safety was threatened, and they were targeted for escalating attacks to the point of murder. This was in effect a form of taxation far more efficient than that of the State.

When his minion's had need for contacts and relationships in the economic, administrative, and political sphere of the outside world it was the Don who was sought out for his widespread contacts, business connections, political allies and influential acquaintances in others towns, districts and cities.

Further empowering the Mafiosi, after unification in 1860 the administration's policy regarding public order was to leave things in the hands of the local power brokers, and if that happened to be the Mafia then it was left to them. In effect, the Mafia left to its own devices duplicated every Italian legal and administrative institution - a State within the State.

This is but a snapshot of the Sicilian Mafia and Sicilian life experienced by the substantial number of Southern Italian and Sicilian immigrants making up the more than one and one quarter million coming to America between 1900 and 1910. In the main they were driven out by poverty, oppression, and lack of hope, seeking the promise of opportunities in the new world. However, life under Mafia rule was an integral part of their culture and mind-set. Others fled due to their criminal activities and criminal associations, and they would bring with them to their new home a unique form of crime and crime society unlike any previously known.

The Protection Racket

Wherever Italians settled in number, establishing what were popularly called "Little Italys," the predators took up shop. By 1910 there were gangs in many large cities, but little unity. Sicilian clans fought Neapolitan Camorra gangs, and each fought among themselves. Not all had been members of secret criminal societies in the old country but they were familiar with them, and whatever their background they preyed almost exclusively on other newly arrived Italians. The inherent distrust of official authority and reluctance to rely on the establishment for protection or help played into the hands of these predators, as did the hostile environment the new comers faced, laden with discrimination and exploitation.

In the newcomer's eyes nothing in their experience in their new home provided any evidence that things would be any different than in the old country. That included the Mafia of which they were all too familiar, though having no part in it. Thus they were vulnerable to threat, extortion and blackmail, often in the form of letters signed with the image of a bloody dagger, a black hand, or the signature, "La Mano Nero" (The Black Hand). Fresh over from the old country where the Mafia ruled, what choice did they have but comply? Who was there to turn to? Why complain when one was certain no one was listening or cared? And, of course, they were terrified.

Much has been written as to the origins of the Black Hand designation for crimes of extortion in "Little Italy." According to one account, the label was coined by the publisher of a New York Italian-American newspaper hoping that by avoiding the use of the term Mafia the criminal acts reported would be viewed as America in origin. Another version attributes the label to a newspaper reporter who in, or around 1903, picked up on it and popularized it in reporting a sensational murder case, and a wave of extortions that followed. For a time this label overshadowed the more traditional ones of "Mafia" or "Camorra." Thus for the American press and periodicals crime in Italian neighborhoods was the Black Hand.

The label, unfortunately, stigmatized Italians as it came to dominate news of the Italian community leading to a distorted image of Italians as the Mafia. Recounting stories of the Black Hand, Mafia, Cosa Nostra, represents an extremely sensitive topic for people of Italian heritage. Although the point has been made it bears repeating. The overwhelming number of Italian-Americans were not, and are not, involved in organized crime, and are innocent of all that has been attributed to that which is most popular referred to as the Mafia. Joseph Valachi, the first to ever reveal the secrets of Cosa Nostra, was taken aback when accused of smearing the good name of Italians. He answered, "I'm not talking about Italians. I'm talking about criminals."

In the early part of the 20th Century there were less formalized groups of individuals who could be described as plying the "mafia trade" along with independents, encouraged by newspaper reports of large amounts of money being extorted who assumed the role of a Mafioso using the Black Hand tag. In either case this criminal element had no real power or standing in the criminal world outside the confines of their neighborhoods. On the other hand, since the language, customs, and culture of the old country were duplicated in "Little Italy" neighborhoods the influence of these predator's in the day-to-day life of the residents was expanded, similar to Mafia societal influence in the old country.

It was clear the methods used were the same as those of the Mafia in Sicily and the Camorra in Naples, and represented a very real problem. However, the Black Hand label more accurately described an extortion racket and not, as sensationalized newspaper accounts implied, a secret Italian criminal organization transplanted here in America. It seems clear there was no singular organization involved solely in sending Black Hand extortion letters. It also seems clear criminal associations were forming, committing crimes beyond extortion, and involved in blood feuds and vendettas. They were quietly expanding in size and influence, as it was in their nature to do so. This dynamic went largely unrecognized, overshadowed by front-page headlines of the Black Hand. Those closest to the scene, the residents of "Little Italy", certainly recognized the true nature of these clans, but knew better than to ever speak of such things.

To further differentiate between Mafia-like criminal factions and other neighborhood American and ethnic gangs, the former maintained social and working relationships with groups and individuals in other cities, as well as with countrymen, relatives, and members of the Sicilian Mafia and Neapolitan Camorra abroad. New Orleans can be cited as one very early example.

New Orleans is the reputed home for one of the earliest Sicilian Mafia members known to have immigrated here. Conflict erupted between two rival Sicilian clans over control of the docks. Chief of Police David Hennessey had been investigating the clans, and on October 15, 1890 he was shot dead, his murder laid at the feet of the "Mafia." Nineteen members of one clan were arrested and charged with the murder. Legend has it that the "Brotherhood" came to their defense, and from around the country money flowed in for bribes, and for the best legal counsel available. The jury was intimidated ending up acquitting all but three. An outraged public stormed the jail where the Sicilians were housed. The vigilante mob killed 11 men including two hung from lampposts, creating a national and international firestorm.

A Black Hand Infestation

Not only was the Black Hand protection racket rampant in Kansas City's Italian community, often drawing front-page coverage, but it was so pervasive the city gained recognition as a center for such activity in national news accounts.

As early as November 1897 the Kansas City Star carried a story of a violent murder in "Little Italy" reporting that whispers of "Mafia" were heard. The story included a description of the prevailing climate in that section of the city, reporting the various nationalities residing there hate one another "with extreme bitterness", and the police have said it is remarkable there are not more murders. The report went on to state, vendettas of the "truest Italian stripe" exists in the area with nearly every gathering breaking out it a fight, "cutting scrapes" a almost nightly occurrence.

Some twenty-one years later a lengthy Kansas City Star article revisiting the topic of community conditions in "Little Italy" described the scene as one "of inscrutable crimes, the lurking places of criminal elements whose sources and ramifications never have been tracked." This finding was based on an interview with an investigator who had spent in excess of ten years following the activities of the Black Hand in both Kansas City, and other cities, both as a government agent and as a special investigator. It was said he was probably the most knowledgeable person in the city when it came to the ways of "Little Italy." This individual was identified only as an "official", as he agreed to the interview on the promise his name would not be used. Hereinafter, he will be referred to as "The Official" when information attributable to him is set forth.

The newspaper report cited prominent citizens of "Little Italy" who minimized the hold the criminal organization had on the community, while others claimed the Black Hand was a myth, a pipe dream of newspapermen and the police. Even some within the police establishment itself claimed they could find no evidence of the existence of the Black Hand. "It is useless to deny the existence of the Black Hand in Kansas City" "The Official" responded in March 1919, and furthermore, "It never was better organized than at the present time."

"There are hundreds of merchants and well-to-do Italians of Little Italy who are paying their tribute today like monthly rent" "The Official" stated, and added, "Not a week passes that dozens of Black Hand letters are not delivered to the selected victims. Some of them find their way to police headquarters, but the majority of them do not. And the men who are getting the letters are coming across. The killings occur only when business becomes slack or there is some trouble over dividing the spoils. Then the sawed-off shotgun is brought into play as a reminder that the threats of the Black Hand are not idle threats, and that its orders must be obeyed."

"The Official" is quoted as saying, "It is true that no direct connection between the Black Hand of America and the Mafia of Sicily has ever been proved." However, he points to a "fragmentatry " diary left by the famous New York Detective Petrosino revealing evidence he had accumulated of a very intimate connection between the Sicilian organization and the different bands of the Black Hand operating in this country.

"The Official" made it clear the American and Sicilian groups were similar in their tactics and operations. "The system is the same, the follow up letters sealed with the dripping dagger, the collectors, the hired killers, the ambush, the sealed lips of witnesses, all these things are identical with the "Mafian system of Sicily."

The mention of New York City Detective Petrosino warrants a further word concerning this legendary police officer who played a prominent role in the story of the Black Hand, and early Italian organized crime. By reason of the pure numbers of Italian immigrants, New York City was the center of the universe when it came to Italian gangdom. By the year 1895 the severity of extortion activities in the Italian community was such that the New York City Police Department assigned Detective Joseph Petrosino to head up a special until of detectives to combat the Black Hand. Petrosino was all of 5'3", had a swathy complexion, spoke English with a strong accent, and Italian fluently, and knew the ways of his countrymen.

The special unit, known as the "Italian Squad", achieved extraordinary success, arresting or deporting more than six hundred criminals. Petrosino's exploits gained him widespread fame and acclaim, while within the criminal element he dogged he was a feared and hated figure, receiving hundreds of threats on his life. By 1904, based on the work of Petrosino and his squad, the New York City Police

Department was certain an Italian criminal organization had formed with branches in every part of the United States. Furthermore, Petrosino had uncovered a network of working relationships between the New York City crime clans and those in Sicily.

Continuing his diligent pursuit of the ever-increasing number of "Little Italy" criminals, a plan was devised that hopefully would establish grounds to deport a number of these predators based on a 1907 law passed by congress allowing for deportation of aliens if arrest records had been concealed. It was agreed Petrosino would secretly travel to Italy seeking information as to arrest records on any number of the estimated five thousand persons of interest operating in New York City. He left in February, 1909, but unfortunately his trip was a poorly kept secret, and on the evening of March 12, 1909 he was shot to death in central Palermo, Sicily. At Petrosino's funeral 250,000 New Yorkers turned out to view the procession, and flags flew at half mast.

As a historical footnote to the story, Don Vito Cascioferro, considered the most powerful and influential Sicilian Mafia chieftain of the time, claimed responsibility for the murder. Cascioferro was a Mafia member when he slipped into the United States in 1900 to join a sister in New York City. He became heavily involved with the Sicilian Mafia-like clans, providing the benefit of his Mafia experience, and was responsible for establishing more formal relationships between New York City clans and those in Palermo. Cascioferro was poised to be a big man in the New York City rackets except for Petrosino, who was on the verge of arresting him. He fled the city, went into hiding for six months and returned to Palermo in 1904, carrying with him a photo of Petrosino. As the boss of all bosses in Sicily he claimed to have personally assassinated Petrosino stating, "In my whole life I have only killed one person, and I did it disinterestedly....Petrosino was a brave adversary, and deserved better than a shameful death at the hands of some hired killers."

Don Vito's statement exemplifies the Sicilian Mafia tenet that the greater the prestige of the adversary murdered the greater the prestige of the man who committed it, and who in Sicily would question such a claim by the most powerful and feared Mafioso of the day.

In addition to establishing the ties between crime societies within the United States and in Sicily, Petrosino had also came to recognize another dynamic of the Mafia-like organization, one that would over time prove a mainstay of organized crime "families." In a visit to the American counsel in Palermo before his murder, he explained he could not trust the legal authorities in Sicily or America as both were corrupt by reason of political ties, and both depended on politicians who sought the support of the criminal element. He had not only discussed his beliefs while in Palermo, but in an official report had written, "A factor to be taken into consideration is that within a short period following their arrival in America, many of the hardened Italian criminals become associated with certain political cliques for which they work, and from which they receive unlimited protection in return."

Nicolo Gentile

"Vita di Capomafia" (Life of a Mafia Boss) are the memoirs of Nicolo Gentile, an admitted Mafioso, and they provide a rare first hand account of the Sicilian Mafia-like clans operating in the early years of the twentieth century. His is the story of a native Sicilian, one of many fleeing the homeland and illegally entering the United States. He traveled first to Kansas City and would later join the ranks of the fledgling Sicilian dominated criminal organization. The memoirs were penned in the early 1960s, and according to the U.S. Justice Department the information, for the most part, was proven accurate by comparing it with intelligence information already on file. His story is particularly pertinent inasmuch as it takes place at a time Sicilian/Italian crime was in its infancy, and yet Gentile, who traveled the country extensively as a liaison man and troubleshooter, establishes the existence of a complex web of inter- connections, working relationships and basic organizational structure, generally understated in historical accounts of those times.

Gentile was born in approximately 1884 in the small Sicilian town of Siculiana that prior to 1900 offered little opportunity for work or secondary schooling, thus limiting the chances for a young person to better their lot in life. There was some potential for youngsters, so inclined, to pick up a trade by means of apprenticeships with local artisans, but it was at the expense of schooling. Even this avenue was closed to those from large families, as necessity demanded older children take up the heavy work in the fields to supplement the father's income. In such cases the mother was also forced to work, taking on the most menial jobs in order to make a few more pennies to keep the family from starvation. The result, illiteracy reigned supreme in the region.

Gentile, a cart driver in his youth, had no trade to rely on and was barely able to read and write. What he possessed was "an uncommon strength of will, with a certainty of purpose and with two eyes which appeared to everybody to be sinister, but with a highly developed sense of justice which I have sought to practice and to make others respect, and to follow a code based on my good sense." In this self-appraisal he describes those traits considered in Sicilian life as "Mafioso."

In 1903, at age 19, he left his village and stowed away on a trans Atlantic ship bound for America. Carrying a battered suitcase, held together by a piece of cord, containing all his worldly possessions, he disembarked at the port of New York City, alone with no one to meet him. A sailor on the ship came to Gentile's aid escorting him to the home of a countryman. He was given a train ticket to Kansas City, Missouri, arriving with a trainload of other immigrants after a hard six-day journey. For the young Gentile it was a "time of bewilderment", still alone, unable to be understood, he was overwhelmed by the rows of buildings, the endless streets, the pedestrian traffic, the style and dress of the people.

He had come to stay with his brother Vincent only to discover the address he had been given was but a mail drop where his brother, and other countrymen who worked outside the city in Topeka, Kansas, came once a week to pick up their mail. Having nowhere to go, tired and discouraged, he sat by the building entrance for hours. With nighttime approaching he was elated to spy someone he recognized walking by. He excitedly called out to his countryman, they embraced, and after exchanging news he was taken to the man's home where he stayed until his brother Vincent came several days later.

His brother, a railroad worker, took Gentile with him to the job site in Topeka where the workers were provided housing in a railroad car. It was brutally hard labor on the work crew, the day starting at sunrise and ending at sunset, all for a $1.25 daily wage. Three months later an unexpected visitor appeared at the railroad work site, his uncle Pietro Piro, accompanied by two young Sicilians who were working as linen peddlers. Upon learning the two peddlers were earning $5 to $10 for 2 to 3 hours of work a day the Gentile brothers urged the young men to teach them the business. An agreement was reached and the brothers left for New York City. Gentile stayed with he job for some 6 years earning enough that he was able to return to Sicily, visit his parents, and meet the woman who would be his wife.

The year was 1911 and Gentile, leaving his wife and a new addition to the family, a baby daughter, behind in Sicily he returned to America, going back to work in the linen business.

He writes, "My temperament was bringing me a life of adventure. The courage which nature had endowed me with, my intrepid spirit and imperious nature and my code, which I thought was right, made me join the "Honor Society." However, Gentile is not specific as to the time, place or protocol of his initiation into the American "Mafia." Never is the word "Cosa Nostra" or Black Hand used in his descriptions, but rather Gentile uses the labels Mafia, Honor Society, and Borgata, the Sicilian term for a crime grouping. He makes it clear that in the early 20th century definite lines were drawn between the Sicilian, Neapolitan and Calabrian clans and there was frequent conflict between them.

Gentile speaks of these Sicilian criminal "associations" forming in cities around the nation, and developing a district structure over time. It was not an uncommon occurrence for members of one Borgata to transfer to another, sometimes in a different city. To accomplish the transfer the member first had to be accepted by the Capo (Boss) of the family he was joining, and then he had to obtain a letter of authority from the Capo of the Borgata he was leaving. For instance, Gentile over the course of his years in America, was a member of Sicilian crime "associations" in Kansas City, Pittsburgh, Cleveland, San Francisco, New York City, and the Porto Emedocle "family" in Sicily, and describes following the procedure of obtaining letters of authority to implement a transfer.

Gentile's view of the Mafia society is highly idealistic and speaks to his Sicilian upbringing. He writes, "The organization had originated many, many years ago in antiquity and it gives the right to defend the honor, the weak and to respect the human law. With these principles as its guide it still operates." On the other hand he describes the "Honor Society" as finding as its reason for existence, force and terror.

He discusses historical aspects of the Honor Society describing its start in the least developed part of Sicily by landowners as a disciplinary force in the community (The Gabellotti). Thereafter, it was brought to America in the sections of the country where Sicilian, Calabrians and Neapolitans lived. At the time he penned his memoirs he speaks of his disgust with what he sees as the abandonment of the basic tenets of the society, describing "scroundrals seizing the well springs of production and have formed somewhat monopolies," and further, "All organizations are born with principles and humanitarian goals, but in their midst the opportunists are never missing and will try to make a profit."

Gentile's complaint is best illustrated by a statement attributed to that Americanized gangster Charles "Lucky" Luciano in the 1930s summing up his view of the rackets, as opposed to two old-line competing Sicilian Bosses in New York City. "To me the whole things was a matter of organizin' a business: for them it was the pride that came first - who was going to be the boss of bosses."

In 1915 while in San Francisco he and his brother received an invitation from a group of friends in Pueblo, Colorado to come and pay them a visit. Gentile met up with the Chiappetta brothers, Marco and Vincenzo, described as old associates, natives of Poggio Reale, Sicily. Vincenzo was a somewhat sickly individual, thin of build and generally in bad health. Unlike his countrymen he was able to read and write and this set him apart, as did his inability to handle the hard labor required in the steel foundry where his brother was employed.

Vincenzo complained he was ill treated by what he described as "ignorant and savage" men, reducing his life to a living hell. Gentile promised to "interest" himself in Vincenzo's cause. Typical of his style he does not always finish a story, however, it would appear by reason of Gentile's interest in the matter Vincenzo Chaipetta relocated to Kansas City, Missouri, where he prospered as a member of the Kansas City Borgata.

Gentile was traveling extensively mediating disputes and resolving problems for "Mafia" families in various cities. In approximately 1921 his travels had taken him to Chicago, Illinois, when he received word that once again his countryman Vincenzo Chiapetta was in trouble, only this time it was far more serious than being ill-treated by a circle of illiterate associates. Once in Kansas City the Mafia "Capo", Paolo (Paul) DiGiovanni, informed him that Chaipetta, now a member of the "Kansas City Mafia" society, had been "placed under charges" by the head of the Los Angeles, California, "family", Vito DiGiorgio

The naming of Paul DiGiovanni as the Boss in Kansas City is contrary to the bulk of historical data available concerning this time period. There were four DiGiovanni brothers all associated with the Sicilian criminal society in one form or the other, with Pete and Joe generally recognized as holding the leadership positions. Gentile in recounting events having taken place some forty years previous, and in dealing with four brothers, may well have confused the names. Another possibility is that Gentile was right, and Paul DiGiovanni played a larger role than that portrayed in historical accounts of the era.

In any event, Gentile was asked to use his influence in defending Chiapetta against the charges leveled by the Los Angeles Boss, a man possessing a fearsome reputation, who wanted Chiapetta killed on sight. Time was of the essence, as DiGiovanni himself could be accused of insubordination, punishable by death, if he failed to take action against Chiapetta.

The story illustrates Gentile's position with the fledgeling Mafia-like society, and how he operated. Seeking to rally support, Gentile first traveled to San Francisco to enlist the aid of "trusted and faithful" associates, meeting with them to outline his mission. However, at the mention of DiGiorgio's name, "their faces turned pale, so great was the dread" of the man, and all were dissuaded from any participation. Moving on to Los Angeles Gentile sought out an old friend from Pueblo, Colorado, Rosario Desimone, seeking his advice on the proper protocol in approaching DiGiorgio. They agreed a preliminary courtesy call was in order as a first step, and this Gentile did, paying his respects to a sitting "Mafia" boss

Several days later, at a dinner arranged by Desimone at his home, Gentile and DiGirgio had an opportunity to discuss the matter at hand. Gentile opened his defense of Chiapetta by stating if the facts, as he understood them, on which the charges were based were true, he too would disapprove of Chaipetta's conduct. On the other hand, the events in question had occurred long in the past at a time when Chiapetta, and apparently DiGiorgio, first arrived in New Orleans. In pleading Chiapetta's case Gentile described him as a very dear friend, using the Italian term "compare", and godfather to his daughter. The Los Angeles Boss was swayed by Gentile's eloquent pleas and by Gentile's reputation within the "Mafia society." DiGiorgio directed Desimone to write a letter to the Capo in Kansas City explaining that in view of Gentile's interest in the matter he was revoking the accusation against Chiapetta, and "consequently he (Chiapetta) was rendered clear." Gentile never reveals what indiscretion Chiapetta had committed.

Gentile moved on to other cities and other entanglements, many similar to the Chiapetta affair, in his capacity as troubleshooter and arbitrator, "resolving many risky situations." His activities are further evidence of the interrelationships between Sicilian clans in different parts of the country. With the passage of time Gentile would find himself back in Kansas City.

Battling Kansas City's Black Hand

Despite enormous obstacles and real danger there were those who dedicated themselves to combating the evil deeds of the Black Hand. Especially so were the heroic efforts of police officers willing to stand up for those good citizens of the North End who unquestionably deplored Black Hand exploitation, but were ill equipped to fight it themselves. The exploits of Kansas Police Detective Louis Olivero and Patrolman Joe Raimo, two Italian police officers who viewed as unacceptable the situation the citizens of "Little Italy" faced, provides a vivid picture of what the early days of the 20th Century were like on Kansas City's north side.

Joseph Raimo, born in Naples Italy in 1879, was appointed a probationary Kansas City Police Officer on June 28, 1909. On July 23, 1910 he was commissioned for a three-year term, assigned a beat in North End section. He was extremely well regarded, characterized by the Captain he worked for as "one of the best men on the department." When it came to discharging his responsibilities as a police officer he arrested everyone believed guilty of violating the law showing no favoritism for any race or nationality, and doing so despite threats on his life.

Among the North End's criminal element Raimo became a hated figure, and threats on his life were indeed numerous. Citing but one example is a letter he received warning, "Mr. Raimo this notice brings you death. Beware. This is the last chance", signed, "La Mano Nero" He simply shrugged off such threats as part of the job, once stating, "If they're going to get me, they'll get me anyway."

As crime conditions on the north side deteriorated Raimo and another officer were assigned to work in plain clothes focusing their efforts on suppressing the crime and violence infesting the neighborhood. North side residents and businessmen faced ever increasing extortion demands typically in the form of a letter in Sicilian, and signed with depiction of a black hand or a dagger dripping blood and a black cross.

Besides Black Hand extortion letters, the specter of murder hung over the community. Paulina Pizano, described as a sharp-tongued woman, was shotgunned to death in front of her grocery store at 301 Campbell Street on the morning of December 14, 1910. Eyewitnesses to the killing saw two men fleeing the scene, but no one could or would identify the assassins. Some said Pizano may have been talking to the police.

One month later, on January 23, 1911, Vincenco Lasaldo would suffer a similar fate. Passing the time of day with a group of friends gathered in front of a restaurant at 408 East Fourth, two shots were fired at Lasaldo from within the group. He was rushed to a hospital mortally wounded where he remained conscience for several hours capable of speaking coherently. He certainly could have, if he knew, identified his assailant or assailants, but all he would say was "They got me." Not one person in the crowd was willing or able to name the murderer or murderers.

These were but two of the crimes occupying Officer Raimo's attention when sometime in February 1911 he was relaxing off duty in a "Little Italy" tavern, and happened to overhear three men discussing the Pizano murder, naming the man who had killed her. One of the men chanced to look up spotting Raimo, immediately recognizing him, and realizing Raimo had overheard their conversation. The consequences of the incident were crystal clear to Officer Raimo. He later confided to friends, the secret knowledge he possessed would someday result in retribution. Undeterred he redoubled his efforts to bringing the killers to justice.

Extortion demands plaguing "Little Italy" continued unabated, most going unreported. In early March 1911 the police did learn of an extortion demand on rooming house keeper Angelo Roma, followed by the surfacing of another similar case of extortion. Following up on this second demand, Raimo and his partner set up a stake out on the evening of March 27, 1911 hoping a dummy money package would lure someone to the pick up spot the officers were stalking. No one showed, and the surveillance was called off at 4:00 a.m.

Tuesday, March 28, 1911, was Raimo's day off, and just as well after spending a long night on surveillance. That evening he enjoyed a friendly card game in a saloon at Fourth and Holmes Streets and then headed home. He was strolling south on Holmes Street when out of the darkness of a vacant lot, half way between Fourth and Fifth Streets, four shotgun blasts rang out. Joseph Raimo, aged 35, father of four, a police officer for two years, was dead.

The next day Joseph Raimo's 10-year-old son Frank approached a visitor to his home, a reporter from the Kansas City Star. Frank asked the reporter if he thought the Black Hand had killed his father, and if so, he had a letter from them. He showed the reporter a note he had hidden behind a loose brick, explaining he had found it that morning crumpled up under his father's bed. The letter, signed with the likeness of a dagger and cross, written in Italian, read, "Mr. Raimo. Traitor. The others want money and you know it, and this notice brings you death. Beware. The last notice."

In the Daily Bulletin of police news posted at police headquarters a special notice was printed, surrounded by a black border, signed by Chief of Police Wentworth E. Griffen:

> Officer Joseph Raimo was assassinated at 11:15 p.m. March 28, 1911, on Holmes Street between Fourth and Fifth Streets. The Officer was noted for his bravery and diligence in the performance of his duties. He had been especially assigned to the various Italian cases,

and his untiring efforts aroused considerable enmity among the criminal classes of that nationality. Officers will use every means to bring to justice the perpetrators of this foul crime.

No one was ever arrested or convicted for the murder of Joseph Raimo. Some four years later Raimo's widow appeared at police headquarters sobbing, asking to see the Chief of Police. Mrs. Raimo was known to have been acting peculiarly ever since her husband was assassinated. The Chief wasn't able to meet with her, and in his place an official, identified as an "Inspector of the Insane", did. He had her detained, pronounced insane and sent to General Hospital, stating her four children probably would end up in juvenile court. Officer Raimo was not the only victim when north side extortionists took his life.

In The Footsteps of Officer Raimo

Luigi (Louis) Olivero was born in the North of Italy, his father a member of the Carabinieri's royal secret service (Italian Police), and shortly after immigrating to America Louis joined the United States Army serving as a non commissioned officer for three years. In 1911 he joined the Kansas City Missouri Police Department and quickly was promoted to detective. His grasp of his fellow countrymen's way of life at a time when Black Hand crime was pervasive made him a real asset to the department. The Chief of Police recognized the need for such an officer as evidenced by his statement following the murder of Officer Raimo. "While the police department has done everything in its power to suppress crime in 'Little Italy', the unfamiliarity of the officers with the language and customs of the people make it impossible to trace murderers and other criminals."

It was said of Olivero's personal appearance and habits he was as well mannered a man as there was in the law enforcement ranks. He was described as gentlemanly, gracious, not too talkative or boastful, and he made a good impression.

Olivero's value was such that he was loaned to the U.S. Immigration Service for extended periods, tracking down criminals who were in the country illegally. His work resulted in numerous deportations and the turning back of criminals from the old country attempting to slip into the United States.

As was the case with Officer Raimo, the police badge offered no immunity, and Olivero received hundreds of threatening letters such as one directed to him in 1915 reading, "We get tired of you now-very. We have $1300 put on you, and if you don't care we will put double that on you. Better stop. Goodbye. P.S. We tell you enough in this. No more." Olivero shrugged off the threats as simply part of the job.

Threatening letters were not the only danger Olivero faced. On one occasion he captured a man lying in ambush with a sawed off shotgun, the favored weapon of these murderers. On other occasions shots were fired at him, certain persons in the neighborhood cursed him, and anyone seen talking with him became a marked man. He pushed on with his investigations, his name seemingly connected to just about every case and roundup in "Little Italy." He was a truly hated man with a price on his head.

The year 1915 proved to be a significant one in this saga of the Black Hand. The new-year literally started with a bang when on January 9th two men shot Mario Ippolito from ambush as he walked with friends at 17th and Oak Streets. Dying in the arms of a companion Ippolito moaned, "Oh mother, I've been killed. They got me. They got me." In the scheme of things such murders were quickly put out of mind, and life went on. In this case, Ippolito's close friend, Luciano Musso, and Detective Olivero were not going to let that happen.

Even though it meant working with the hated Detective Olivero, Musso would not rest until his friend's murder was avenged. What made the situation so improbable, Musso was not only a criminal but was considered a major player in the Black Hand. He had prospered greatly owning a pool hall at 408-1/2 Locust Street, and lived in a big brick house in the north end. His decision to team up with Olivero most likely cost him his life.

The day following Ippolito's murder Vincent Tortorici and Sam Vanza were arrested by Olivero, both having been seen in the company of the murder victim. A third companion, Sam Jennusa , could not be located by the detective. It was at this point Musso joined up with Olivero in the search for the missing Jennusa. Five days later the efforts of this odd couple paid off when Jennusa was located and arrested. The Olivero-Musso team pushed on continuing to search for new evidence, but here their efforts came up short.

On the morning of January 23, 1915 Jennusa and Vanza appeared in court, and upon a finding by the judge that the evidence was insufficient to bind them over, they were released. Tortorici had been released previously so that no one was in custody for the murder. Musso made it known he was still in the hunt, and would not give it up until the guilty men, whoever they were, paid the price for the murder of his friend.

On the afternoon of the same day Jennusa and Vanza were released, Musso was making his way home to his residence at 416 Locust Street, and just as he was crossing Locust a man with a heavy mustache, wearing a dark brimless hat, and dark overcoat came up behind him. At a point some ten feet behind Musso the man brought out a sawed off double barreled shotgun from under his coat discharging both barrels into Musso's back. He collapsed and died on the pavement in front of his home. His wife ran from their home, fell on him and in vain called for him to speak to her. The assailant fled on foot throwing down the shotgun, his false mustache falling from his face.

It was also in the year 1915 that Detective Olivero's enemies tried another tact in their efforts to eliminate him. A fire was discovered in a four room, second floor apartment at 615 Independence Ave, the residence of Detective Olivero. The fire was raging in the kitchen of the apartment, and tenants discovering the blaze found all the doors locked. Fireman were called and had to break into the apartment to put the fire out. An inspection of the scene indicated the kitchen had been soaked with oil, an obvious case of arson. Fortunately the apartment was unoccupied at the time.

On July 29 and 30,1915 front-page headlines in local newspapers heralded the arrest of nine men suspected of being members of a Black Hand gang. Those arrested were alleged to be members of one group of 17 responsible for sending extortion letters to residents of the Italian community. The police described them as all Sicilians coming to this country several years ago broke, and in the span of two years their operations netted them sufficient monies to accumulate real estate, other property, and start them all in businesses. There were high hopes this would be the breakthrough case where successful prosecutions would be achieved.

The arrests came as the result of police efforts concerning letters written to Frank Babara, a saloon keeper, and Samuel Brancato, described as a wealthy grocer, demanding $5000 and $2000 respectively, threatening death and destruction of their property should they choose to resist. The letter Brancato received was published in the newspaper with a translation and reads in part, "Dear Friend, The Noble Black Hand is in a desperate condition and asks you for $2000 because the Black Hand knows you can afford to pay this sum;

otherwise your life will pay the penalty." Brancato was also warned if he went to the police, "you and your family will be assassinated."

The police were successful in identifying the leaders of the gang as two "saloon keepers", John Cirrincone, aged 36, a tall powerfully built man with red hair, red bushy mustache and black eyes, and Salvatore Tripitaro, aged 29. The police also let it be known that as a result of their investigation information was developed indicating the gang was associated with similar groups in cities such as New York, Chicago and San Francisco.

The reason for police optimism was twofold. Most important, the police had developed a well-placed "spy" who was cooperating with them. Additionally, their efforts received a substantially boost by reason of the gang's ever-increasing boldness and greed. They had become bold to the point of no longer demanding protection money be left at a drop site to be picked up anonymously, but instead collected it in person, their identities made plain to the victims. Their greed led to a doubling of the sums of money demanded for protection, creating a burden the victims could no longer bear, leading them, despite the fear, to seek the aid of the police. In a month's time the police had received over 100 complaints.

Of those arrested two names are of particular note, Joseph DiGiovanni, described as a 27 year old grocer, and Paul Cantanzaro, aged 30, a shoe shop operator. By the time the Black Hand was but a dark memory both of these individuals would remain on the scene playing prominent roles in the story of organized crime in Kansas City.

Joseph DiGiovanni was born February 23, 1888 in Sicily immigrating to the United States in 1903, arriving in New Orleans, Louisiana. He also resided in Chicago, Illinois, for a period before coming to Kansas City. It is believed upon arrival in Kansas City he quickly became involved in Black Hand activities moving up to a position of leadership, a position he would maintain for years to come.

Paul Cantanzaro was born November 9, 1884 in Sicily, and after immigrating to the United States became a naturalized citizen in July 1924. He had arrests in this early era for extortion by bombing, malicious destruction of property and burglary, however his full arrest record is unknown as in later years police records of many racketeers were removed from department files.

By reason of his courage, persistence, and extraordinary skills, Detective Olivero accomplished what at the time was thought to be impossible. He had successfully penetrated the veil of secrecy surrounding the Black Hand. It was Olivero who developed the "spy" within the organization leading to the unmasking of Black Hand methods of operation. Olivero's "spy" successfully gained the confidence of the gang to the point he was permitted to attend their meetings, held in various business locations in the north end. According to the informant, these gatherings start out on a social note and then its down to business. A name of a potential extortion victim would be thrown out for general discussion. Everything that was known about the prospect was batted around, to include a decision on the right amount of money to demand. The attendees then voted on whether or not to send a demand letter with the majority ruling.

A set procedure was followed entailing three letters. The first was a demand and warning letter signed with the depiction of a pierced heart. If the demands were not met a second letter went out signed with a stiletto. The third letter, if required, outlined the violence that could be expected upon continued non-compliance. If the letters failed to achieve the desired result the gang would meet to decide whether or not violence was called for, and a unanimous vote was required before turning to actual violence. According to the "spy", when violence was approved, whether it was destruction of property or an assassination, the gang would contract it out to someone from another city. Utilizing people from outside the area meant no gang member had to commit murder on his own turf, and there was little chance the assailants would be recognized.

Upon receiving a request from compatriots in another city for a job to be done the gang members in Kansas City would draw numbers to decide who would carry out the assignment. The gang in the city where the deed was to be carried out paid the expenses for the visiting black hander.

Olivero's informant also revealed that out of town Black Hand operatives played a role in mediating an internal conflict, further illustrating the working relationships between Black Hand operatives in various cities. A rift developed as the result of the January shotgun murder of Luciano Musso, described as a leader of the gang. Following the murder six members split off to go out on their own. Some believed Musso was killed due to internal strife, while others believed Musso had become far too close to Detective Olivero. Musso knew too much and was too involved to have any sort of relationship, for any reason, with anyone in law enforcement, especially Louis Olivero. According to Olivero's source, shortly before the July police roundup of gang members the dispute was resolved when visiting Chicago Black Hand leaders interceded, and were successful in getting the two groups back together.

These inner workings of the Black Hand society were further exposed by "The Official" in the newspaper account of his interview. He speaks of an underground connection running through every city where the Black Hand was active. Furthermore, in an effort to avoid handwriting identification Black Hand letters were written in other cities and then sent to Kansas City to be mailed or delivered to the intended victim. "The Official" described the protocol when murder was called for: "Very few of the Black Hand murders are the work of local killers. When a victim has been selected, and a time set for the job, expert shotgun operators are sent here for a stipulated price, there is a market quotation on gunman, bombers, collectors, kidnappers and thieves, and a system of reciprocity governs their exchange. They generally travel in pairs, always two killers to a victim. When they shoot they drop their shot guns on the ground and make their get-away the same night if possible. If the assassins happened to be rounded up in a quick raid, the local organization is bound to set defense machinery at work and to finance it. Bondsmen are furnished, the habeas corpus mill started and the 'omerta' does the rest."

He explained that the refusal of dying men to identify their attackers is to a large degree understandable when considering the use of out of town killers. "As a matter of fact they do not know. Most of them will say 'they got me" that means they know it is the Black Hand but who did the actual killing they do not know, they were strangers imported for the work."

Taking into account Nicolo Gentile's revelations, there seems to be little question that as early as the 1920s these Sicilian clans were part of a loosely knit national confederation governed by certain rules and protocols. Gentile describes the Sicilian clans as subject to the rulings of what he labeled alternately the "Consiglio of the Onorata Society" (Council of the Honored Society), and the "General Assembly." He speaks frequently of "commissions", a type of investigating committee formed preparatory to bringing a matter before the "General Assembly."

In his words the General Assembly, "As it has always been shown, since the beginning, the General Assembly which functioned in truth like a Court of Assize, was composed of elements who were nearly all illiterate. The eloquence was that which impressed the ears, and the more one knew how to speak the more they (were) heeded, and it ended by your will being imposed on that "mass of boors." Gentile characterizes those leaders who sat on the General Assembly as placing more importance on oratory and grand style than on the merits or on the intelligence and toughness of the presenter. He alludes to the general assembly as a manipulated system stating, "once a General Assembly is named, the matters for discussion are presented with the program already fixed by the Capo, assisted by four or five "caporioni" (heads of families), and they put you in a position to vote solely on that which is to their liking.." He complains that any voice of dissent would serve only to anger the assembly members whose response would be to disgrace the dissenter and maybe even have him killed.

Besides "commissions" and general assemblies there were what he labeled "interstate" meetings attended by "representatives" from the various "families" throughout the United States. Gentile speaks of one such meeting held in Buffalo, New York, in 1919 or 1920, and of another held in Boston, Massachusetts, in late 1930 or early 1931.

A "family" Capo had the power to order the murder of an individual who had violated, or was perceived to have violated, certain recognized rules, or committed personal insults. When the intended victim was outside the reach of the Capo's "family" a system of notification was in place that all other "families" were duty bound to honor. Gentile alludes to the fact this power was at times misused by "family" Capos, and he was called on often to defend the subject of a death sentence.

Illustrative of the workings of the general assembly system, Gentile recounts a case where he was asked to interest himself in a matter impacting the Kansas City "family." A young man named Scaglia was murdered in Pueblo, Colorado, and the fallout from the killing caused internal conflict, more murders, and a split in the Pueblo "family."

Following the murder Pellegrino Scaglia, a younger brother of the victim, along with the victim's father-in-law, and a nephew transferred to the Kansas City "family." A man named LaRocca, of the Pueblo "family", leveled "grave accusations" against the three men and requested a meeting of the General Assembly, then headed by a

New York City "family" boss recognized as the top man in the city.

The Pellegrinos were called to New York City to appear before the General Assembly at which time LaRocca enumerated all the "misdeeds", many of which Gentile labeled as untrue but cunningly presented to the assembly. The recommendation of the assembly was a death sentence for the three, and charges of insubordination on the part of the Kansas City "family", apparently for having failed to take action against the three despite the outstanding charges.

Gentile was allowed his say, and to an extent was able to discredit LaRocca causing sufficient doubt on the part of assembly members that they agreed to postpone implementation of the death sentence. Fifteen days later in Pittsburgh, Pennsylvania, the assembly reconvened. Pressure was brought to bear on Gentile to back off in his defense of the three men or face the threat of a death sentence. Gentile plowed ahead "eloquently" presenting a credible defense of the three, and won the day. Despite LaRocca's refusal to considered the matter settled, the Pellegrino group was acquitted by the assembly, the death sentence removed, however, the three men were ordered expelled from the Kansas City "family."

The Black Hand Exposed But Undeterred

In rounding up the gang of Black Handers in July 1915, and uncovering the inner secrets of this criminal society, the police department no doubt had done an outstanding job. It was now up to those victimized to do their part if convictions were to follow. Chief of Detectives Ghent made a public statement asking, "Is Little Italy going to free itself from the Black Hand or is it going to let the men now under arrest go without being prosecuted? ....If you don't testify against them they will get out and resume their operations, bolder than ever, because they have defeated the law. What will you do?"

Responding to Chief Ghent, a group of 15 citizens of the north end gathered in his office but they were not prepared to provide an answer to the challenge, instead asking for a delay until the next day before disclosing their decision. "You have the right men, but we do not know whether we dare prosecute" a spokesmen for the group stated. There was a promise a meeting would be held that night to decide, and Chief Ghent would be advised of their decision the next day. The citizen's meeting never took place, and none of the victims appeared at police headquarters the next morning. They had made their decision. The extortionists once again escaped prosecution.

Chief Ghent's warning proved all too accurate, and the Black Handers, to no one's surprise, resumed their operations, emboldened by the lack of citizen support for police efforts.

Having received two Black Hand letters, one resident of "Little Italy" offered an explanation for the lack of action on the part of his countrymen. "Many of these men under arrest have political pull and might get off. If they were convicted they probably would receive light sentences and soon be back to avenge themselves on those who talked. If they would be sent back to Italy that would be a different matter." The cozy relationship between politicians and organized criminals, described by New York City Detective Lieutenant Joe Petrosino, was indeed a fact of life in these early times, and would remain a continuing dynamic throughout the ensuing years.

Much of the violence associated with this era was the direct result of gang feuds, internal discipline, and dissension within the ranks. Again quoting "The Official", "Not every killing is that of a blackmail victim, in fact the goose that lays the golden egg is not often sacrificed, but they will kill somebody near to him to let him know that they mean business...sometimes they kill for revenge, one of their own members has defaulted with money belonging to the gang or has done some injury to the family of another member or perhaps has been appointed to do some job and weakened. He must pay the penalty."

The murder of Luciano Musso was just such a case, however, he was but one of many who ran afoul of their own kind. Joe Cancialose earned the reputation of a man to be reckoned with, an important cog in the operations of Little Italy's criminal organization. On the night of June 14, 1915 Cancialose was walking south on Tracy Street at 11th when a man ran up behind him wielding a sawed off shotgun gunning him down, the assailant throwing the weapon to the street as he fled. Detective Olivero reached Cancialose before he died but could illicit nothing from him except for a reminder it is not their custom to talk to the police no matter what.

The killing was attributed to the climax of a developing feud within Black Hand circles over the division of spoils, Cancialose alleged to have pulled a double cross on members of the gang. Olivero commenting on the assassination said of the victim, who had many prior arrests, "Joe goes to his grave with many murders on his conscience and many secrets of the Black Hand in his heart."

John Cirrincone the Black Hander recognizable by his red hair and impressive red mustache had been identified as one of the leaders of the gang rounded up in July 1915. He had walked free when his victims failed to stand up and give testimony, returning to his criminal ways. A little more than a year after that arrest, on the night of August 19, 1916, he was strolling along East 5th Street when from a darkened alley a shotgun blast came his way. He was fortunate that night and escaped with his life. Once again the shooting was attributed to gang dissension, the motive apparently a quarrel over the distribution of money collected from extortion victims.

Joe DiGiovanni, another of those rounded up in July 1915, would cross paths with Detective Olivero's on at least two more occasions. On October 9, 1918, DiGiovanni was arrested by Olivero on charges of murder. According to a news account, on that date, following a dispute in the grocery store of Pete and Joe DiGiovanni, Mrs. Ella Smith, "a Negro", was shot and killed, and her sixteen-year old daughter "dangerously wounded." The police alleged Joe DiGiovanni did the actual shooting, but once again the detective was unable to secure a conviction. Then on March 23, 1919, Olivero's investigations led to the arrest of 14 individuals, including DiGiovanni, on charges of "Investigation-Black Handers" but no one went to jail.

Despite the periodic arrests and roundups the lack of convictions obviously emboldened the gangsters and frustrated the authorities. In a newspaper report dated March 24, 1919, Chief of Detectives Robert E. Phelan described the criminal problem in the north end:

> More than $100,000 has been extorted from Italians in Kansas City by the Black Hand system in the last year. Kansas City has become the western headquarters of the extortionists. The conditions in Little Italy are worse than at any time in the history of the city. The situation has reached a crisis and something must be done. If the victims would assist in prosecutions I could take five men and run every Black Hander out of Little Italy in twenty-four hours. We are determined to break up the Black Hand, but our success to a large degree depends on the cooperation of the good citizens of the Italian section.

It was several weeks prior to the Chief of Detectives' observations that the interview of "The Official" was published wherein he offered his view regarding the scope of the criminal organization. "There are not all told probably over fifty members of the criminal gang operating today in this city, but all the influences that are linked with the underworld everywhere are hand in glove with them." Furthermore, he saw the job of combating the organization as a " ...big job and one that must be hammered on systematically, persistently and fearlessly, for it is a subtle and terrible organization that you have to deal with."

As a postscript, it would appear a good case could be made for the proposition the "The Official" was in fact Detective Louis Olivero. On the other hand, if it was Olivero why would he, a well-known and recognizable police figure of the day, request anonymity for the interview?

Four days after the Chief of Detectives published statement Olivero was faced with yet another murder on the north side. This time the victim was eleven-year old Frank Caramusa Jr. On March 28th the youngster was riding on one of his father's delivery trucks driven by an 18 year old. At Independence and Charlotte Avenues the truck struck, and slightly injured, a 6-year old boy. Quickly a hostile crowd gathered at the accident site, and from out of the gathering a shotgun blast rang out. Young Frank Caramusa was hit and would die later at General Hospital. The shooter was said to be Paul Cantanzaro, well known to Olivero as a member of a Black Hand gang. As legend has it he was caught by the crowd and nearly beaten to death. Although this makes for a good story, documentation is lacking that it ever happened.

Caramusa's father initially had nothing to say, but later opted to speak of his son's murder, admitting to being on the outs with the Black Hand. He spoke of the events leading up to the killing of his young son. "I had a fruit cart peddling business and the Mafia came to me and demanded 20% of my profits. I simply could not meet these demands, but I was told if I did not pay the money they would kill my 8-year old son. I could not put together enough through the profits and loans to pay what they said I owed them so they killed my boy with a shotgun."

After the murder Cantanzaro disappeared, and it took Olivero over a year to catch up with him. On April 30, 1920 Olivero arrested him on charges of 2nd Degree Murder. The brotherhood came to Cantanzaro's aid methodically terrorizing a host of witnesses. Any chance of a conviction evaporated. As fate would dictate, in years to come the names Caramusa and Cantanzaro would again be linked, this time as part of a major narcotics case.

The Outfit Never Forgets

The winds of change were blowing through the city and the nation. Forces were in play that would have a profound impact in the criminal sphere, namely the coming of prohibition. Coincidentally Black Hand activity was on the wane. Detective Olivero left the police force in 1920 taking a position with the United States Immigration Service. The years slipped by and in 1929 Olivero opted to take a job with the Jackson County Sheriff's Office as a booking clerk in the jail. Years may have passed but Olivero's enemies were still out there, and he was well aware of it. He remained cautious and wary, keeping the blinds in his home closed, and rarely venturing out at night.

On the evening of November 28, 1930, Maria, his wife of 18 years, and his 7-year old son, Albert, were spending the night at St. Joseph's Hospital in anticipation of Albert's sinus operation the following morning. At 7:10 am Saturday morning November 29th, dressed in an overcoat and wearing a black derby hat, Olivero left his brown frame home at 808 Lydia Street. He often walked to work at the Sheriff's office, not that far from his residence. On this particular morning he may have planned a visit to the hospital to look in on his son. Smoking a cigarette, hands in his pockets, he was walking west on the south side of the 8th street. He had reached the 1300 block when a new Ford sedan with three men inside, coming from the east, veered to the south side curb pulling up next to Olivero. One of the men shouted something causing Olivero to look over to his right. At that moment a shotgun blast from the car struck him tearing away his lower jaw and piercing his throat. Louis Olivero fell to pavement where he died.

Just a week prior he had received a threat, but who it was, if he knew, he never said. Memories are long on the north side and some person, or persons, had not forgotten Detective Olivero. The murder was intended as a message for Olivero, as well as others, that the dark forces of the north end did indeed remember.

It was no secret that certain prominent members of the north end criminal rings had never forgotten or forgiven Louis Olivero. On the other hand, the vicious and cowardly deeds of these predators are also long remembered. Some twenty yeas after the murder of Olivero a U.S. Senate Investigative Committee, headed by Senator Estes Kefauver, tasked with uncovering the scope of organized crime activity in America, selected Kansas City to kick off its inquiries. Committee hearings gained national attention exposing gangsters and racket activities in the nation generally, and Kansas City specifically.

Joseph DiGiovanni, identified to the Committee as one of the two most prominent leaders of the criminal organization in the city at the time, was called to testify and answer for his criminal history. It was no stretch to say he was one of those who had a score to settle with Detective Olivero.

He denied he had ever been arrested for bootlegging. His memory improved slightly when shown a record of a guilty plea in 1928 resulting in a $500 fine on liquor charges. He then remembered the fine, but not the arrest. He explained it away claiming that some unknown person had put a still on some property of his and the agents took him to the post office (The location of the Treasury Agent's offices). He protested it certainly wasn't his still. Neither could he recall having been arrested with 4,000 gallons of liquor in 1927, nor an arrest on liquor charges in 1930.

The committee turned their attention to the days of the Black Hand asking DiGiovanni to recall his early years as a member of that group.

> Q: Weren't you arrested with Paul Cantanzaro in 1915 and others on charges of sending Black Hand letters?
>
> A: I never heard of the Black Hand
>
> Q: Never even heard the word?
>
> A: No
>
> Q: Ever heard of the Mafia?
>
> A: No sir
>
> Q: Did you know an Italian detective Louis Olivero?
>
> A: Yes, I knew him.
>
> Q: Don't you remember that he arrested you in connection with these Black Hand letters?
>
> A: You got the wrong Joe DiGiovanni.

To refresh DiGiovanni's memory his birth date, various home addresses, and physical description were read off, and a photo taken by the police displayed. DiGiovanni admitted to all of the identifiers but still could not remember whether he had ever been arrested. Twenty minutes of questioning followed concerning the arrest for the murder of Mrs. Ella Smith on October 9, 1919, but to no avail, as he didn't remember that arrest either. When asked to look at the pertinent arrest record he explained he couldn't - he had not brought his glasses with him. He was shown his police arrest photo and admitted that it was his photo. "How do you think we got it?, asked committee counsel Rudolph Haley, to which DiGiovanni answered, "I don't know." "Weren't you arrested at the time this picture was taken?" DiGiovanni responded, "Maybe I was."

At this point Senator Estes Kefauver took over the questioning pressing DiGiovanni as to the murder arrest, but he insisted he couldn't remember.

> Q: Now Mr. DiGiovanni you might as well understand right now we are not going to take that kind of answer.
>
> A: Well, I was. (arrested)
>
> Q: Why didn't you tell us a few minutes ago?
>
> A: I didn't remember then.

DiGiovanni explained he now remembered being arrested at 5th & Gillis Streets, and spending 24 hours in jail, and being released when the case was dismissed.

> Q: Who was the victim?
> A: A colored girl

As ordered he returned the following day with his glasses. DiGiovanni was shown photos of all the subjects arrested in the 1915

"Black Hand" roundup. He once again testified he did not remember this arrest. He was reminded that on the prior day he had finally admitted to this arrest. A photo of Pietro Agnello was shown and DiGiovanni was asked if he had been arrested with Agnello in 1915. Apparently the photo jogged his faulty memory as he now admitted he had been arrested but could not remember the charge.

> Q: Yesterday you said you had never heard of a
>   Black Hand Letter.
> A: I didn't know
> Q: Do you now?
> A: Yeah, sure
> Q: Tell us what it is.
> A: It mean they got a black hand; I don't know
>   what it is.

The 1919 slaying of young Frank Caramusa, Jr, was yet another event DiGiovanni had no memory of. Hadn't he employed Paul Cantanzaro, the man arrested for Caramusa murder, DiGiovanni was asked. Yes he had hired Cantanzaro as a night watchman in 1936, and Cantanzaro had worked for him for 7-8 years. Senator Keafauver:

> Q: Do I understand you to say you were a friend of
>   the Caramusa family?
> A: Yes sir.
> Q: Then how can you reconcile hiring this man,
>   who was thought to have killed the boy, as a
>   night watchman?
> A: I needed a watchman in my place.

The totality of DiGiovanni's testimony before the committee led

Senator Kefauver, upon adjournment of the hearings, to announced the committee would strongly recommend that he be indicted for perjury. The matter apparently was considered by the United States Attorney's Office in Kansas City but no indictment was forthcoming.

In later years, Senator Kefauver summarizing the results of committee hearing in Kansas City remarked, "Witnesses before the committee believed to be Mafia members claimed to be completely ignorant of the organization and its operations. Joseph DiGiovanni refused to even admit to having heard of the Mafia, which is patently incredible since all persons of Sicilian extraction are at least familiar with the existence of the Mafia, but when confronted with his criminal record he admitted that he had been involved in a Black Hand charge," The explanation for such answers is simple. Senator Kefauver and his committee witnessed first hand the code of Omerta.

Clash of Cultures

A natural ingredient in the melding of immigrant masses into American society was a clash of cultures, a societal fact common with the foreign born struggling to cope with the unfamiliar. Coming out of Kansas City's "Little Italy" is just such a story. It is pertinent not only because this book is about Kansas City, but also because it exemplifies how the Sicilian mind-set and old world outlook contributed to a climate in which a Sicilian Mafia-like criminal clan could gain a foothold, and thereafter prosper. It is the story of American law versus the Sicilian vendetta, and reflects on a common human trait - cultural traditions and beliefs are difficult to alter and slow to die.

Joe Guzzardo and Sam Brancato, both born in Sicily, had been long time friends. Guzzardo was described as a good mixer with lots of friends, character traits that more than likely led him into politics.

To say the least, his was an unusual political career. In 1919 and 1920 Guzzardo was the Republican "boss" for the north side's old fifth ward responsible for lining up votes for the party. He was Chairman of the Republican ward delegation at the 1920 county convention. In what seems an unusual move, in the same year he also was a delegate at the Democrat city convention. Not unexpectedly, this did not sit well with the Republican County Committee, and Guzzardo was "convicted" of party treason and tossed out of the party.

In the eyes of Guzzardo's wife Julia there was a fundamental difference between the two friends. "Both came from Sicily. But there was this difference in them. Joe (Guzzardo) became assimilated in the American melting pot. He made progress in American methods. Sam Brancato continued to be a Sicilian. He profited in only one way by living in this country. He made money and he has lots of money." This was the same Sam Brancato who in 1915 had received a Black Hand extortion letter demanding he pay $2000 because, as the letter stated, he could afford it.

Brancato owned a grocery store and a drug store and he brought Guzzardo into his drug store business located at 6th and Locust Streets. Brancato put up the money to operate the store as Guzzardo had little to offer except the good will and friendships developed as a political figure. The drug store was an outlet for drug sales and Guzzardo was swept up in a police dragnet of drug dealers in 1921. Family members alleged Guzzardo had taken the fall for Brancato who was equally involved in the drug operation, but never charged. They described how Brancato hid the drugs in a hole in the floor in a space under his grocery located next door, the two businesses connected by an interior door. Guzzardo was convicted of violating federal narcotics laws, and sentenced to a two-year prison term at the Leavenworth Federal Penitentiary.

After serving 19 months and 8 days he was released from the penitentiary in 1923 and he, Sam Brancato and Victor Brancato partnered up in the operation of the swimming pool, hot dog stand, and café concessions at Fairyland Amusement Park. Each partner put up $21,000 for a one third interest.

As the result of a falling out between Guzzardo and Sam Brancato, sometime toward the end of the 1920s, Guzzardo was frozen out, barred from further involvement in the business. Guzzardo valued his share of the business at $52,000, and to be made whole he opted to follow what he considered "the American way" by going to court and filing suit. It may have been the American way, but it was not the Sicilian way, and his decision was generally frowned on in "Little Italy." Thereafter the two men did not speak.

Taking the dispute outside the closed world of the north end brought on the expected response. In a telephone call to the residence, answered by Julia Guzzardo, the anonymous caller threatened to blow them up. Following the threat, Guzzardo was paid a visit by an "Italian" urging him to sign some papers in connection "with his trouble" with Brancato, but he refused, insisting the matter would be settled in court. Several months later he was invited to visit a grocery store at 8th and Harrison Street to talk about the lawsuit. After consulting with his brother-in-law, a lawyer, he stayed away. In January 1930 Guzzardo was pestered by any number of north end people, including at least one of Brancato's relatives, pressing him to settle his differences out of court. He paid them no heed.

Guzzardo was nobody's fool, familiar with the ways of the north side he recognized the repeated runs made at him as an bad omen. He expected trouble and became nervous and edgy, but had no intention of giving in. On the night of January 11, 1930 Julia Guzzardo had after dinner plans to attend a lecture, so her husband decided a relaxing night at the movies might just be what he needed.

Leaving the family residence at 3638 Indiana Street he strolled the few blocks down to the Baltic Theatre at Indiana and 35ᵗʰ Street. At around 9:00 p.m. the movie let out and he started his short trip back home walking south, on the west side of Indiana Street. He was just about to walk past 3616 Indiana, his house a few doors away, when a car, traveling south, came abreast. From inside the car a shotgun blast felled Guzzardo, his body riddled with what were described as thirty "slugs." Rushed to the hospital he lived about an hour, time enough to tell the police he knew who shot him but unwilling to furnish names or a motive. But before he passed away he whispered to his wife "Sam, Sam." Mrs. Guzzard provided the police with Sam Brancato's name as the Sam her husband accused with his last breaths.

Brancato, brought in by the police later that night, denied involvement in the murder, and furnished an alibi advising the authorities he was home from 6:00 p.m. till the police came for him at midnight.

The very next day, before the shock wore off, a casket selected or funeral arrangements made, the widow and four of Guzzardo's sisters appeared at the offices of the county prosecutor accusing Sam Brancato as the man responsible for Guzzardo's murder and demanding action. Mrs. Guzzardo, displaying none of the normal fears accompanying such cases, proclaimed there would no adherence to the usual methods of vendetta — "We are not going to use sawed-off shotguns or stilettos in dark alleys or hire anyone to do that. We are going about this in the American way."

"Brancato told me once that as long as he had money and James P. Alyward as his attorney he could do anything he wanted to do in Kansas City," the widow proclaimed, and added, "I intend to see just how far that influence will extend." There is an old Sicilian peasant saying that seems to apply here, "He who has money and friends can sneer at the law."

A Crime Family Develops

As criminal types infesting the north end, and "Little Italy" neighborhoods in other cities, joined together and took root their organizations mirrored the Sicilian Mafia, Neapolitan Camorra and Calabrian 'Ndrangita secret societies. Routinely escaping prosecution the criminal clans prospered, their numbers swelled, consolidation progressed, political alliances expanded and they took on an increased role in the Italian community. Just as in the old country these men, the Amici, besides their nefarious activities, provided protection and other services, and to this end it was advantageous to preserve the distinctive Sicilian culture where they operated as power-brokers.

Carried over to America was the love-hate dynamic as these Americanized predators were at the same time givers and takers, protectors and violators, hero and villain, just as it had been in Sicily. The Amici certainly were recognized for what they were, thus feared and detested, but at the same time respected. They displayed a combination of brutality and old world gentility. They possessed an inbred sense for public relations displayed in their dress and bearing, always a smile, a wave, a tip of the hat for the neighbors. A man of influence one could talk to, nothing too minor for his consideration, he made your problems his problems. Friendship and favors, all to be repaid one day.

They came to monopolize the goods and services, the necessities of Italian life, and extracted a price for permitting their distribution. They ran the Italian lotteries, and other gambling games viewed generally as innocent pastimes by the people, but unlawful in America. They insured a man could make his own red wine in a home distillery, another illegality that made no sense to these immigrants. They were bankers and moneylenders to the poor who either were prevented from borrowing from legal institutions or distrusted them. However, there was a price to paid, an interest rate that would keep the borrower indebted forever. They arranged for relatives to come to the United States legally and illegally, again at a steep cost.

As in the old country, they positioned themselves as the people to see for contacts with the outside world, utilizing their political influence and ability to intervene with various establishment agencies, the police, landlords, etc, to solve various personal and neighborhood difficulties. They had a vested interest in perpetuating the long held distrust of legal and governmental entities. They were the neighborhood facilitators, the fixers whose stature was enhanced by their ability to get things done. The Mafia in Sicily gained power by inserting itself in that space between the populace and the State and the same was true in America. Mafia type criminals were parasites in the Old Country and it would be the same in America.

On the other hand it was impossible to duplicate exactly the old world ways and alterations would have to be made within the criminal organization to account for existing societal, governmental and cultural conditions that made up the prevailing environment. In America they faced a population far different from that of the old country. A population unfamiliar with a "Mafia mentality", one that did not inherently abide by the code of omerta, or personal revenge, and did not generally have contempt for the State and the establishment. Eventually these criminal organizations became a meld of familiar old world models adapted to new world conditions. The Italian criminal organization that developed in America was Mafia-like in essence and in the comportment of its leaders and members, but at the same time was an Americanized product that came to be known as Cosa Nostra.

Chapter III

Prohibition

THE 18TH AMENDMENT ushering in prohibition was passed in January 1919 followed in October 1919 by the Volstead Act the law implementing the prohibition on the manufacture, sale, and transportation of liquor. Enforcement of the law was to commence in January 1920.

Sentiment for prohibition in America dated to the 1820s. The Prohibition Party was founded in 1869, the Woman's Temperance Union in 1874, the Anti Saloon League of America in 1895, each launching a campaign against alcohol. Women were actively recruited into the anti-liquor movement and played a leading role. At a time when women did not have the right to vote the attraction to the cause was substantial. In fact, the anti liquor movement was the forerunner and impetus for mobilizing women in the campaign for the right to vote. Of local note, a teenager named Carrie Moore, an Irish lass raised some miles south of Kansas City was greatly influenced in her formative years by the preaching of a fundamentalist Baptist minister railing against the evils of that demon liquor. In later years she would return to Kansas City as Carrie Nation, a prominent name in the prohibition movement, wielding a hatchet in attacks against saloons.

Between 1900 and 1920 many other individuals and groups agitating for various economic, political and social reforms lent their voices in favor of ban on alcohol. In the eyes of the reformers a prohibition law would close the saloons thereby saving scarce family resources, reduce the number of those abusing alcohol and contribute to domestic tranquility. Instead the result of the 18th Amendment was a bewildering era for the nation. It was a law generally un-enforced and, contrary to the hopes of the abolitionists, outlawing a product so widely in demand resulted in an unparalleled opportunity for the criminal element. Prohibition was the beginning of a two-decade period when Kansas City operated as a wide-open town.

Underworld elements seized on the opportunity prohibition afforded, and prohibition is generally accepted as the catalyst for the development of organized crime in America. Rather than solve a social problem, prohibition created one far different and more dangerous than the consumption of alcohol.

Overnight, across the nation, the rush was on to capitalize on this new and unpopular law. Bootlegging became a major industry and Kansas City was no exception. For years innumerable home distilleries operated in Irish, Polish, Italian, and other ethnic neighborhoods providing their inhabitants a running start in the bootlegging industry. In Kansas City's north end the majority of residents derived income from illegal alcohol production. It was an opportunity that could not be ignored, and people were willing to pay the price, whether it be arrest, imprisonment, physical injury, even death, to reap the benefits.

There were few families in the poorer sections of the city that did not have at least one male member arrested for bootlegging. Thousands of stills were operating, many, many discovered yet no amount of raids could stem the tide. To the masses bootlegging was not considered a crime, but rather was viewed as some kind of folly. For others, such as the young middle class, consuming illicit booze was a flaunting of convention, a snub of those who frowned on it, a poke in the eyes of those who said you can't drink, and an expression of independence. Besides, since the law only prohibited the production and sale of liquor there was little, if any, risk for those who simply consumed it.

Although extortion in one form or another would remain in the arsenal of organized criminals, the Black Hand racket that indiscriminately targeted and victimized a whole ethnic community was on the wane. The opportunities presented by prohibition for making money with little risk far outweighed that of sending Black Hand letters. Additionally, trafficking in illicit liquor opened vistas far beyond the boundaries of an ethnic neighborhood.

Graduating from the Black Hand racket, Joe and Pete DiGiovanni had established themselves as powers in one criminal faction operating on the north side, Joe the more recognized of the two. Joe and James "Big Jim" Balestrere were regarded as the top two men in a budding criminal organization. In this period, criminal operations had not fully coalesced into one dominant organization but rather other factions and individuals were in the mix. Especially when it came to bootlegging the Italian racketeers were not alone in the quest for a piece of the action. There was a mad scramble to cash in by individuals of all stripes.

Opinions differ as to which of the two, Joe DiGiovanni or Jim Balestrere, wielded the most power. Balestrere was recognized as playing the role of "arbitrator" on the north side. Not that far removed from life in the old country, the north side immigrant was not only wary of the establishment but also ill prepared to face what seemed a bewildering system. Most often the north side citizen chose to bypass the legal establishment, and other institutions of government, and instead looked within, opting to have disputes, grievance and problems solved in their own community by their countrymen.

In the footsteps of the Sicilian Mafia Don, Big Jim Balestrere was that person people looked to. He held informal hearings, summoned witnesses, acted as judge and jury in resolving neighborhood problems. His edicts and judgments were followed explicitly. While known to his criminal peers as a vicious individual, to the populace of the North Side he showed a different face, that of a humble man, polite, tipping his hat to everyone, a man you could talk to. This was a man who could get things done, and, therefore, a man to be respected.

Balestrere was born June 24, 1891 near Palermo, Sicily, in a village of stonemasons, immigrating to America on April 15, 1903. He went first to Milwaukee, Wisconsin, where a large contingent of his family had settled. He visited Kansas City in 1905 and returned in 1908 to stay. By trade a stonemason and bricklayer he built his own five- bedroom home at 5421 Brooklyn in a modest residential area of medium-income families. When asked how he came to live in Kansas City as a teenager he replied, "My brother-in-law, he was a contractor here, and my mother had come here because my sister was going to have a baby, and so when they come back (to Milwaukee) she like Kansas City better than Milwaukee, so we come here".

Immediately upon arriving in Kansas City he went to work for Henry F. McElroy, Sr., a real estate man engaged in various building projects and later was the Pendergast Machine's choice for City Manager. Balestrere became foreman of McElroy's bricklayers. Balestrere subsequently tried his hand at various employments operating a north side saloon and a grocery store.

Practically until the day he died of natural causes in 1959 he would remain a man of extraordinary influence, at the top of the criminal organization, operating mainly in darkness behind the scenes.

Black Market Sugar

In a time before prohibition, during World War I, the DiGiovanni brothers and Jim Balestrere, along with other North Side figures, were engaged in black market sugar operations. With the end of the war they found themselves with a huge supply of sugar for which there was no longer a market. The warehouse storing this excess sugar burned down in what the fire department described as an intentionally set fire for insurance purposes. It was widely believed that Joe DiGiovanni himself set the fire and in the process had been caught up in the inferno. The "proof", his horribly scarred face, neck, and hands, earning him the nickname "Scarface Joe". He steadfastly denied this allegation claiming he was scarred as the result of an accident with an oil heater.

With the advent of prohibition sugar was once again in demand as an essential product in the illicit manufacture of alcohol. Several "sugar houses" sprung up on the North Side to service bootleggers. Four of the major ones were those run by the DiGiovanni brothers, Pete, nicknamed "Sugar House Pete", Paul, and Vincent, along with Vincent Chiapetta, located in the 500 block of East 5th St. The Lusco brothers, James, Joseph and "Tudie" were another of the four, as was a smaller operation run by Marion Nigro and Jack Lesner.

The largest sugar house, having the majority of business, belonged to Charles Carrollo, joined by brother Frank, and father Anthony, located at Harrison and Missouri Avenues.

Besides the big four operators there were rival Italian criminal factions and other individuals actively engaged in the alcohol business leading to rivalries, numerous hijackings of liquor shipments, undercutting of prices, spot murders, other acts of violence. Of particular note was a young man displaying great potential by the name of John Lazia who along with a group of rising stars represented the future of the organization. There were other renegade north-enders who despised the element they referred to as the "Greasers" or "Mustache Petes", referring those early immigrant gangsters, lacking in language skills, clannish, and welded to old-world thinking and protocols.

Operating with abandon, Frank "Chee Chee" DeMayo, came to be known as the "King of Bootleggers. DeMayo and his partner Robert Carnahan were headquartered right across the street from the offices of the revenue agents. They were servicing customers in Missouri, Kansas, Oklahoma and Nebraska. DeMayo later admitted to having spent vast sums during these times fixing public officials.

Another notable of the era was George W. "Slim" Goode the owner of a "soft drink" establishment at 6917 Independence Avenue. In 1925 a police official characterized "Slim" as being "one of the most arrested and persistent bootleggers the department has had to contend with, having been arrested 16 times in the last two years with no convictions." Despite many gallons of whiskey having been confiscated from Goode's establishment, and purchases made with marked money, he always escaped punishment, even when charged federally. On several occasions, when arrested by the police, Goode offered to bet $100 he would not be convicted. He would have won every bet.

The Return of Nicolo Gentile

The lure of prohibition brought the roving Mafioso Nicolo Gentile back to Kansas City. Picking up on his adventures, he had successfully defended Vincenzo Chiapetta against a death sentence issued by the Los Angeles "family" boss. Chiapetta, identified to the Kefauver Committee as a "Mafia member", was prospering as part of the DiGiovanni's sugar operation. His next stop was Pittsburgh, Pennsylvania, where he had been urgently summoned to assist "associates" there in a political matter. His efforts on their behalf had put him in a deep hole financially so he was only too happy when offered the opportunity to join Tony Ferrantello in Kansas City in his barber supply company. In truth Ferrantello's business was a front for an illicit alcohol enterprise.

Ferrantello's business sold perfumes and barber supplies, the perfect business to use as a cover to traffic in illegal alcohol. With prohibition the law of the land a special license was required in order to acquire the pure alcohol needed to produce the perfumes, and a portion of the alcohol obtained was put that use. However, the majority of the alcohol drawn from the legal warehouse was sold to bootleggers. To cover their tracks they got their clients to agree to keep the legitimate bottles of perfume prominently displayed in their barbershops for show purposes in the event Federal agents made an inspection. They acquired the alcohol at a price of $15 a gallon while the original cost to the business was $5 a gallon, translating into a sizeable profit.

In addition to the lucrative alcohol business Gentile garnered sizeable earnings from a jewelry business opened in Kansas City at the behest of jeweler friend, a transplant from Palermo, Sicily. His good fortune allowed him to make a "contribution" to the Kansas City criminal "society." He claims this was done to show his gratitude for the assistance the outfit had provided him, including allowing his participation in the "society's" activities, which he described as "already prospering." Here Gentile is alluding to his having been made a member of the Kansas City outfit.

To further enhance his position in the "society", and to make money for it, he followed his venture in the jewelry business with the opening of a front business, a wholesale grocery, supplying bootleggers with items required for the manufacture of illicit alcohol such as corn sugar, yeast, and tin cans. Gentile claims that within a short period of time 75% of the bootleggers were his customers, and he was contributing $2000 a month to the "society."

His alliance with the criminal "society" in Kansas City had made him a sizeable amount of money, and in 1925 he opted to return to Sicily for a visit. He turned over the wholesale grocery business to his "compare" Vincenzo Chiapetta who according to Gentile profited handsomely during the ensuing years of prohibition. Independent of Gentile's story, there is information that he was backed in the grocery store by Big Jim Balestrere, and Joe DiGiovanni joined in later.

Churning Out The Booze

In the early days of prohibition bootleggers relied heavily on innumerable home stills operating throughout the community. A portable one-gallon still was generally available for under $10.00, and how-to instructions could be found in government documents and in books and publications available at the local library. In some cities the criminal outfits seized on the potential of home manufacture by organizing the neighborhoods, distributing portable home stills, making it clear a refusal to go along was not acceptable. On first glance it might appear an operation of this kind had limited potential in generating a sizeable quantity of bootleg liquor, or making money for the outfit. To the contrary, in Chicago, Illinois, the home stills distributed by the Genna Brothers bootlegging operation produced liquor generating gross sales of $350,000 a month, while they paid the home cookers at a rate of $15 a day.

One step up from the home still was the commercial still, larger, more costly but capable of a production rate whereby the price of the still was recouped in approximately 4 days. A still costing $500 could produce from 50 to 100 gallons of liquor every day. The cost to produce a gallon of liquor selling for $4.00 was but 50 cents

Other methods of obtaining product was limited only by the ingenuity and cleverness of the traffickers. The Gentile and Ferrantello phoney barbershop supply operation was made possible by reason of the fact the law permitted the use of alcohol in certain specified areas. Doctors were allowed to prescribe and druggists to dispense intoxicating liquors for medicinal use. As a result, in the early days of prohibition, when demand outstripped supply, doctors were prescribing whiskey as a universal remedy for laryngitis, flue, insomnia, back pain and a host of other ailments. Soon enough there was no longer a need for a doctor visit to get ones fix of booze as a vast array of speakeasies sprung up to service the public.

Combining theft and collusion prohibition gangs found another source of alcohol in the warehouse stocks of liquor on hand prior to passage of prohibition. Burglarizing these warehouses was one way to get at the liquor, but an even simpler and safer way to tap into this ready made source of product was working in collusion with the liquor warehouse owners. Another method involved collusion with the owners of pre-prohibition breweries who took in racketeers as silent partners, or set them up in front operations, to take advantage of a legal product labeled "near beer." "Near beer" was beer having an alcohol content of no more than one half of one percent, and the bootleggers edge came as a result of the production process. To produce "near beer" the first step involved the manufacture of the genuine product followed by a process to reduce the alcohol content to the legal limit. It was an easy matter for the gangster, working with dishonest owners, to divert the genuine product before that final stage of the "near beer" process.

"Prohibition is a business" that titan of industry, Alphonse "Scarface" Capone, was quoted as saying, and as time progressed crime syndicates did in fact employ business principles in the operation of the bootlegging racket. Existing crime outfits, and new ones, recruited heavily to fill manpower needs necessary to handle the multiplicity of tasks associated with the business. Unsophisticated gangsters became experienced administrators running multi-million dollar enterprises, requiring they manage payrolls, security, transportation, production, distribution, and establishing smuggling contacts and procedures.

By the late 1920s smuggling had become a major source of illegal alcohol. Major smuggling routes were established, and the liquor was brought in by boats, automobiles, trucks, aircraft and any other form of transport the gangsters could arrange. The largest source of smuggled liquor came from Canada, and by 1929, by one account, 80% of the entire production of the Canadian liquor industry ended up in the United States. The demand was such that a Canadian liquor firm established a subsidiary to exclusively produce popular American types whiskeys for sale to bootleggers. In future years the expertise in smuggling gained during this time would be put to use in narcotics trafficking.

The Sugar House Syndicate

In this era labeled the Roaring 20s, Kansas City quickly gained a national reputation as the wettest city in the nation, and the budding Italian criminal organization would come to dominate the bootleg industry.

The early 1920s was a time of intense competition in the field of bootlegging as the irresistible attraction of easy money with a modest investment lured petty criminals, small businessmen, otherwise law-abiding citizens, and assorted others, into what was then a wide open arena. For the more established criminal outfits this was not an acceptable situation.

In the late 1920s, most likely 1928, Joe DiGiovanni approached Charles Carrollo outlining a plan to consolidate the north side sugar houses on the basis of ten shares divided among six entities. The DiGiovanni group, the Carrollo group, the Lusco group, and the Joe Filardo-Joe Cusumano Roma Bakery group, each holding two shares. James Balestrere and Gaetano Lococo would each have one share. An agreement was reached and the "Sugar House Syndicate" was born.

The consolidation controlled competition and raised the price of sugar to $5.00 a sack, a $2.00 a sack profit, with thousands of sacks sold each week. Sugar was also sold on credit to anyone wanting to set up a still thereby encouraging more production and increasing the customer base. Rather than taking cash in repayment they took the whiskey, paying $5 per gallon, then turning around and retailing it for $15 a gallon. To further increase profits the outfit arranged for the theft of boxcars full of sugar.

The Sugar House Syndicate came to control the illegal liquor business from start to finish, raw product to finished product, and the equipment needed to deliver it. No one else could sell supplies to the bootleggers, and no one else could sell the finished product without a payoff to the syndicate. They controlled the sale or financing of all automobiles used by the group to deliver the finished product. Cops of the day recall that before an individual bootlegger could make a payoff to a beat cop, Sergeant, Lieutenant, or Captain they first had to obtain permission from Joe DiGiovanni.

Human nature dictates there will always be those whose ambition or greed drives them to defy the odds, step outside the law of the mob, and then pay for their mistake with their lives. Lost are the actual numbers of those who suffered beatings, other acts of violence and murder as the result of involvement in the illegal liquor trade. The following are but two examples.

Ralph Faranella was a bootlegger and his criminal history substantiated that fact. In March 1927 he was arrested on liquor charges, but was released by the prosecutor. In June 1929 he was again arrested, and again released by the prosecutor. In that same year he did serve a short jail term on a liquor conviction. He was again arrested on November 1,1930, when police seized 30 gallons of liquor from his car. He was turned over to federal authorities, charged, and then released on $2000 bond.

Faranella was an ambitious bootlegger with visions of becoming a big time dealer, and that was not always a healthy thing. He should have realized he was stepping outside the lines, and he should have heeded the warnings that came his way, but ambition blinded him. He was told to forget about plans of expanding his modest Independence Avenue liquor run, and warned against selling 5 gallon lots to out of town customers, and told to stick to pint and quart residential deliveries the outfit was willing to tolerate.

At 8:30 p.m. the night of November 25, 1930 gunshots rang out attracting the attention of a witness who spotted two men running from a car parked on Kersey Coats Drive. Inside the car, a Ford Roadster, was Ralph Faranella shot and dying. From what the police could determine Faranella had been set up, lured to the spot for a meeting or a possibly a potential liquor transaction. Faranella overriding dream of the big time had cost him his life.

Jimmy Howard was considered small potatoes as a criminal figure, but when it came to the liquor business he dealt only in the best, importing cases of beer and alcohol from Canada. It was a good business for Howard but it put him at odds with certain powerful competitors inasmuch as trafficking in the good stuff hurt the local trade. An emissary paid Howard a visit explaining there was a syndicate operating, and the idea was if everyone worked together prices could be raised meaning more money for all. Howard wasn't much for sharing with any syndicate, and to make his feelings crystal clear he gave the emissary a beating.

On the afternoon, February 12, 1931, Howard stopped by the A.B.C. Auto Livery Company at 1111 Broadway, a location he used as a contact point for messages and telephone calls. He chatted up the part owner of the firm while standing in front of the plate glass window casually observing the activity on the street. At 2:20 p.m. two men, one tall one short, exited an automobile and walked north on Broadway approaching the livery office. The shorter man was armed with a revolver while the taller man pulled a machine gun from under his coat and proceeded to fire directly into the window of the livery company where Howard was standing. Howard, 38 years of age, was riddled with 14 bullets and fell dead.

The syndicate's message was abundantly clear. Howard had crossed them and had to pay. As a historical footnote, the Jimmy Howard murder was put in the books as the first in Kansas City where the victim was killed by a machine gun.

The Sugar House Syndicate ran efficiently, effectively and profitably, the members becoming wealthy, none ending up in the penitentiary, while hundreds of their employees, and those running the stills, went to jail.

Now Big Jim Balestrere, a prime mover in the bootlegging rackets, would have you believe he certainly didn't become wealthy during prohibition. Balestrere, appearing before the Kefauver Committee in 1950, provided the committee members with his view of the era. Yes he had sold corn sugar to bootleggers during prohibition, but when it came to how much he had benefited from the business, it was no big deal:

> Q: How much were you worth when repeal came in?
> A: I don't remember.
> Q; Well, $50,000?
> A: Oh no (throwing up his hands in shocked surprise) I had a family to feed, it wasn't anything like that.
> Q: What did you make out of the sugar business?
> A: Some months $800, some $900, sometimes maybe $1000.

The impact and consequences of prohibition were enormous locally and nationally. A general disrespect for the law and the law enforcement establishment fermented. A climate was created whereby ordinary citizens and racketeers where thrown together, rubbing shoulders in illegal speakeasies, leading to an acceptance, even admiration, of gangsters. The public shook off gangland bloodshed, an earmark of the bootlegging rackets. Despite Big Jim Balestrere's protestations, mobsters reaped hundreds of millions of dollars using the money to expand their horizons, buy protection and insure their viability for years to come.

During this period existing relationships with other criminal elements nationally were cemented while others came into being where there had been none before. For organized crime this was the beginning stage of consolidation. At first it was an informal national syndicate made up of groups of various ethnicities. However, many of the old line Sicilian gang leaders resisted inclusion in a cartel that included "outsiders." Eventually "Americanized" elements would prevail bringing forth a modernized national Italian crime organization known as La Cosa Nostra, and as the evolutionary process continued Cosa Nostra would eventually come to dominate all of organized crime.

Former Kansas City Missouri Police Chief Lear B. Reed writing in 1941 summed up prohibition this way:

> The Eighteenth Amendment to the Federal Constitution and the Volstead Act did more toward making crime a business than any other curse this country has ever suffered. It brought into existence the worst gangs the world has ever known. It caused more corruption in high places than anything else could have done. It resulted in more killings than we like to admit. Nothing has ever resulted in as much graft in law enforcement. No other one thing ever poured as much cash into the coffers of gangdom. The attempt to enforce it brought forth a horde of incompetent, insincere, untrained and uncontrolled men, in many places. The "alky" racket led to a far more flagrant and widespread traffic in narcotics. The Prohibition era taught the underworld what it did not already know about organizing and opening a business. The outlaw army of the land wanted prohibition to remain. The Repeal meant the loss of the most lucrative source of money crime has ever know.

Chapter IV
The Political Machine

THE POLITICAL MACHINE was part of the American experience from very early times. History is replete with names of machine Bosses in cities around the nation who exerted extraordinary and usually corrupt influence in their domains. Enoch J. "Nucky" Johnson of Atlantic City, New Jersey; James Michael Curley of Boston, Mass.; Frank Hague of Jersey City, New Jersey; Huey Long of Louisiana; Edward J. Kelly of Chicago; Boss Tweed of New York City's Tammany Hall, to name a few. Ranking right up there was the name Pendergast of Kansas City.

There was a definite pattern to the development of these political machines. At a time when this was still a young nation, in the neighborhoods of our cities the saloon keeper, gambling house operator and politician were often the same person. The saloon was the center of neighborhood activity and entertainment. It provided its patrons with a myriad of social services not available anywhere else in the city. This was especially true in the ethnic neighborhoods where the immigrant population was unfamiliar with societies' customs and the workings of the legal establishment and government institutions. A perfect illustration of this dynamic was Big Jim Pendergast's Kansas City west bottoms saloon, a neighborhood center for the hard working, underpaid, Irish immigrant. One could warm himself in the winter, read a newspaper, cash his pay check or leave money on deposit with Big Jim who would monitor the funds insuring the patron didn't go overboard on liquor or gambling.

Who was in a better position than the Saloon keeper to deliver votes, and votes translated to political power. In the days before public welfare it was the local politico who provided jobs, food, assistance with public agencies, the police and the courts. In return he expected loyalty when election time rolled around. Members of the community were not viewed as nameless, faceless voting blocs, but rather as individuals having specific needs and desires that had to be tended to.

The political movers and shakers came to recognize the potential of existing neighborhood criminal gangs. To the politico it was clear these criminal groups could be utilized for broader purposes outside of their normally limited sphere of street crimes, and put to work in the political realm. For one, criminal gangs consisted of numbers of members, and in numbers were power. If the potential for violence existed among those making up the numbers, then the power they represented was even greater. If at least some of the energy of the organization could be channeled into politics, the power of politicians could be multiplied. A bargain was struck between corrupt politicians and the underworld that became a fact of life in the urban setting. The power of the organization would be put at the disposal of the politicians to perpetuate them in office, and enrich them in the process.

By means of violence, or the threat of it, voters could be forced to the polls to vote the correct line. Potential challenges could be rebuffed, and reformers cowed into submission. In return, the power of the politician would be placed at the disposal of the underworld to ensure its survival and prosperity, protecting it from arrest or official harassment. Each would be dependent on the other.

In the beginning the politician was the master, the hoodlum his servant. As time passed the roles would be reversed, the politician becoming the servant on the payroll of the underworld at its beck and call.

Kansas City's organized crime "family", its most famous leader John Lazia, and those who followed him, are as much the product of this dynamic as anything else one can point to. The development of a homegrown criminal organization that became part of the La Cosa Nostra syndicate represents the melding of many factors and influences. Clearly politics was a key ingredient. There is little doubt organized crime in Kansas City benefited and prospered by reason of the fact the city was home to one the most powerful political machines this country has known.

It began in 1876 when 20-year-old James Pendergast moved from St. Joseph to Kansas City settling in the west bottoms starting out as a "puddler" in a local iron foundry. Big Jim was a thick necked, friendly sort, prone to whistling, singing Irish tunes and telling jokes. Ironically in the same year, 1881, gambling was outlawed Pendergast is said to have used the winnings from a horse bet to open a combination hotel-saloon on St. Louis Ave.

Politics seemed to come naturally and the position of saloon keeper/politician fit him like a glove. His saloon became a west bottoms meeting place where small time politicians and locals would congregate and spend time. He became interested in politics in 1884 attending a March Democratic primary. Pendergast was elected city alderman in 1892, and although he dominated first ward politics (west bottoms), he sought to extend his power to the north side (second ward) where he had opened another saloon one block from the courthouse and city hall.

In most cities the immigrant population tended to live in cohesive neighborhoods making it easier for the local party leaders to deliver their votes in a bloc, and that translated into political power. This was exactly how it worked out for Big Jim.

Pendergast saw no need whatsoever to comply with anti-gambling laws, operating gambling games upstairs at both saloons he owned. His attitude was in conflict with that of the police department, which at this time was under State rule. Kansas City's Police Chief followed an anti-gambling policy calling for crackdowns on gambling activities. In August 1894 thirty-eight men were arrested in a big dice game held at Pendergast's north end saloon. However, change was just around the corner. In April 1895 a new board of police commissioners, appointed by the governor, selected a new chief of police, L.E Irwin, whose attitude was in sync with that of Big Jim. Gambling would run without police interference.

Pendergast continued to lay the groundwork for political control of the north end. His tavern became HQ for city officeholders, lawyers, and gamblers. Pendergast's ties were strong with men of influence in the north end who maintained liquor and gambling interests there. Supported by Marcy K. Brown, a political ally, police protection for organized gambling was insured. By 1895 if you didn't join with Pendergast's gambling combine you were raided. Gambling was a large-scale business in Kansas City, one reform group claiming $800,000 was the annual gross by the combine. The accuracy of these numbers is unknown.

The alliance between gambling and politics, one relying on the other, called for the politicians to provide protection while gambling interests provided the money the machine required to perpetuate itself. This dynamic would be in play throughout the early history of Kansas City, as it was in large cities around the nation.

As it were, the issue of gambling would enable Pendergast to gain complete control of the north end and become its political boss. The catalyst was Pendergast's opposition of District Attorney Frank Lowe's policy against the expansion of gambling. His political east side rival, Joe Shannon, was supporting Lowe whose crack down on gambling created a furor within north end saloon and gambling interests. As a major player in the gambling cabal, Jim Pendergast waded in, lending his considerable clout to the conflict. North end political leaders were now motivated to follow Pendergast's lead if they were to defeat Shannon at the next convention, and rid themselves of District Attorney Lowe.

Joe Shannon, an ambitious Irish Democrat politician, operated across town on the east side in the 9th ward and was working his way up the ranks. His ward was growing as the number of people leaving the squalor of the West Bottoms escalated. The Democrats had split into two factions, Pendergast's "goats" and Shannon's "rabbits". The divide was not based on differing political philosophies but rather a simple struggle for control of patronage jobs, a prime source of power for political machines.

Aligned with Shannon was another tough Irish politico, Casimir John Joseph Michael "Cas" Welch who was destined to play a significant role in Kansas City's political history. Welch was a plumber by trade but in 1909 he went into business with Big Jim's brother,

Tom Pendergast, establishing the Hurry Messenger Service. It lasted a year before the two parted ways. In later years Tom Pendergast would became the political boss of the "goats" and Welch would emerge as kingpin of Shannon's east side "rabbit" faction. Welch was flashier, bawdier, more careless than Tom, prone to fist fighting even after he became a justice of the peace. In 1924 Welch broke with Boss Joe Shannon aligning himself with Tom Pendergast.

At the 1898 Democratic convention Big Jim Pendergast was successful in unseating District Attorney Lowe and getting his man, James A. Reed, nominated for District Attorney. With this victory under his belt Pendergast seized the mantle of new leader of the north end, while remaining undisputed boss of the first ward. He followed this up by beating his rival for a seat on the city council by a 5 to 1 margin.

Two years later Pendergast's man, James A. Reed, won the primary election for the post of Mayor and Pendergast's growing political machine went into action pushing for the election of the remainder of his slate of candidates. This marked the first campaign where a major effort was made to organize the Italian community. Working hard for Pendergast was Joe Damico, known as the "King of Little Italy", making campaign speeches in Italian. Black gambling interests were promised that a vote for Reed would mean less police interference. For the German voters there was the promise of free beer from the Heim Brewery people. Something for everyone could well have been the motto.

Reed won the Mayor's office and the resulting patronage was immense, allowing Big Jim to become the most powerful political boss in the city. Between 1900 and 1902 he named 123 of 173 patrolmen on the police force. By the close of 1900 Pendergast and fellow Alderman, John P. Lynch, founded the Jackson County Democratic Club located at 716 Delaware. Thirty years later an offshoot of the club, The Jackson Democratic Club would serve as the base for Boss Tom Pendergast's machine.

In 1906 Big Jim was re-elected to the city council, however with his health on the decline for a number of years he began the process of delegating management duties to his younger brother Tom. Tom and two of his brothers, Mike and John, had come to Kansas City from St. Joseph in 1890. After graduation from St. Mary's College and turning down a contract to play professional baseball Tom was given a job as cashier in a booth at the racetrack owned by his brother Big Jim. He was also put to work, along with a brother, as bookkeepers in one of Jim's saloons. Tom Pendergast was said to have shown far more interest in running around with his Irish mates than being with his family. He was described as rough and tumble, capable of fighting with the best of them, gaining a well deserved tough guy reputation.

For 16 years Big Jim tutored Tom in the ABCs of machine politics. He preached the importance of showing concern for the people's day-to-day problems, helping them when necessary, and in lieu of thanks you collected votes. The true source of power for these political factions was the ability to provide jobs through patronage rather than the philosophy of ideas. The heart of a political machine was taking care of the people in return for votes.

Tom's first political office was an appointment in 1896 as deputy Jackson county marshal. In 1900 Mayor Reed selected Tom for the patronage-laden job of Superintendent of Streets. In 1902 Tom won election as County Marshal, but lost in subsequent elections in 1904 and 1906.

Big Jim retired from politics and passed away on November 10, 1911. Tom succeeded him as Alderman from the first ward, the only elected position Tom Pendergast would ever hold. Tom took aim on expanding the political organization showing a willingness to go to almost any lengths to accomplish it. Illegal voting was but one tactic in his bag of tricks, not that this was anything new. In the mid 1890s, fueled by anti Catholic feelings, Republicans gained control of the city council and the patronage that came with it. In response the Irish politicos simply manufactured more democrats by vote rigging, and the Irish community had no trouble in ignoring the outcries that followed.

The political factions were entrenched in the older, poorer, seamier, harsher sections of the city, a fact that a enhanced their political power. For the resident who needed something taken care of or a job it was the ward boss who had the ear of Big Jim, or Boss Tom or Joe Shannon, and that was how things got done. As with the Sicilian Mafia Don, holding sway in his rural town or district, getting things done translated into power and respect. Their districts and wards were inhabited by the working class and immigrant population who did not have the time, or patience to study the political landscape, figure out who to vote for, and decide what was what. In the Irish conclaves, for example, that was left to the ward boss, that friend to all, to decide.

Each district or ward had a political leader, commonly called a precinct captain. On election-day club owners, gamblers, and the like, took care of the captain by arranging for carloads of associates to travel the precincts voting in each. In return the ward boss ensured no one would cause trouble for those who did the machine's business. In hard times the ward bosses distributed food to thousands, found jobs for the needy, and helped pay resident's taxes. He could get tax assessments lowered, tax penalties waived, obtain liquor permits for those with arrest records, arrange for the authorities to overlook liquor violations, void traffic tickets, cause records to be destroyed or altered. The beneficiaries of the machine's largess were certainly grateful, and they repaid with their vote.

Four years after taking control Tom Pendergast expanded the machine becoming a major political force to be reckoned with. However, his interest lay not in the politics of an elected official, but rather that of a behind the scenes power, and in 1915 he left public office.

Boss Tom set his sights on the leadership of the local Democratic Party and his plan called for the ousting of rival Joe Shannon. His succeeded in doing so, and by 1916 was at the helm of the party. He immediately put his position, power and influence to work. With control of the police department he insured that prostitution would be protected. With the power to appoint excise commissioners liquor interests were served. Contractors benefited, receiving special consideration on county road projects. Brother Big Jim had fully supported local gambling interests and it would be no different now. North side gambling interests continued to work for Tom and he for them. The indigent were provided Christmas dinners, fuel handouts, food and clothing, all on the machine's dime.

Boss Tom

One writer described Tom Pendergast as a "blued eyed, light haired, heavy weight, carrying 220 pounds on a stocky 5'9" frame. His rumbling voice emphasized his rugged appearance, as did his massive face with a powerful jaw, broad nose and wide mouth." He resided with his wife and daughter in a lavishly furnished mansion costing $175,000 at 5650 Ward Parkway. He dressed neatly in tailored suits sent to him by Wolf Brothers clothier. He was devoted to his family and spent his nights at home, away only if business called.

In contrast to his mansion his headquarters, the Jackson Democratic Club at 1908 Main Street, where he had moved to from the north side in 1926, was located in a shabby business district. His dingy office was one of three rooms on the second floor of a brick building. Often arriving before the sunup, traveling in a chauffeur driven car - unbelievably Boss Tom did not know how to drive - he would find people already lined up waiting, sometimes 100 to 200 in number. Businessmen, bankers, job seekers, office holders, panhandlers, politicians, anyone seeking assistance or a favor. This was the political center of the universe, so much so that the State Capitol in Jefferson City, Missouri, was referred to as "Uncle Tom's Cabin."

In 1922 the co-owner of a downtown haberdashery, a good democrat, was on the verge of closing down the shop, a failure. As it turned out Boss Tom had plans for this individual, tapping him to run for a position on the three-member Jackson County Administrative Court. Harry S. Truman won the election, and as the saying goes the rest is history.

Boss Tom's day at 1908 Main normally ended at noon. He would have a light lunch sent up from a restaurant next door. Then his attention was focused on his passion, horse race betting. After carefully studying the racing forms Tom would place his wagers on races at various tracks around the country and listen to the races using a private race wire service hooked up in the office.

The rest of the afternoon was taken up with his other interests including concrete, wholesale liquor, asphalt, paving construction, and hotels. Many of these companies relied on municipal contracts, and as he saw it his product was as good as any, voicing his opinion, "why haven't I got as much right to do business with the city as any one else?" By six o'clock he was home for dinner with the family, wife Carolyn, a son Thomas Jr., daughters Marceline and Aileen Margaret.

Tom continued to run the North End's "Little Italy" district until 1926 when he moved his headquarters from the north side to 1908 Main, putting his man, and business partner in Ross Construction Company, Mike Ross in charge. Ross, an Irishman, had a group of young Italian men working for him including a young man with a bright future by the name of John Lazia.

Chapter V

John Lazia
The Outfit & Politics

F OR MANY LIVING in the squalid and substandard conditions of the north end, suffering discrimination, terrorized by the Black Hand, having limited opportunities for honest jobs, the prospect of easy money and a way out was too tempting to pass up. Pendergast machine ward Captains wielded great influence in the awarding of concessions for illegal operations to selected leaders, including limited local monopolies over the selling of narcotics. Other promising candidates working under the tutelage and control of the ward boss were given spots in bawdy houses, gambling operations, and tasked with enforcement duties. All in all it was an especially corrupting influence on the younger generation.

With the prospect of easy money and the risk of prosecution minimal, the young men of the north side quickly and readily joined up, submitting to a form of servility, impelled to follow the orders of the political functionaries and their allied criminal bosses. In far too many cases these young men came from good families and had bright futures. One of them was John Lazia.

John Lazia, known to many as Brother John, has been described as the most successful and probably the most discussed Kansas City figure of the time, drawing even more attention than his ally machine boss Tom Pendergast. His criminal background and underworld reputation were not solely responsible for the fascination engendered in a curious public. He had personality and charm. He looked amiable and modest, spoke good enough English, told humorous stories, chewed gum constantly, and smiled often behind his rimless glasses. There was little about his appearance and manner to mark him a gangster, other than his ever-present burly bodyguard Charlie Carrollo. He was described as the first north end gangster to come out of that section of the city wearing a white shirt, as his underlings were recognizable in their customary black shirts, and the armored touring cars they drove.

Lazia was not the normal secretive, mysterious figure operating within the confines of the North End neighborhood. Instead he made a point to be seen in public, a man about town, frequenting night spots, sports events, gambling establishments, racing a high powered speed-boat around Lake Lotawana where he maintained a villa type residence. He was out there for all to see rubbing shoulders with a cross section of the city to include many people in high places.

Appearances aside, force remained the instrument by which he ruled, as it had to be in his world, but force alone did not account for his success. He is said to have commented that he had met with Al Capone of Chicago and denounced Capone's methods. "There is little need here in Kansas City for violence. In Chicago it may be different, but we can keep things pretty straight without bloodshed. We're not going to have out of town men muscling in here. That would cause war." Lazia reputedly had met with Al Capone, the Boss of organized crime in Chicago, to work out an informal, and mutually beneficial, arrangement based on Capone's desire to use Kansas City as a bootlegging distribution center.

Lazia possessed organizational, executive and leadership abilities enabling him to operate on a level beyond simple threats and violence. During his time the criminal organization would experience more stability leading to a reduction of internal conflicts, and a prohibition against killings amongst themselves. Disputes and grievances were to be sorted out by the organization. Criminal activities such as gambling would be organized and controlled. He insured that his followers profited, and were taken care of when in trouble. However, for those who would oppose him or stand in his way he could be ruthless, and there were those who would try.

The most common birth date for John Lazia is 1897, however one official document Lazia personally filled out showed a date of birth of September 28, 1895, at New York City. He was the son of an immigrant laborer, and his schooling took him through the 8th grade. He found work as a clerk in the office of a reputable law firm, studied law, and seemed destined for legitimacy and a legal career, but it was not to be.

A Rocky Start For Brother John

There is a rite of passage for the prospective mob member, a type of proving ground where the prospect establishes his worthiness and displays the qualities the upper ranks of the crime family are looking for. As the young men brought over from the homeland as children or those born here mature, moving beyond youth gangs or engaging in street crimes, they form a pool from which the organized crime outfits recruit new members. It is a pattern that repeats itself over and over in the progression of those who made it in the mob. Studies of the gangsters who played major roles in the growth of organized crime in America show the majority got their start in the rackets before 1920. John Lazia was one of those.

As a young man of 20 or so, Lazia was known to the authorities as a the chief lieutenant of "Black Mike" McGovern, leader of a gang of "motor car thieves" and hold up men that terrorized the city in the mid 1900s operating out of the north side. Lazia's criminal exploits had led to any number of arrests but no prosecutions. His good fortune ran out in the year 1916.

The new year of 1916 was just six days old when "Black Mike", Lazia and Tommy Bosco paid an evening visit to the Saloon owned by Herman Allman at 2513 E. 15, and robbed Allman and his customers of $200 and some diamonds. Shortly after the robbery they were arrested by Police Captain John Ennis, but not before engaging the officer in a gun battle. Free on a $5000 bond the charismatic Lazia made it known that he was ready to change his ways. He was reported to have begun following the revival meetings of noted preacher of the day Billy Sunday, and as a result he had seen he light. That promise quickly fell by the way side when he was arrested on February 29, 1916 charged with brandishing a revolver in a 12th Street restaurant.

On an early Sunday morning in March 1916, burglars broke a window at the Parker Machinery Company, 709 N. 6th Street, Kansas City, Kansas, entered the premises, and made off with a variety of tools. The burglars then moved down the street to the George Miller Produce Store at 509 N. 6th Street. Using the stolen tools they attempted to crack the safe but were unable to get it open.

The frustrated bandits fled, abandoning the stolen tools on the floor of the produce company.

Police responding to the scene at the produce company quickly traced the stolen tools back to Parker Machinery. Scouring that crime scene police found little in the way of clues except for the shards of broken glass under the window where entry had been made. Lazia may well have gotten away clean except for the fact he left a fingerprint from his right ring finger on one of those fragments of broken glass.

Based on the fingerprint identification police picked Lazia up at 12th and Grand, and upon waiving extradition he was brought to City Court, Kansas City, Kansas, for arraignment. Bond was set at $500, and Lazia was remanded to the county jail. His stay would be short. Certain friends appeared to make his bond securing his release. The authorities claimed to have forgotten exactly who those friends were, and who had come up with the $500 bond money.

Lazia still had to answer for the charges filed in February of brandishing a firearm, and he indeed had the perfect defense when appearing in court. At his preliminary hearing he displayed a deputy constable's commission issued to him by Clarence Stephens, a constable in the court of Justice Charles Clark. The fact that at the time the commission was issued Lazia was free on bond on charges of felony robbery apparently was not a good enough reason to deny him this privilege. However, this time the authorities seemed determined to see justice done. Upon dismissal of the charges in the lower court the authorities immediately refiled them in the higher criminal court, and upon arraignment bond was set at $2000. Lazia found himself back in jail when he failed to come up with the $2000.

When the time came for Lazia to face trial on the armed robbery charge stemming from the hold up at Herman Allman's saloon he was back in the Wyandotte Kansas County jail. Lazia figured he had a hole card to play, refusing to come up with bond money for his release, and even refused release without bond, letting it be known he was happy to remain in jail on the Kansas side. His strategy was obvious. He would take his chances on the Kansas burglary charge based on fingerprint identification, a new science, against serious felony charges in Missouri based on strong evidence, plus participating in a shoot out with a police captain.

Lazia's hole card was trumped when negotiations between Missouri and Kansas authorities resulted in the Wyandotte County District Attorney agreeing to dismiss the charges. Missouri authorities took custody of him on May 1, 1916, returning him to Jackson County to stand trial.

The events that followed would prove John Lazia was no ordinary youthful common criminal. He undoubtedly had caught the attention of certain "influential" forces recognizing in young Lazia an uncommon potential. The police reported the discovery of a plot to shoot up Justice Casimir Welch's court at the time of Lazia and "Black Mike" McGovern's arraignment, and yet another plan to break them out of jail.

The jury that convicted Lazia and McGovern of robbery received death threats, and had to be given special protection. Initially both were sentenced to a prison term of 15 years, however the presiding judge apparently saw some redeeming features in these two and cut three years off the sentence.

Newspaper accounts reported Lazia, while free on $10,000 appeal bond, receiving the aid from "powerful" allies in north side political circles who provided jobs for him while he awaited the decision of the appeals court. Lazia again ran a fowl of the law when on January 4, 1917 he was arrested in connection with the assault of a woman occurring that morning. The woman reported Lazia and others forced her to enter a "closed motor car" and attempted to "attack" her.

On December 10, 1917, his appeal rejected by the Missouri Supreme Court, Lazia reported to the Missouri State Penitentiary to start his prison sentence. He ended up serving only 8 months and 7 days. His parole was recommended by the Jackson County District Attorney, a probation officer, other party members, and was granted by a Pendergast connected Lt. Governor, Wallace Crossley, acting in the Governor's absence. Crossley described his decision as coming within the category of a "war measure" stating, "When men are needed as badly as now it seems wrong to keep them in prison."

On August 17, 1918, Lazia was escorted home by several north side political figures, taken to a barbershop for a shave, and feted to one of the biggest "blowouts" ever staged by his political friends. Meanwhile "Black Mike" McGovern remained in prison, apparently the Lieutenant Governor did not see the same need for McGovern to serve the country as he did with Lazia.

Upon returning to Kansas City, rather than military service, Lazia opted to take advantage of the political forces that had come to his support. Under the tutelage of Pendergast ward boss Mike Ross he moved up quickly. Another important political ally was James P. Aylward, a Kansas City lawyer tied closely to Joe Shannon while at the same time acting as a political advisor to Shannon's rival, Boss Tom Pendergast. Aylward was one of six boys, five of whom became lawyers, raised in humble circumstances in a five-room cottage on East 4th Street. He served as Chairman of the Democratic Party in Missouri, and was a widely respected and influential political figure. Lazia is alleged to have handled "some enforcement duties" for the machine through Aylward.

On top of his political successes he aptly applied his talents to criminal operations becoming involved in gambling and bootlegging activities. His leadership qualities proved substantial, developing a following among some up and coming toughs such as,

Gaetano Lococo, Charles Gargotta, Tony Gizzo and Charles Carrollo, all names that for many years in the future would be associated with the leadership of the criminal organization. Each of these individuals followed the same pattern, racking up criminal records involving "ordinary" crimes before graduating to the rackets.

Lazia Makes His Move

The fast rising John Lazia was putting together a political juggernaut so that by 1924 he laid claim to control of some 7500 votes in the north end ward. In 1926 he broke with his mentor Mike Ross forming the North Side Democratic Club. By 1928 Lazia's position, influence and backing had reached a point where he was ready and able to make a truly bold move to seize complete control.

Both Boss Tom Pendergast and his ward boss Mike Ross had moved out of the old neighborhood. Ross was running things in the north end as an absentee landlord, and Lazia resented having an Irishman controlling things on his home turf. He capitalized on the situation justifying his opposition of the established order as move for "home rule" for the Italian community. On bond election day in 1928, employing strong-arm tactics, Lazia took over. His men roamed the precincts in curtained sedans kidnapping several of Ross' lieutenants, inflicting other mayhem on Ross' ward healers, and threatening voters. When the polls closed the results showed Lazia's boys had delivered the greatest number of votes. Within a week Ross resigned his claims to the north end and his defeated ward heelers threw in with Lazia, or quit altogether.

The political waters were further muddied when in the wake of Lazia's takeover Pendergast's man James A. Reed, by now as U.S. Senator, received an unsigned letter alleging political chicanery led to Lazia's coup. The letter writer alleged, " This rebellion was led by an Italian by the name of Lazia. Lazia is the henchman of Jim Aylward, who in turn is Judge Welch's very close political friend." According to the writer Judge Cas Welch had ambitions to expand his political role to a level matching that of Boss Tom and Joe Shannon, and the rebellion had been instigated by Welch as a means to undercut Pendergast.

Whether or not there was any foundation for the anonymous allegations the information outlined in the letter coincided with reports that Lazia, prior to his take over of north end politics, was working for Aylward. In turn, north end racket boss Big Jim Balestrere was known to have ties to Aylward, and certainly would have had influence over Lazia. From these links one could construct a scenario wherein Balestrere, liking what he saw in the young Lazia, hooked him up with Aylward. Balestrere then used the alliance in orchestrating the north side political takeover, undercutting Boss Tom. All in all a plausible theory, the type of Machiavellian scheming that may well have propelled Lazia's political and criminal rise, for there is no question that Boss Tom's position was substantially altered following the coup.

Lazia proceeded to organize and grow the new North Side Democratic Club signing up 2500 members. Boss Tom Pendergast was not at all pleased with developments on the north side, initially making known his displeasure in an newspaper interview, proclaiming he would stand by the deposed Mike Ross.

Whatever Boss Tom's displeasure may have been Lazia was standing his ground. Either by reason of his charm or his power, or both, Boss Tom came around, and an alliance was forged. More than likely Pendergast understood fully his need of the north side votes Lazia now controlled along with the power of the criminal organization.

Lazia emerged as not only the recognized political leader, now staunchly supported by Tom Pendergast, but as the outward boss of the Italian criminal syndicate. Lazia's larger than life persona complicates the question of who truly wielded the power within the North End criminal outfit at this time. In this regard theories are plentiful, the real answers lost in antiquity.

It is clear that Joe DiGiovanni and Jim Balestrere remained powerful, influential figures, and with the passage of time their positions as behind the scene powers would be confirmed. Their outfit, composed of many Sicilian born members and former Black Hand extortionists, was the dominant force on the north side. A theory proposed by a knowledgeable source had Lazia paying off Jim Balestrere in return for being allowed to operate, as Lazia was not an inducted member of the DiGiovanni-Balestrere outfit. That some later time he, and his followers, became members of the outfit.

Another source, having personal involvement in north end activities, stated it was not until Lazia's death in 1934 that the old-line group became aware of the true extent of Lazia's activities and the amount of money he had been generating. It was at that time the two factions, Lazia's men and the old-line outfit, came together.

Other historical reporting of that time period speaks of Lazia as responsible for affecting a consolidation by reason his obvious talents, personality, political clout and leadership qualities That Lazia pulled the various factions together and gained the support of the old guard, who in turn approved of Lazia holding the position of boss, handling day to day activities. Under Lazia's leadership rules governing membership were established, and all criminal activities came under the control and scrutiny of the organization. Gambling was put on a business basis with territories outlined and prominent members selected to oversee these operations.

Still another possibility is that outfit leaders early on recognized Lazia's talents and had recruited him, making him a member of the organization. The unusual amount of support the 20 year old Lazia received when facing armed robbery charges, and then prison time, tends to support this proposition. With the support and guidance of the leadership he developed a strong political power base, attracting a following of his own. Lazia was groomed for the leadership spot, recognized as the perfect man to operate in the public realm, something men like DiGiovanni and Balestrere were not comfortable with. Orchestrating the north side political coup was the final step in elevating Lazia as the out front outfit boss.

Whatever the case may have been, Lazia emerged publicly as the leader of the local underworld, was accepted as such , and personally made no bones about who he was and what he represented.

The combination of prohibition, the continued growth, organization, and consolidation on the part of the Kansas City crime "family", and the growth of the Pendergast political machine, set the stage for a city wide open for all forms of vice and corruption. A political-criminal alliance became a fact of Kansas City life when Tom Pendergast and John Lazia forged their partnership in 1928, and there was no where to go but up.

The Lazia Reign

Evidence of Lazia's stature came the year after he assumed the role of north end political/criminal Boss, and Pendergast partner. Historically, the reign of John Lazia in Kansas City coincided with a period of growing sentiment in the underworld for some form of national crime syndicate. In furtherance of the concept a meeting of racket leaders from around the nation was scheduled for Atlantic City, N.J. on May 13, 1929.

As a backdrop to the Atlantic City meeting, in 1928 democrats nominated New York governor Al Smith to run for President. At this time he openly voiced his disdain for prohibition and he campaigned for its end, convinced it was unworkable and bad for the nation. Even though Smith was defeated the signs were apparent, prohibition's demise was a just a matter of time. This led to sentiment for a national conference to plan for the end of prohibtion on the part of syndicate bosses emerging from prohibition and expecting to maintain their position in the future. Nucky Johnson who ruled over Atlantic City would host the meeting, insuring one and all he could guarantee a safe haven.

By way of background, as a by-product of prohibition a myriad of criminal organizations developed made up of racketeers of all stripes and ethnic backgrounds. The lineup of men attending the Atlantic City meeting were some of the top men in what was truly the gangster era. The names of these racket figures are important, as there has been a tendency for many to equate organized crime strictly as "The Mafia." During this period these men often over shadowed Italian organized crime clans. Some of these syndicate figures worked in conjunction with Italian organizations, and in other cases they were bitter rivals. Many old line "Mustache Petes" were not prone to cooperative efforts, and became a bone of contention between them and the Americanized elements within that sphere.

On May 13, 1929, the crime delegates arrived taking over the President Hotel on the famous Atlantic City boardwalk. Those in attendance included Al Capone and Jake "Greasy Thumb" Guzik from Chicago. King Solomon represented Boston. After he was murdered in 1933 Hyman Abrams took over. Philadelphia's Max "BooBoo" Hoff, Waxey Gordon, and Harry Stromberg, aka, "Nig" Rosen were present. "Mo" Dalitz, Louis Rothkoph & Chuck Polizzi (true name, Leo Berkowitz) were Cleveland's representatives. Abe Berstein from

Detroit and Longie Zwillman of New Jersey were in attendance. Coming from New York City were Meyer Lansky, Louis Buchalter, Frank Erickson, Dutch Schultz (true name, Arthur Flegenheimer). Also from New York City were Lucky Luciano, Frank Costello, Frank Scalish, and Albert Anastasia considered Americanized hoodlums in favor of cooperation. John Torrio, formerly Chicago Boss and John Lazia, of Kansas City were present. The meeting would last three days.

Other prominent figures of the gangster era included Benjamin "Bugsy" Siegal; Frank "Buster" Wortman, influential St. Louis, Missouri, and East St. Louis, Illinois, gangster; James Michaels, leader of a Syrian gang in St. Louis; Irishman Dion O'Banion, and Polish racketeers George "Bugs" Moran and Hymie Weiss, bitter rivals of Al Capone; Dandy Phil Kastel of New Orleans; Owney "Killer " Madden from New York City and Hot Springs, Arkansas; and Isadore "Kid Cann" Blumfield of Minneapolis.

In what has been reported as "Lucky" Luciano's memories, he states cooperation in various areas of the illegal liquor racket was agreed on at the meeting, representing the start of a cartel where a group of organizations would operate jointly, decisions made by equals at the top, to develop a national monopoly beneficial to all. There were discussions as to a course of action if prohibition were to end, and much talk of entering the legitimate liquor industry if that were to happen, since they knew more about it than anyone else.

It is clear the conference was unsuccessful in ending all existing divides between the ethnic syndicates. At this point in time the concept of a formal National Crime Syndicate was probably too much for many of the delegates to grasp. The meeting was a big step in an unstoppable movement toward some form of syndication, and Kansas City's John Lazia was right in the middle of it.

Cosa Nostra

In cities across the nation, various factions within the Italian organized crime sphere were consolidating. This did not come without violence or happen simultaneously, but rather, depending on local conditions, in stages over a period of time. For instance, the situation in Kansas City differed from that in other cities by reason of the fact there were no rival criminal organizations or influential racket figures to be dealt with. Whereas in other areas various ethnic based criminal outfits and other prominent gangsters were in a struggle for underworld dominance. For an Italian crime organization to dominate it was imperative that internal strife be put aside, and unification achieved.

The year 1931 would prove pivotal in finalizing this process of coalescence. The final product came about as the result of a violent struggle for supremacy involving two prominent New York City crime outfits. Masseria, charged with murder in Sicily fled to America in 1903, and had fought his way to a position of number one among the New York City "families" in the early 1920s. On the other hand, Maranzano, a member of the Mafia in Sicily, was a relative newcomer arriving in this country in 1927 with a plan to take control of organized crime activities. He immediately began his campaign to wrest leadership away from Masseria. In character and style the two men were direct opposites. Masseria, in his mid 30s, was a vile, brutish man while Maranzano at 43 years of age was educated, refined, and scholarly, displaying those traits recognized in Sicily as "Mafioso."

Much has been written of these times and, as is often the case, historical accounts of the events are divergent, contradictory, and at times erroneous. Fact and legend mixed together. A detailed and lengthy account of the conflict is not helpful, as it is enough to say the rivalry deteriorated to the point Masseria sought to wipe out all of

Maranzano's followers, whether in New York City or anywhere else, known as the Castelmarrese, the region in Sicily they hailed from. What followed has been labeled the Castelmarrese war, and it ended up costing the lives of some 60 members of the two clans during 1930 and 1931.The bloodshed generated heat not only within law enforcement, but also within the Italian underworld. Sides were taken with some clan leaders remaining neutral.

Thirty-four years old Charles "Lucky" Luciano had been relentlessly recruited by both Masseria and Marranzano, so highly was he regarded. Although reluctant, he finally joined up with Masseria and was made the Boss' number one man. Luciano had his own following, and they represented the younger, more Americanized element within these outfits. They had no use for the "greasers" like Masseria and Marranzano and many of their Mafia beliefs. According to Nicolo Gentile the only reason Luciano decided to throw in with Joe the Boss was his belief that of the two warring bosses Masseria would be the easier to unseat as part of his modernization plan.

A critical element in this saga is the apparent lack of recognition by Masseria or Marranzano of the gap existing between their old world, clannish philosophies and the innovative, expansionist views of the younger "Americanized" element. A perfect example of this clash of cultures can be found in the apparent refusal by these two heavyweights, or any of their old-line counterparts, to attend the 1928 Atlantic City meeting that included "outsiders."

Luciano represented those men born in the United States of immigrant parents, or brought here as infants or young children, growing to maturity in a city environment, exposed to the influence, opportunities and variety of American culture. John Lazia was one in that category. They attended school only as long as they had to, their departure hastened by ridicule for their lack of language skills, dress and cultural differences. Besides, the real action was out on the streets, and they turned to crime as their way up and out of their squalid surroundings.

As youthful criminals they often ran with non-Italians, as was the case with Johnny Lazia, Tony Gizzo, and many other of Kansas City's racket figures. They came of age in time for the prohibition era and served as recruits for expanding criminal outfits, led by the older immigrant gangsters referred to as "Greasers" or "Mustache Petes."

The Lucianos and Lazias of this era were a different breed with different values, not as connected to old world mindsets, protocols, or concepts such as pride honor and vendetta, They were not as suspicious and distrustful of the outside world as were their elders who believed it unwise to venture outside their "Little Italy" domain. They saw the rackets for what they were, a means to big money without the risk of conventional crime, and sought to expand them beyond the limited borders of an Italian community, employing efficient, businesslike methods of operation. On one hand they viewed the Mafia-like culture as too restrictive and outdated, but on the other hand realized there were many powerful people still welded to it and that there were beneficial aspects that had to be retained.

Recognizing the Masseria-Marranzano conflict as a golden opportunity to purge the old line "Mustache Pete's", Luciano, as a first step secretly approached Marranzano with a proposition. He would orchestrate the murder of Joe Masseria on the condition there would be no reprisals against members of the Masseria organization.

On April 15, 1931, Luciano invited his boss to lunch at a Coney Island restaurant. After a lavish meal, a tradition when a Boss is to be removed, the restaurant now empty, Luciano excused himself to use the restroom. Four gunmen entered the restaurant and executed Joe the Boss. Luciano explained to the police he had been in the restroom, and upon hearing shots returned to the dining room where he found Masseria shot dead. Luciano, of course, had no idea who may have committed the murder.

Maranzano, now at the top of the heap, moved quickly to consolidate his position, and several meetings were held, one in Chicago and one in the Bronx, New York attended by representatives of the various "families" around the nation. Among the many in attendance at the meeting in the Bronx was a young member of the Marranzano clan named Joseph Valachi. Some thirty years later Valachi would turn on the mob spilling the secrets of his organization to the FBI. In 1963, in dramatic testimony before a congressional committee investigating organized crime, the first insider ever to go public, he described the events of the Castelmarere war, the gathering called by Maranzano, and the nature of an organization called La Cosa Nostra.

Valachi testified there were 400 to 500 Italian crime "family" members from around the country in attendance at the Bronx meeting. In a lengthy oration Maranzano frequently used the term Cosa Nostra (Our Thing) when referring to the criminal organization he was forging. The name stuck with the members and was the name they used amongst themselves. Marranzano set forth the structure, hierarchy and organization of what he referred to as a Cosa Nostra "family." New York, as the largest city, would have five distinct "families" and he rewarded Luciano for his treachery by appointing him as Boss of one of them. Crime families were recognized in some 26 other locales, and together formed a national crime organization

In some circles Maranzano is given credit for recognizing the impracticality of attempts to duplicate the Sicilian Mafia in view of the vast differences between American society and culture and that of Sicily. The Sicilian Mafia of that time was a loose knit largely rural conglomeration of clans operating independently, its foundation a Sicilian culture defined by a "Mafia mentality", bound by a code of silence, distrustful of legal authority, and affording the Mafiosi respect. This was not the case in America, and therefore Marranzano's blue print called for a formally structured organization with a governing constitution.

Marranzano saw himself as an American Caesar and thus anointed himself "Boss of Bosses", overlord of the entire organization, with the right to a cut of everything. This did not sit well with many of those in attendance, especially the younger element. He also discouraged outside alliances, another rule invoking disagreement, as it was viewed as shortsighted and smacked of old world clannishness.

In Luciano's eyes consolidation would not be complete, nor would his purge of the "greasers", until Maranzano was eliminated. It was clear to Luciano and his allies they were not the only fish in the underworld pond, but rather one element in what hopefully would become a national crime syndicate. If Cosa Nostra was to survive, prosper, and eventually dominate, the current climate called for cooperation with outsiders. This would never occur with Marranzano at the helm. At the same time Marranzano realized his hold would never be secure until Luciano was eliminated.

On September 10, 1931 Luciano, employing non-Italian outside gunman, had Maranzano killed preempting Maranzano's own plot to eliminate Luciano.

Lucky Luciano could easily have laid claim to the title of Boss of Bosses but he rejected the idea, as it had no place in his scheme of things. Instead he proposed a ruling commission made up of the Bosses of the five New York families, the Chicago Boss, and the Bosses from two other cities. In the commission system each Cosa Nostra "family" is independent, generally free to operate without outside interference. The commission is in place to arbitrate any disputes or conflicts between "families" and enforce certain rules and edicts that all families must abide by.

The label Cosa Nostra, in vogue on the east coast, did not take hold with "families" everywhere, however following Joe Valachi's testimony it became the accepted name publicly for the national Italian crime syndicate. In Kansas City crime "family" parlance the term outfit or clique was most commonly used.

The passage of time would prove Luciano and his Americanized peers, who took control were right, as Cosa Nostra held together as other syndicates fell apart, and emerged as the dominant force in organized crime in America.

Troubling Times For Brother John

In May 1931 Lazia dodged a bullet, not an assassin's, but rather one fired by the government. Lazia was one of 47 individuals indicted in a bootleg liquor conspiracy allegedly involving Capone backed liquor products. Included in those indicted were his close associate Charlie Carrollo, and two Wichita, Kansas liquor and gambling operators aligned with Lazia, Max Cohen and Bobby Carnahan. Seeing that Lazia's name was on the door as President of the North Side Finance Company, a firm that provided motor cars for rum runners involved in the bootleg operation, it was enough to get him indicted. Stepping up, Lazia's pal Charlie Carrollo, although carried as an officer in the firm, admitted to the Government he was more than that, he was in fact the president regardless of whose name was on the door. Carrollo's "confession" was sufficient to get Lazia off the hook. Carrollo stood the conviction paying $3500 in fines, a small price for the boost in stature that came with taking the heat for the Boss.

Lazia may have skated on the bootleg conspiracy case, but his North Side Finance Company drew the interest of other federal authorities. In the fall of 1931 U.S. Internal Revenue Agent Harry D. Beach became very interested in the company along with the North Side Distributing Company, both integral parts of the Sugar House Syndicate, and both connected to John Lazia. Agent Beach scrutinized Lazia's taxes and uncovered income for the years 1929 and

1930, including income from gambling interests, and that Lazia had failed to file any returns for those years.

The time came for Agent Beach to call Lazia in for an interview and it took place on March 9, 1932 at the offices of Intelligence Section of the Internal Revenue Service. During the interview Lazia explained it all away claiming he had gambled away far more than any income he had for those two years.

Three days after the interview, at 11:30 p.m., two men appeared at the apartment-hotel where Agent Beach resided informing the night clerk they were looking for Beach, providing the clerk with an apartment number. The night clerk explained they had the wrong apartment number, and besides, Beach was not home. The two then departed.

Agent Beach, a bachelor, had placed an advertisement for a room-mate but the ad did not reveal his name or that of the apartment/hotel where he resided, only a telephone number to call. The following day at 2:15 p.m. the same two men appeared and called up to Beach's apartment referring to the advertisement. Beach invited them up. He was curious how they could have known his name and how to find him. The two men not only had no logical answer to those questions, but also were vague and evasive about who they were. Beach played along providing little about himself, claiming he was an accountant, mentioning only the building where he worked. In fact it was the building housing the offices of the Internal Revenue Service where Lazia had been interviewed, and the two mystery men knew it.

Beach sensed something was wrong and was not at all comfortable with the situation he found him self in. It appeared the two were about to leave when one asked if he could have a glass of water. As Beach went to the kitchen he heard one of the men say, "He's the one we want". Whereupon Beach was violently assaulted, beaten and kicked repeatedly, left for dead. Rushed to a hospital, it was found he had multiple factures of the jaw, and a fracture of the skull behind his right ear. He was not able to return to work for several months. In fact Beach never fully recovered, and passed away on September 9, 1936, partially as the result of the beating.

There was no doubt whatsoever robbery was not the motive, nothing having been taken from Beach or the apartment. The Internal Revenue Agents were convinced the motive for the attempted murder was Beach's investigation of the gangster element.

Fellow agents weren't going to let the investigation die and they stepped in to take it over. Not surprisingly they met with staunch resistance in their attempts to secure the cooperation of potential witnesses who were being asked to provide information about racketeers like John Lazia. Despite these hurdles they made progress uncovering Lazia's ownership of a greyhound racetrack and the Cuban Gardens gambling club. Lazia disguised his ownership by using the names of employees of the Merchants Bank for record purposes. The locations were then leased out, the rental income collected by a Merchants Bank cashier, some $6000 a year, and distributed to Lazia.

Other hidden sources of income were located and eventually sufficient evidence of a tax liability developed to support a charge that Lazia failed to file income tax returns for 1929 and 1930. The agent's investigation disclosed Lazia had net income of $82,042.25 for 1929, and $98,290.83 for 1930 resulting in a tax liability of $26.909.01 that was due and owing. It would be fair to say, as substantial as these numbers were, they were by no means all of the Lazia's income, rather only that which the government was able to uncover.

To put these income figures in perspective, the average annual income in the 1920s for postal workers was $2128; federal government employees in executive departments, $1809; coal miners $1691; telephone company employees $1117; teachers $1277; iron and steel workers $1687.

The statute of limitations for the tax year 1929 was due to run out on March 15, 1933. On March 14, 1933 the United States Attorney filed a criminal information charging Lazia with intentional failure to file a tax return for the year 1929. Charges for the year 1930 were held in abeyance pending presentation of the case to the next Federal Grand Jury scheduled to be in session in September 1933.

In a repeat of the events of 1916, when Brother John faced armed robbery charges, the politicians once again were there for him. In a letter dated May 12, 1933, Boss Tom Pendergast wrote to Postmaster General James A. Farley as follows:

> Dear Jim,
>
> Jerome Walsh and John Lazia will be in Washington to see you about the same matter that I had Mr. Kemper talk to you about. Now, Jim, Lazia is one of my chief lieutenants and I am more sincerely interested in his welfare than anything you might be able to do for me now or in the future. He has been in trouble with the Income Tax Department for some time. I know it was simply a case of being jobbed because of his Democratic activities. I think that Frank Walsh spoke to the proper authorities about this. In any event, I wish you would use your utmost endeavor to bring about a settlement of this matter. I cannot make it any stronger except to say that my interest in him is greater than anything that might come up in the future. Thanking you for any and everything you can do, I remain,
>
> Sincerely your friend

During the summer of 1933 Lazia, and his high powered attorneys, Frank Walsh, of New York City and his son, Jerome, had several conferences with government officials as efforts continued to resolve the matter in Lazia's favor.

September 1933 rolled around and the United States Attorney in Kansas City had yet to receive his marching orders from Washington D.C. authorizing him to present the tax case to the grand jury. The grand jury session was about to commence and the jurors made known to Federal Judge Merrill E. Otis their desire to proceed with an inquiry into the Lazia tax matter. The judge informed the grand jury they did not need authorization from the United States Attorney, and were free to look into the matter. All was resolved when the U.S. Attorney received permission to proceed with the case.

On September 16, 1933 Lazia was indicted for the willful failure to file a return for the year 1930, and for tax evasion for the years 1929 and 1930. The case went to trial before Judge Otis on February 5, 1934. Brother John's allies rallied to his defense. Each time the trial jury was taken to the Pickwick Hotel for meals, automobiles filled with menacing looking men cruised slowly down the street keeping pace with the jurors as they walked to and from the court house. No talk came from the cars, but sufficient signs were made to leave an impression on them. Near the end of the trial as the jurors were returning to the court house a youngster playing the role of news boy waiving one lone newspaper ran past them shouting, "Extra, Extra. Jury does its duty and acquits Lazia."

Lazia's allies may have won a partial victory. On February 14, 1934 Lazia was found guilty on misdemeanor charges of failure to file tax returns for 1929 and 1930, but acquitted of the felony counts of tax evasion. Fourteen days later he was sentenced to 12 months jail time and a $2500 fine on each count, with the prison sentence and fine on the second count suspended, plus a 5-year term of probation.

Lazia filed an appeal petition and was released on $5000 bond. With the conviction and one year of jail time hanging over his head Lazia went back to work.

Home Rule

At a time prior to Lazia's running a foul of the I.R.S., reform strategies, as they often did ended up backfiring. In an effort to eliminate patronage, recognized by all as the lifeblood of the machine, the reformers pushed to rewrite the city charter. Part of their proposal called for the hiring of a city manager who would be required to evaluate city employees based solely on performance. Additionally, they pushed to reduce the 31 member city council down to a nine- member council. Although the reformer's efforts proved successful, the strategy backfired when in the November 1925 election Pendergast's candidates won a 5-4 majority on the council handing control to the machine. Pendergast quickly hired Henry McElroy as city manager, and he took office in April 1926. McElroy, despite a city charter prohibition, openly announced the city would be run on a strictly partisan basis. Corruption at city hall became rampant with McElroy manipulating the books in a system he labeled "country bookkeeping."

Another coup for the political-criminal alliance came in 1932. Since before the turn of the century the police department had been under State of Missouri control. In 1932 the State Supreme Court ruled the police department should be under city control, or what was popularly known as home rule. Following the court's decision, at the direction of Boss Tom, John Lazia and his constant companion Charles Carrollo, representing the crime syndicate, were given a major say in the Kansas City Missouri Police Department. With Lazia as one of three people awarding positions on the force, men with criminal records, even convictions, were hired on. Officers of Republican persuasion were fired, the criminal records of some 300 outfit associates and others were erased from the files, and a policy was forged protecting vice and gambling interests. To top it off Lazia was instrumental in hiring as police chief a former used car salesman.

Police Officers were told where they could reside, how to vote, and were required to deliver their quota of votes on election day or lose their job. Police employees had to give up half their salary to the machine, and of, course, officers had to look the other way when crimes were committed by those who bought themselves protection.

The system was so corrupt that the police department had a squad whose function was to ensure that no protected establishments were raided. Police Officers were used to drive cars for the gangsters, and motorcycle officers were used by the underworld to deliver narcotics. Despite such disgraceful conditions there were still honest, dedicated officers, and for them this was their worst nightmare. However, their day would come.

The same corrupt system was in place for other city departments, the district attorney's office, and the courts. In the grips of the political/criminal machine dominating every aspect of city life, Kansas City was indeed an open city.

In a 1932 speech Rabbi Mayerberg fired a broadside at the Pendergast machine in a scathing attack pronouncing the city had been given up to a band of crooks and racketeers, and it was time for action. It was one of the earliest such attacks by a prominent citizen and religious leader. There was risk involved in speaking out and Mayerberg was certainly cognizant of the threat, installing bullet proof-proof glass in his automobile. Fortunate it was that he did so, as an attempt was made on his life, his car sprayed with bullets. His call for action did not go unheeded It was directly responsible for the formation of the National Youth Movement composed of young professionals and women. Although they were forced to meet in secret and had little early success, seeds were sown that would eventually take root for a future time when the movement would play an important role in effecting reform.

Rough seas were ahead for Brother John. Besides the tax conviction and jail sentence hanging over his head, his role in formulating a new police enforcement policy, one that overlooked minor infractions and concentrated on major crimes, would come back to bite him. The policy did not, as anticipated, result in a noticeable reduction in the level of crime. In fact, there were still numerous major crimes taking place, and expected cooperation on the part of some important underworld elements did not materialize. Competition for gambling and liquor concessions seemed to be increasing despite a policy of tolerance, and seemingly more control by the north end criminal outfit. This put Lazia in a bad light and besides that he, along with other prominent underworld leaders, still had various threats to contend with.

One such threat came from out of town criminals who viewed Kansas City under home rule as a safe haven. It was no secret that a policy had been hammered out by the political-criminal syndicate whereby the police would in effect grant protection to wanted fugitives. The consequences of this dynamic would not bode well for Lazia or the home rule doctrine. Similar to the Sicilian Mafia Don who controlled all crime in his domain, nothing of any significance occurred in Kansas City without Lazia's knowledge. However, that did not prevent him from taking the heat in the wake of so many sensational crimes that came with an open city.

The Midwest was inundated with dangerous men and women who individually, or in teams or family groups, roamed from state to state robbing, kidnapping and murdering. The names have been immortalized in books and films. John Dillinger, "Pretty Boy" Floyd, "Machine Gun" Kelly, the Ma Barker gang, Wilbur Underhill, Harvey Bailey, Bonnie Parker and Clyde Barrow and many others. They left their small town Midwest homes and farms adding their crime sprees to the roaring twenties era and the wide-open thirty's. FBI Director J. Edgar Hoover referred to the Midwest as "The cradle of crime." These desperados were not connected with any of the big city organized crime cartels, however their sensational headline grabbing crimes, flamboyant conduct, and over the top violence, overshadowed the big city racketeers. Kansas City represented a safe oasis and many would find their way to the city for some R&R.

A notorious bank robber and fugitive, Harvey Bailey had been living well, under an assumed name, in a luxurious apartment bordering the Country Club Plaza district. Left alone by the police and feeling secure, a pleasant round of golf seemed in order. It was the 11th day July 1932 when Bailey, and three other wanted criminals, hit the links. At the conclusion of the round Federal Agents were there to meet the foursome, arresting Bailey and two of his golfing partners, mail train robbers and prison escapees out of Chicago. One of the foursome escaped arrest. He would return to Kansas City a year later and play center stage in possibly the most infamous crime in the annals of Kansas City, the Union Station Massacre. His name was Frank Nash.

Kidnappings abounded in this era. Michael Katz, Chairman of the Board of the Katz Drug Company, was kidnapped in 1930 and released after payment of a $100,000 ransom. On December 16, 1931 Nell Donnelly was the victim of a kidnapping having a most unusual and unexpected ending. The story is recounted in a movie, "Nelly Don: A Stitch in Time" and a companion book, by local Kansas Citizen Terence M. O'Malley

Nell Donnelly was the founder of The Donnelly Garment Manufacturing Company operating under the trade name Nelly Don, a firm that grew to be the largest of its kind in America. On the evening of December 16, 1931 she was returning home from her Nelly Don office in downtown Kansas City with her driver, 28 year old George Blair at the wheel. As the car attempted to pull into the drive of the Donnelly mansion at 52nd and Oak they encountered a car blocking the driveway entrance. Three men rushed Donnelly's car, seized Mrs. Donnelly and her chauffeur and drove off. They were taken to a remote farmhouse where Mrs. Donnelly was forced to write a ransom note demanding $75,000, and threatening Mrs Donnelly would be blinded and George Blair killed if the money was not paid.

Long time Pendergast ally James A. Reed, by this time a former U.S. Senator from Missouri, had secretly fathered a child with Nell and would later marry her. Upon news of the kidnapping Reed rushed to the Donnelly home. He focused his ire on John Lazia who denied any involvement on the part of the criminal organization explaining such a crime would only focus unwanted attention on the syndicate. Reed gave Lazia 24 hours to find Nell or he would use his considerable influence in exposing to the nation the full extent of Lazia's operations.

Lazia's men, turned detectives, were able to identify a local restaurant owner who had knowledge of the crime. Their powers of persuasion well honed, the local man provided a map to the farmhouse where the two kidnap victims had been held for some 34 hours. At 4:10 am December 18, 1931 the Kansas City Missouri Chief of Police, waiting in his office for word of developments, received an anonymous telephone call advising him where they could pick up Nell and her driver. Lazia's men had rescued them, but true to the code Lazia would not reveal any other facts or identify the culprits, leaving that to the police to sort out.

The ringleader of the scheme was identified as 39 years old Martin DePew. He may well have felt secure in far away South Africa where he had fled, but he was eventually located, arrested and returned to the United States. His two accomplices were 31 year old Walter Werner and Charles Mele. All three were convicted and sent to prison.

In yet another headlines grabbing kidnapping, the victim this time was Mary McElroy, 25 years old daughter of Boss Tom's City Manager Henry McElroy. On a Saturday morning in late May 1933, four men, having big time ambition but little in the way of criminal talent, hatched the plot to snatch Ms. McElroy. Two of the kidnappers posing as delivery men took Mary from the McElroy residence delivering her to a hideout where she was secured with chains. The kidnappers demanded $60,000 ransom from her father but he was successful in bargaining it down to $30,000. As the story goes, it was John Lazia who took on the task of getting the ransom money together.

The $30,000 ransom was paid, and 34 hours after she was taken Mary was released, picked up by her father and brother on the Kansas side not far from the state line. Four kidnappers were identified and tracked down, convicted and sent to prison. The ringleader received a death sentence, commuted to life based on Mary's plea to the Governor. Mary was apparently badly damaged by the experience, suffering nervous breakdowns, and in 1940 shooting herself to death. .

The notorious George "Machine Gun" Kelly was the mastermind behind another kidnapping, one involving a wealthy Oklahoma City, Oklahoma oil man Charles F. Urschel. On July 23, 1933 Urschel was kidnapped from his home and held for a ransom of $200,000. Urschel was hid out at the home of relatives of Kelly's wife in Paradise, Texas, awaiting payment of the ransom. The ransom instructions called for an Urschel family friend to bring the ransom money to Kansas

City. There was speculation Kansas City was chosen as the payoff site due to the city's reputation as a safe haven. On the afternoon of July 30, 1933 the ransom courier, as instructed, was walking near the LaSalle Hotel when an unknown individual approached him and relived him of the ransom money.

Urschel was released unharmed, and played a major role in unraveling the case. While in captivity he remained alert to his surroundings and was able to document for the FBI Agents the time each afternoon a plane flew over the place where he was held. The agents working with this information were able to pin point the farmhouse in Paradise, Texas, where Urschel had been taken. Harvey Bailey, arrested the prior year on a Kansas City golf course, was nabbed at the farmhouse in possession of some of the ransom money. Kelly was tracked to Memphis, Tennessee, where in the early morning hours of September 26, 1933 as he was arrested by FBI agents he shouted out, "Don't shoot G-Men", a label that would forever attach to agents of the FBI.

June 17, 1933 marks the day of what is probably the most infamous crime committed in the history of the city. Frank Nash a notorious killer and bank robber was a hunted man wanted as an escapee from Leavenworth Penitentiary three years earlier. His luck had held when federal agents just missed him in July 1932 after finishing a round of golf in Kansas City. Almost a year later federal agents caught up with him arresting him at Hot Springs, Arkansas. Immediately upon Nash's arrest the word went out to his criminal brethren, and the authorities escorting him realized there could be trouble.

Nash was transported by train arriving at Kansas City's Union Station on June 17. He was then to be driven to the U.S. Penitentiary at Leavenworth, Kansas. As he was being transferred in broad daylight from Union Station to a waiting auto for the trip to Leavenworth, three men attempted to free Nash engaging the escorting FBI Agents, local police detectives and an out -of-town Chief of Police, in a gun battle. In a hail of machine gun fire two Kansas City Missouri Police Detectives, an FBI Agent and the McAllister Oklahoma Chief of Police were killed. Two other FBI Agents were wounded. The escape attempt was unsuccessful as Nash was also killed in the melee.

Names of numerous suspects were proposed as perpetrators of what came to be known as the Union Station Massacre. Eventually three noted desperados, wanted fugitives of the day, Charles "Pretty Boy" Floyd, Vern Miller and Adam Richetti were identified as the responsible parties. They would all meet with violent deaths. Miller was the first, his severely battered, naked body found on November 29, 1933 in Detroit, Michigan. He had run afoul of local gangsters. "Pretty Boy" Floyd was run down by FBI Agents and local authorities and shot to death after a gun battle in an Ohio cornfield. Of the three only Richetti stood trial, and he was convicted and executed at the Missouri State Penitentiary.

The events of the afternoon of February 27, 1934 were described in one news account as the most daring and ruthless holdup in the history of Kansas City. On that cold afternoon, the temperature had dipped to 9 degrees below zero earlier in the day, Webster Kemner, Assistant Teller at the Commerce Bank at 10th & Walnut, accompanied by a bank guard, were making a routine trip to the Old Post Office at 9th and Grand. Kemner a young family man, slight of build, wearing horn- rimmed glasses was carrying a satchel containing $207,294, mainly in non-negotiable bonds. It was 3:40 p.m. when they turned east up 9th Street from Walnut, the bank guard several steps behind Kemner. A 1934 Ford westbound on 9th with four occupants pulled up and stopped next to the two bank employees.

Three men, all about 30, each wearing a different colored felt hat, jumped out of the car brandishing weapons. The man in the brown hat was carrying a machine gun, his job was to cover the street. The other two men threw the bank guard up against a building holding him in check. Kemner turned in their direction and one of the two holding the bank guard pointed his revolver at Kemner firing one shot hitting him in the chest, the satchel falling to the sidewalk. The shooter scooped up the satchel and dived into the waiting car, driven by the youngest of the four. The two other men got back in the car fled the scene. It had taken all of thirty seconds. Kemner staggered to the corner falling inside the doorway of a clothing store and died.

There were any number of witnesses to the murder, but the one person who could have made a difference unfortunately was of no help. A police officer was standing on the southeast corner of 9th and Walnut, opposite the shooting scene, was unaware of the events unfolding. He had not seen anything nor had he heard the shot. Because of the cold he had donned a pair of earmuffs.

The police believed they had solved the case identifying the four men as Sam DeCaro, Charles Tiabi, Phil "Foolie Babe" Lascuola, Meyer "Ace" Berman, and a man using the name Jimmy Bove. About two weeks after the murder the police searched Bove's apartment at 11th and Pacific recovering a Lugar machine pistol, two sawed-off shotguns, a .25 caliber automatic, a machine gun, pistol and shotgun ammunition, a blackjack, and a Bowie knife.

DeCaro was tried and convicted of murder receiving a life sentence. Indictments were secured for the remaining three who had fled, becoming fugitives. Almost three years later, in December 1936, Lascuola surfaced and was brought in by the police. It was apparently safe to come back to Kansas City, as by this time witnesses had suffered loss of memory or refused to appear at police headquarters to make identifications. In April 1936 "Ace" Berman was arrested as he walked on a downtown street.

The police were forced to inform the prosecutor there was insufficient evidence to support the murder charges pending against Lascuola and Berman, and they were dismissed. On May 11, 1937, two detectives stopped in at the pool hall at 1108 East Fifth Street looking for a burglary suspect. Instead, they happened upon a well-tanned, and relaxed Jimmy Bove reading a racing form. Bove acknowledged his tan, claiming he had been down south for the winter. Bove was taken into custody, but the case had fallen apart, one witness having been placed in a mental institution, and the charges had to be dismissed. The man's true name was not Bove. In future years the person behind that alias would play a significant role in Kansas City's organized crime scene. His real name was Carl James "Corky" Civella.

All of these high profile events were laid at the doorstep of home rule and John Lazia.

The Lusco-Welch Faction

Lazia would also have to deal with internal threats emanating from ambitious wannabe gangsters seeking their own piece of the action, and from certain established factions on the north side, such as the Joe Lusco crew. For those with ambition it seemed the deck was stacked against them with Lazia's followers getting the lion's share of the vice concessions.

Tall, heavyset, physically strong, Joe Lusco had spent his life in the north end earning the reputation of a man more likely to rely on his fists than a gun. He was on John Lazia's side when Lazia seized control of the north end political apparatus, establishing the North Side Democratic Club in 1928. Lusco later split off from the Pendergast-Lazia coalition, politically aligning himself with the Cas Welch "east side" faction.

As was common for north end figures, Lusco had business interests including a partnership role in the Lusco-Noto flower shop at

1039 Independence Avenue. The police considered Noto a suspect in the machine gun murder of bootlegger Jimmy Howard, bringing him in for questioning in February 1931. A search was conducted of Noto's residence at 546 Harrison turning up a stolen shotgun, a high powered rifle, two pistols, ammunition, five feet of fuse used in making homemade bombs, and miscellaneous items of merchandise. Some three months prior to the murder of Howard police officers found the door to Noto's home left open, and upon entering they observed machine gun ammunition but no machine gun.

Of further interest, four hours before Howard was killed on February 12, 1931 the flower shop building was raided by Federal agents and 500 gallons of whiskey was seized from rooms adjacent to the flower shop. A police official described the flower shop as a "rendezvous for racketeers." Lusco and Noto were using the business as a headquarters for a major bootlegging operation in the 1930s. As if it were not notorious enough, a violent confrontation between law enforcement and gangsters would mark Lusco's flower shop location, along with Union Station, as an infamous landmark in the city's history.

The brewing confrontation was fueled by the fact illegal liquor continued to be stored in the building housing the flower shop and federal agents knew it. A search warrant was obtained, and on the night of July 20, 1931, sometime after 8:00 p.m., five federal agents and 4 police officers raided the location catching the bootleggers by surprise. The agents and police officers fanned out searching rooms in the upstairs portion of the building. What follows is an account of the events of that evening as contained in official law enforcement reports.

Federal agents E.G. Havens and Curtis C. Burks, upon entering one room at the west end of the building, encountered John Calio (also listed as John Calia), aged 20, and Havens relieved Calio of a

.45 caliber automatic. Undiscovered by the agents was a second gun Calio had secreted on his person. Pulling this weapon Calio starting shooting. Agent Burks was hit in the stomach and went down. As Calio dashed from the room police officer Clarence Reedy, responding to the shots, was coming up the stairs. Calio fired at Reedy hitting him in the face, the bullet traveling down to his spinal column. Fleeing down the hallway Calio ran into Agent A.C. Anderson, and Calio shot and wounded the agent.

A call went out for assistance and Police Lieutenant E.L. Nelson quickly made it to the scene entering the building with his riot gun. He found Agent Burks lying on the floor badly wounded, and Agent A.C. Anderson, also wounded, directed him down the hallway where Calio had disappeared. Accompanied by another police Lieutenant, Nelson started down the hallway, kicking in the locked doors of rooms as he went. In one of the darkened rooms they found a large box filled with artificial flowers and rags. Nelson poked around in the box with his shotgun, felt something move and ordered whoever was hidden in there to come out. The man coming up from the box grabbed for the shotgun attempting to wrest it from Nelson's grip. Jerking back on the weapon it discharged hitting the man in the left side. John Calio, identified by the other officers as the man who shot the two federal agents and a police officer, died instantly.

The night's violence would claim one more life, that of an innocent bystander. Mumsford P. Wilson, 23 years of age, had just arrived in the city from Bessemer, Alabama, and by pure chance was walking down Independence Avenue. He arrived in front of the flower shop just as the gunfire broke out inside, and he was struck by what was believed to be a stray bullet. Just as he was hit a male figure burst from the building and fled the area. Eleven days later Wilson died of his wounds.

Later it was reported the person fleeing the scene, and may well have been Wilson's killer, was none other than Charles Floyd. Better known as "Pretty Boy" Floyd he would return to Kansas City a little less than a year later to reek further havoc as a participant in the Union Station massacre.

Federal Agent Curtis C. Burks shot twice, was able to hold on for two days after an operation to remove the bullets. Before he died he had one last chance to see his 3-month-old son, Curtis Jr. At 10:00 p.m. July 22, 1931, he passed away.

It is more than likely this episode, added to the other acts of violence, kidnapping and mayhem, characterizing the home rule period, did not sit well with John Lazia.

It was no secret that as early as 1930 there was dissension between Lazia and Joe Lusco over gambling concessions, political patronage, and other issues. Lusco broke away from the Lazia-Pendergast alliance and joined the Fifteenth Street faction headed by Cas Welch. One theory was the split had to do with Lusco's growing influence and ability to attract the younger generation of hoodlums. The political split is alleged to have grown into a feud.

By 1933 word was circulating that the "north side element", most likely a reference to Lazia, had made heavy financial demands on east side vice spots, and was enforcing them. The reference to east side vice spots probably meant Cas Welch and Joe Lusco. Politico Welch had been for years running his own mini machine on the near east side that included the most popular vice emporiums in the city. Furthermore, competition in the bootlegging arena, a racket Lusco was heavily into, was heating up, and strong protests were made concerning the levies imposed on various vice spots.

Caught up in the conflict was an individual named Ferris J. Anthon, and his name would be attached to one of the most sensational events in Kansas City's history of crime. Described by one author as a member of the Lusco faction, and in a news account as a member of an "east side gang", and bodyguard for Guy Given, a worker in the Welch political organization.

Anthon, whose alias was Tony Kansas, was considered a relative "small fry" in the scheme of things. He was a business partner of Given in the operation of the Arena Buffet, then located at 15th and Troost Streets. Anthon had an extensive police record and among other criminal activities was known as a "torch", an arsonist for hire. In August 1933 he was under investigation for an arson fire of a building at 10th and Troost Streets. One Kansas City Star news article reported there was evidence that in 1926, in Richmond, Missouri, Anthon set fire to a whole block of the business district just to destroy one building.

Anthon either was an unlucky crook, or simply inept. In Chicago two motorists stopped for speeding explained to the arresting officers they were on their way to pick up some alcohol for "Kansas City Tony." Capitalizing on this unsolicited bit of information, prohibition agents put together an undercover operation leading them to a gang of boot-leggers, including Anthon and 6 other subjects. On September 29, 1932 Anthon and his confederates were indicted and charged with being members of an "alcohol syndicate" selling $10 million worth of alcohol in the mid west over a five-year period. It just goes to show what prohibition did for otherwise "small fry" criminals like Anthon.

One night approximately a year later, Anthon, accompanied by his wife, mother-in-law, and brother-in-law, pulled his car up in front the Cavalier Apartment Hotel, 1109 Armour Boulevard in Kansas City where he was residing. It was 1:15 a.m. the 12th day of August 1933. As he exited the car two men approached Anthon and shot him eight times, killing him.

At that very moment Jackson County Sheriff Tom Bash, accompa-nied by his wife Jennie, and a 15 year old girl who would be staying at the Bash residence overnight, along with Sheriff's Deputy Lawrence Hodges, were nearby, proceeding in that very direction. They had attended a lawn party, and with Hodges at the wheel of the Sheriff's Department car, were heading south on Forest Avenue on the way to the Bash residence in 3400 block of Woodland. As they approached Armour Boulevard they spotted flashes, heard gunshots and screams. Bash ordered the car stopped, grabbed the shotgun carried in the car, and both he and Deputy Hodges got out.

Coming from Armour Boulevard a Buick automobile sped around the corner onto Forest, gunshots coming from the car directed at Bash and Hodges. Bash moved toward the Buick unloading two shotgun blasts into the windshield of the car causing it to career out of control, crashing into the Sheriff's car. Out in the Street Deputy Hodges was exchanging shots with a subject fleeing east on Armour Boulevard past Forest Avenue. Bash, now aware of more gunfire coming from Armour Boulevard, looked up to see another subject running directly at him firing a revolver in his direction. Bash had the gunman in the shotgun's sights and was about to fire when the gunman threw his revolver down screaming, "Don't shoot me! My God, man, don't shoot me!" Bash would later reflect, not shooting the gunman down was probably a mistake. He explained, "I had my gun trained on him. I was ready to cut loose. But when he dropped his revolver and pled, 'My God don't shoot me" a feeling came over me I was about to kill a defenseless man."

Inside the Buick Sam Scola, the driver, and Gus Fasone were dead, the tops of their heads blown off. Upon opening the car door a .45 caliber automatic fell from the hand of Fasone onto the pavement. The man Sheriff Bash now had pinned up against the building on the northwest corner of Armour and Forest was no longer pleading for his life, but was anything but comfortable. Bash had no trouble recognizing the man. He was Charles Gargotta, a key Lazia lieutenant.

The subject shooting it out with Deputy Hodges fled into an alley between Forest and Tracy Avenues, and eluded the deputy. Hodges did recover a .45 caliber automatic discarded by the fleeing gunman. Sheriff Bash recovered a similar weapon, the one Gargotta had been firing at him and threw to the pavement. Ballistics tests conducted identified it as the one used in the murder of Ferris Anthon. In all, five U.S army .45 caliber automatics were recovered at the scene, later identified as part of a batch of seventy -five .45s that had been stolen from a National Guard Armory in Kansas City, Kansas on October 23, 1932.

As expected, Gargotta's version of events varied drastically from that of Sheriff Bash. He had been visiting a woman who lived in the Cavalier Hotel Apartments, leaving her at 1:15 am. Just as he reached the lobby he heard shots fired and ran outside to see what was going on. Suddenly Sheriff Bash was advancing on him yelling for him to put his hands up. That is when he shouted, "My God, don't shoot me!"

The police pegged the gunman eluding capture as Tano Lococo, another of John Lazia's crew. Lococo had been seen a few hours before the killing sitting in a car with Charlie Gargotta watching Anthon's bootleg joint. Lococo and the deceased Gus Fasone had a history together, associates in a 1928 business venture, the Ringside Athletic Club at Independence Avenue and Locust. Lococo was one of the owners of the two-story brick building, and Fasone ran the bar. Insured for $42,500 the building was destroyed by an explosion on November 19, 1928.

Some three months following the explosion, a suspect named Tony Micelli confessed to the police he was the go-between arranging for the club to be blown up. Micelli served a twenty-month sentence, and not long after his release from prison was murdered on the sidewalk in front of his home.

Sheriff Bash attributed Anthon's murder to competition in the bootlegging racket that he claimed had become intense since the repeal of prohibition. The murder tended to corroborate word on the street that the north side organization had placed heavy levies on east side vice operations that had caused a good deal of anger. Considering that Gargotta, Scola, Fasone and Lococo were all aligned with John Lazia, the man most likely responsible for the push against the Lusco-Welch east side faction, it was only natural the killing was seen as an message for those who would resist Lazia's demands

Remarkably, the Anthon murder is considered unsolved. The reason is Gargotta was acquitted of the murder charges filed by a Jackson County Grand Jury. His acquittal came as the result of a fixed trial. Kansas City Police Officer L.L. Clairborne had intentionally switched a police property room evidence tag on the gun Gargotta had dropped at the murder scene with that of a different weapon. He compounded his misdeeds by offering other perjured testimony. Clairborne was subsequently charged with perjury, and convicted in July 1934. Despite the fact the trial had been fixed, the acquittal had the effect of invoking the double jeopardy rule, and Gargotta could never be tried again for the Anthon murder.

To correct this miscarriage of justice Federal authorities charged Gargotta with possession of stolen government property, the .45 caliber revolver he threw down at the scene of the killing. This trial ended on June 23, 1934, the jury finding Gargotta guilty. He received a three-year prison sentence. However, good fortune shined down, and Gargotta's appeal of the conviction was upheld resulting in the charges being dismissed. Once again Gargotta walked free.

Gargotta would still have to deal with the ghost of Ferris Anthon. Some five years later, the case was revisited as part of a "clean up" campaign that focused on the fact Gargotta had gotten away with murder. The case was resurrected and Gargotta was charged in State Court with assault with intent to kill Sheriff Tom Bash. After 27 continuances, Gargotta finally, in June 1939, pled guilty and received a prison sentence of three years. He reported to prison on June 19, 1939. Lightening struck again when after serving a grand total of seven months he was released from prison, his sentenced commuted by Governor Forrest Donnell.

Years later Donnell was called upon to justify his actions. He explained that Governor Lloyd Stark, who preceded him in office, had granted Gargotta a conditional commutation. "Sometime after I became Governor the board of probation and parole recommended Gargotta's citizenship restored. This was made along with scores of others, and I signed the order. There would be no time for a governor to do anything else if he were to make a personal investigation of every case the parole board recommended favorably." Donnell must have been one of the few people unaware of the sensational events that led to Gargotta's conviction, and of his status in the underworld.

Although the murder of Ferris J. Anthon was indeed a spectacular event it was by no means the only one involving Cas Welch's east side faction. Jimmy Howard, whose murder in February 1931 was attributed to competition in the bootlegging racket, had been affiliated with Welch.

John "Jack" Dalton, a former Jackson County Deputy Sheriff turned gangster, was a member of the Cas Welch faction. On July 15, 1931 he was shot dead while playing cards at his 103rd & State Line cabin. His murder was attributed to reports of his attempting to muscle rural restaurant owners into using the brand of near beer he distributed. Two other Welch lieutenants, Mike Katz, city pool hall inspector and gambler, and Roy L. Shephard, deputy constable in Welch's magistrate court, were killed by another Welch lieutenant Sam Bachman, a gambling house operator. The killings were apparently the result of an argument involving Bachman and Katz stemming from Bachman's accusation that Katz was attempting to muscle in on Bachman's gambling operation. Second Degree murder charges filed against Bachman were dismissed when a local grand jury returned a "no true bill."

Possibly the most colorful character associated with the Welch faction was Charlie Bell, labeled by the police as the "bad boy of 12th Street." Reportedly Bell had been the target of some twenty shootings, including having been shot by a police detective for resisting arrest. Bell had killed a man in 1913 during an argument over a straw hat, and served a 30-month sentence for the crime. In December 1932 he killed again, this time a former friend, and during the shooting suffered a gunshot wound to his foot. Bell was charged with second-degree murder and freed on bond. He worked as a bouncer in speakeasies, provided security at card and crap games, and loved to fight just for the fun of it. It was said of Bell his troubles were so numerous the authorities had lost count.

At approximately 4:30 am January 31, 1933 a car coming east on 12th Street pulled to the curb directly across from the Muelhbach Hotel Coffee Shop at 111 W. 12th Street. The man emerging from the car was around 30 years of age, wearing a light felt hat, light topcoat and a brown suit. Seemingly in no hurry, he took two or three drags on a cigarette before discarding it and nonchalantly walked across 12th Street toward the coffee shop. At this very time Charlie Bell was approaching the coffee shop still limping slightly from the gunshot wound suffered a month earlier, and the man in the brown suit fell in behind.

As Bell, followed by the other man, headed for the coffee shop, inside "golden haired" Betty Berry, a waitress, was cleaning tables located by the front window. As she looked out she spotted the two men pass by. Shockingly, unfolding right in front of her, the man walking behind displayed a revolver and proceeded to shoot the other man in the back, and as the victim turned toward his assailant he was shot three more time. One wild shot shattered the front window where the terrified Ms. Berry was standing, sending her scurrying to the rear of the coffee shop.

The first bullet struck Bell in the back, the second below the neck, and the last two in his chest. Bell, 45 years old, married with children, fell dead in the doorway of the coffee shop, one his favorite early morning stops on his favorite street.

The police did not believe the killing had anything to do with any of Bell's past problems or old enemies, but rather someone he had recently made angry. Although definitive proof the killing involved Bell's connection to Cas Welch was lacking, it was clear these were dangerous times for those associated with that faction. In fact, there would be continuing ramifications of the conflict between Lazia and the Lusco-Welch faction.

Troubles Mount for Lazia

1934 definitely was not a good year for John Lazia. Although still free on bond, he was facing a jail term resulting from his tax conviction in February 1934. It would be the least of his troubles.

His legal entanglements prevented Lazia from attending another significant meeting of the nation's top racketeers. In the early spring of 1934 a meeting reportedly was held at the Waldorf Astoria Hotel in New York City attended by leading syndicate figures from around the nation. A grand plan for the formation of a national crime syndicate was on the table. It was said of the nation's major underworld players only Kansas City failed to have representation due to Lazia's tax problems, and what was described as a "runaway" grand jury pressuring machine boss Tom Pendergast.

The meeting was described as the brainchild of John Torrio, former Boss of the Chicago syndicate, considered in the underworld as an organizational genius. Torrio fled Chicago following an attempt on his life at a time the city was immersed in violent bootleg wars, and turned over control of the rackets to Al Capone. Still influential, and greatly respected, Torrio proposed a streamlining of organized criminal activity by means of a system of cooperation, while at the same time maintaining intact Cosa Nostra and other organizations, leaving them free to handle internal affairs as they saw fit.

The plan called for a board or panel of leaders to act as overseers having the authority to iron out differences between organizations. It was at this conclave that Murder Incorporated was conceived, a crew of killers available to any of the cartel members to carry out contract murders. The aim of Torrio's plan was to reduce violence and establish a process where competition would become manageable. The plan apparently was well received and the attendees agreed on a second meeting to be held in Kansas City, when things cooled down there to, tie up loose ends.

Ominous dark clouds were gathering, and three days before city elections, on March 24, 1934, 7000 people attended a meeting of the Citizens Fusion party. Russell Griner, who in early 1934 headed up a grand jury investigation of crime conditions in Kansas City, was campaigning to bring down T.J. Pendergast and the machine. Griner, recalling his grand jury experience, informed the crowd "We found Kansas City infested with gambling, racketeering, vice and other forms of lawlessness, and so dominated by the intimidation and threats of reprisal by the underworld that witnesses were afraid to tell the truth to the grand jury." He had harsh words for the police, City Manager Henry McElroy and John Lazia, described by Griner as a racketeer and Pendergast's partner on the North Side. Griner went on to say, "McElroy hires an automobile salesman as commissioner of police whose chief sponsor was John Lazia at the highest salary ever paid anyone connected with the Kansas City Police Department." He told of Judge Page warning grand jury members, "Unfortunately you will not have the assistance of the police department."

At stake in the election were the Mayor's office, and nine city council seats. For many the contest was looked on more as a test of Tom Pendergast's power than an election. For two years reformers had been chipping away at the machine's influence resulting in some 88,000 names being stricken from the voting rolls prior to the election. Employing a tried and true tactic the machine responded by simply creating new voters, evidenced by the fact tens of thousands of votes in the 1934 election were later found to be "ghosts" votes.

Vote fraud was a way of life in the city, and, as the machine politicos saw it, there was no reason to change. Dead men voted, often more than once. Voters arrived at the polls only to find someone else using their name had already voted. Violence was an integral part of the standard machine formula, and John Lazia's operatives were out on the streets in force.

On election day, March 27, 1934, gangsters roamed the streets in black cars bearing no license plates beating voters and machine opponents with baseball bats and brass knuckles. Four men were killed, 11 severely beaten, and dozens injured. Inmates were let out of jail to vote, vagrants were paid to go to the polls, women were verbally assaulted, embarrassed, and frightened away from voting. The events of this election day were scandalous, described by the national press as the bloodiest in U.S. history.

A bloodied Kansas City Star reporter returned to his office after checking out reports of machine backers transporting prostitutes from precinct to precinct to vote repeatedly. Two reformers were passengers in his car when it was attacked, and the occupants beaten. Bullets riddled the headquarters of the reform party headquarters. A driver for a Kansas City Star editor was shot and beaten as he drove reformers to a voting place. A black democratic reform precinct captain died in a hail of bullets as he attempted to defend a black election judge. All without any police intervention or concern.

Late that afternoon Jackson County Deputy Sheriff Lee Flacy was relaxing playing cards at a deli on Swope Parkway, next door to a polling place. John Gadwood, a Joe Shannon rabbit faction lieutenant, accompanied by three carloads of toughs arrived at the deli. Gadwood entering the deli confronted Flacy, a neighborhood political leader also aligned with the rabbits, angrily accusing him of ignoring the demands of Gadwood's faction that he work against a rival candidate. Flacy stood his ground, whereupon Gadwood shot him in the stomach. Despite the gunshot wound Flacy got to his feet chasing Gadwood outside, whereupon a gun battle broke out. Flacy fired from the doorway while return gunshots came from inside and around the cars.

P.W. Oldham, a 78 years old hardware store owner, was closing up his shop only to be caught in the crossfire. Oldham was shot in the head and died. Seated in one of the faction's cars was Larry Cappo a member of the Joe Lusco crew aligned with Cas Welch. The car overturned while attempting to flee the gun battle scene, and when it came to rest, wheels spinning, Cappo was found to have suffered a gunshot wound. Both Cappo and Flacy were hospitalized, but succumbed to their gunshot wounds.

In the aftermath of this bloody election day the police director was fired, and John Gadwood was convicted of murder, and served a three year prison term. John Belfonte, a 26-year-old associate of Joe Lusco, employed at Lusco's Dante's Inferno nightspot, was charged in murders of Lee Flacy and P.W. Oldham. Later the charges were dismissed at the request of the district attorney. In 1939 Belfonte was shot dead in his car on a downtown Kansas City street. Although the machine successfully returned Mayor Brice Smith to office and maintained control of the city council the public outcry, along with disenchanted Democrats, made it clear the machine was vulnerable.

As a historical footnote, decades later the existence of a phone tap placed in the Jeffersonian Democratic Club, 15th & Troost Street was uncovered. Excerpts from the phone tap were made public by the Kansas City Star to include the following conversation between the just elected Mayor Smith and political faction leader Cas Welch discussing the implications of the bloody election:

> Welch: Well, are they (the reformers) leaving you alone or still giving you hell?
>
> Smith: Oh, I'm getting all kinds of hell. I hardly know what to do about the damn thing?
>
> Welch: Here's the way I feel about it: You squeeze all those fellows (the vote fixers) who had a poll book in their pockets in March, and they know how the election was won.
>
> Smith: Say, they better keep together, hadn't they?
>
> Welch: We can't do in November what we did in March...We'd have been elected this time with out those (padded) votes ... You'd have been elected - I figured it out - by 10 or 15 thousand votes.
>
> Smith: I don't doubt it.

Taking into account Mayor Smith was elected by a 59,000-vote margin it would follow, taking into account Welch's comment, the padded votes amounted to more than 40,000. The recorded exchange between Smith and Welch made it clear the machine politicos realized they were in trouble and fearful that if enough pressure was brought to bear on those who participated in the vote fraud they just might cooperate with authorities.

Also at stake during the 1934 ghost vote primary was a Senate seat from Missouri. Leading up to the primary the candidate favored by the Kansas City and St. Louis political powers was Kansas City lawyer James Aylward. However, by May 1934 Aylward was unsure whether he would run or not.

Another conversation picked up on the telephone tap at the Jeffersonian Democratic Club involved Missouri Governor Guy Park and Cas Welch discussing the Aylward situation. Welch informs the Governor that Aylward had told him that it was more than likely he would not be a candidate for the Senate seat. The Governor indicates they will be in "an awful crisis" if Aylward didn't run, and both agreed Joe Shannon didn't have a chance of winning. Asked who he had in mind as a candidate, Welch said he had no idea, but asks, "how would Truman do? After a long pause, the Governor answered, "I don't know, he's a nice fellow....nice fellow."

Truman was well known in Jackson County, but pretty much unknown around the State. The matter was settled shortly after these conversations when Boss Tom weighed in. Aylward declined to run, and Pendergast, unwilling to back any candidate outside the purview of his machine, flexed his considerable muscle and personally handed the nomination to Harry Truman.

Truman's ties to Pendergast would be a continuing issue during the Senate campaign. However, Truman won the August 1934 primary handily garnering 137,000 of the 148,000 votes cast. In November Truman won the general election and was on his was to the Senate. His ties to Pendergast would haunt him his entire political career, prompting him to comment he was sick of being treated like Tom Pendergast's office boy.

Chapter VI
Taps for Johnny Lazia

J ULY 1934 ROLLED around, and on a beautiful clear night, the tenth day of the month, a witness observed two men get out of a car parked in an alley behind the Park Central Hotel on Armour Boulevard and walk to a spot behind a clump of bushes on the east side of the hotel. One was taller than the other, and they were armed with a shotgun and a machine gun. A third man remained in the car. The witness figured they must have been police officers. It was three o'clock in the morning.

Charlie Carrollo rolled up in front of the Park Central, the residence of John Lazia and his wife Marie, pulling the car up at the front entrance canopy. Lazia emerged from the back seat and was opening the door for his wife when the two men emerged from the shrub-bery and opened fire, gunning Lazia down. Lazia shouted to Carrollo he had been hit and to get his wife out of there. Carrollo sped back out onto Armour Boulevard. With Carrollo gone, the men advanced to where Lazia lay, stood over him and pumped more bullets into his body.

Lazia, wounded 8 times, was rushed to St. Joseph's hospital where a team of doctors worked over him, but had little hope. At 2:06 p.m. July 11 Lazia died. Despite who he was and what he represented Lazia couldn't comprehend what had happened to him. He is reported to have asked an attending doctor, "Doc, what I don't understand is why anybody would do this to me. Why to me, John Lazia, who has been a friend to everybody. I don't understand."

Seven thousand people attended funeral services for Lazia. Those serving as pallbearers included many notables of the crime family, including James Balestrere, Thomas Lococo, Anthony Gizzo, Charles Carrollo, Charles Gargotta, Charles Binaggio, along with Dominic Binaggio, Joe Patito, Vincent Arena and Joseph Galucci.

The sensational murder gave rise to numerous theories regarding the identities of the culprits and the motive for the killing.

The police proposed as one possibility Fred Barker and Alvin "Creepy" Karpis, members of the infamous Ma Barker gang. The the-ory here was they were angered by reason of the fact their good friend Charlie "Pretty Boy" Floyd had been denied permission to open a booze and gambling joint in Kansas City. Even if true, this did not appear to be a very credible theory.

It was only natural there would be speculation the crime "fam-ily" itself had been behind the murder as this was the traditional way changes in leadership came about in Lazia's world. However, there was very little to back up the theory. An obvious suspect was the Lusco faction in view of its history of conflict with Lazia, and Lusco, along with members of his crew were brought in for questioning. Contradicting this idea were reports that following the bloody 1934 election Lusco severed his ties with Cas Welch and had reconciled with Lazia.

Yet another theory had Lazia being killed due to rumblings he had provided police with information identifying the robbers, and killers, of Webster Kemner, the Commerce Trust Bank messenger murdered in a February 1934 robbery. Had Lazia been sufficiently stung by the headline grabbing robbery-murder that he would have tipped the police to relieve some the heat the case had generated? It appears doubtful this proposition holds water.

Following the murder the crime "family" threw itself into solving the mystery, and it soon became clear they had come up with the answer in the person of Michael James LaCapra, aka, Jimmy Needles. LaCapra was one of the wannabe gangsters of the day, a minor criminal figure, a bookmaker who dabbled in narcotics, managed prize-fighters, and harbored the dream of a gang of his own. LaCapra along with Jack Griffen, better known as Jack Gregory, one of several thugs Lazia had imported , had been put to work as labor goons organizing cleaners and dyers, and milk truck drivers. It didn't take these two long before they recognized the money making potential in the labor rackets, leading them on a dangerous path. They decided to go out on their own and compete with Lazia and, of course, this did not sit well with the Boss-man. It was not the only beef he had with these two.

Prior to coming up with the bright idea of competing with Lazia, they had muscled in on the Saratoga Horse Room, a gambling joint located at Armour and Troost Streets, operated by Dominic Binaggio, a brother of Charlie Binaggio. Binaggio cried foul and took his case to Lazia. This was not right, Binaggio protested, as he had been paying protection money. Lazia agreed, ordering the two upstarts out of the joint. As an accommodation he gave LaCapra and Gregory the okay to pick some other location to open a gambling spot. This they did, starting up an operation in the 1900 block of Main Street, and opening a second place directly across the street in the shadow of Boss Tom's headquarters.

Thus, when the two wannabes decided to compete in the labor racketeering arena, Lazia had had enough, and not only nixed their ambitious plan, but ordered them out of the city. His dreams squelched by Lazia, rather than getting out he allegedly went to the Lascuola brothers with a plan to murder Lazia.

Hunting Down the Assassins

As legend has it, LaCapra and his associates were put on the spot after Lazia's men paid a visit to a local nightclub figure and friend of the Lascuolas and "Ace" Berman. Under duress he gave up LaCapra and Jack Gregory as the plotters. Whether this is fact, speculation, or rumor, what transpired thereafter is compelling evidence of just who the outfit believed was responsible.

Fearing an attempt on his life Jack Gregory hid out following the murder of Lazia. On the night of July 30, 1934 as he walked up the steps of the Buckingham Hotel at 3045 Forest a man exited a black Ford parked across the street, while three others remained inside. He approached Gregory, yelled out, "Hey Jack", and as Gregory turned he was shot three times.

Gregory survived the assault and was taken to General Hospital. On August 17, 1934, Police Lieutenant Jeff Rayen appeared at the hospital with an arrest warrant, and took custody of Gregory. The first clue something was amiss, Rayen bypassed police headquarters, the booking desk and all the other normal procedures followed upon the arrest of a subject. Instead Gregory still clothed in a bathrobe, his leg in a cast, was transported directly to the court of Justice of the Peace Louis J. Mazuch. Gregory was charged with the year old robbery of the Merchants Bank.

A word is in order concerning the various individuals playing roles in this well orchestrated scheme. He was active in northside politics from the age of 14, serving for many years as a first ward precinct captain and president of the North Side Democratic Club. In January 1930 he took office as Second District justice of the peace at a time when John Lazia was the power in the North Side Democratic Club.

Another of the players was Jackson Count District Attorney W.W. Graves. He had filed the charges against Gregory the prior day. The criminal complaint Graves presented to Judge Mazuch, rather than naming the bank teller, who supposedly had been held up, named himself as the complainant. No witnesses identifying Gregory were named, his photo had never been shown to potential witnesses, and he had never been a suspect in the robbery. He pled not guilty, and bond was set at $10,000.

Entering the stage were two more of the players, bondsmen Frank DeLuca and Paul Ferrantelli, both crime "family" members, who just happened to be in court for Gregory's appearance, and signed for his bond. They had not been asked by Gregory to be there, nor did he even know them. In fact, being freed on a bond was the last thing he would have hoped for in view of his predicament. A hearing date was set for September 18, 1934.

Gregory left Mazuch's courtroom and was never seen again. There was no record of any attempt by the District Attorney, or anyone else, as was the norm, to obtain forfeiture on the bond signed by DeLuca and Ferrantelli. The property backing the bond was two residences owned by DeLuca, and a building occupied by Ferrantelli housing a drug store. It was a perfect set up, as Gregory's failure to appear for the scheduled hearing cost DeLuca or Ferantelli nothing.

A story, that may or may not be true, has Gregory driven away from the court accompanied by two men who informed him it would be his "last ride". Gregory was allowed a last cigarette, and after enjoying several drags reached over and drove the cigarette into to the left eye of one of the men. Gregory was driven to an apartment building on Independence Avenue, and still alive, forced into the building's furnace.

The mob's purge was nowhere near over. Next up was LaCapra, the man the mob identified as plotting the murder, and believed to have driven the murder car. Less than a month after Lazia's murder LaCapra was walking along Independence Avenue, approaching Benton Boulevard, when assassins caught up with him intent on taking his life. LaCapra was apparently faster on the draw getting off the first shots, chasing off the would-be killers.

What happened next begs the question, did LaCapra have one more act of defiance left in him before he gave up the ship and fled the city?

Upstairs over the North Side Democratic Club, 123 East Fifth Street, a large group of men, including the new crime boss Charlie Carrollo, had gathered to listen to election return reports on the radio. It was a summer night, August 8, 1934, and the club's founder John Lazia had been dead less than a month. Here and there some of the group opted to go downstairs to catch a breath of fresh air out on the street. Some were seated in lounge chairs in front of 117 E. Fifth, while seven or eight men were standing in front of the stairs leading up to the club rooms.

Two men were seen at the corner of Grand Avenue and Fifth Street, but no one paid them any heed. Despite the late hour, about 11:30 p.m., it was not unusual to find people out on the street on a nice summer night. The two men quickened their pace as they proceeded up Fifth Street, and when they came to a point opposite the men lounging outside the club one of the men threw a bomb in their direction. Shouts rang out, lounge chairs were tipped over as the group scattered in all directions. The blast could be heard throughout the north end. The second man drew a pistol and started spraying shots at the fleeing men, the bullets shattering plate glass windows along the row of buildings adjacent to the club. Miraculously none of the men came away with injuries.

Chief of Detectives Thomas Higgins was quoted stating, "We have received no aid in our investigation from the members of the club, and we've talked to a lot of them." Asked what had he expected, he responded, "Just what we got." Chief Higgins did have an opinion as to the responsible parties, claiming the motive involved certain persons disgruntled over failure to receive a favor asked. He did not expand on what that favor was, if he knew. Chief Higgins, in what was a far more plausible motive, pointed to the shooting of Jack Gregory on July 30, 1934, and an attack at Independence and Benton on a Gregory associate as possibly connected, with the bombing representing an act of retribution. Although the victim of the attack was not identified, it obviously was James LaCapra. Not surprisingly, Big Charlie Carrollo was unable to provide the police with any suggestions helpful in solving the case.

Discretion being the better part of valor, LaCapra decided the time was ripe to pay a visit to relatives in Argonia, Kansas. It didn't take long for the mob to catch up with him. On August 30, 1934, three men caught up with him on a rural Kansas road firing a shotgun at LaCapra's car. He was struck but survived, and placed under arrest by responding police officers, jailed at Anthony, Kansas. The three assailants were captured and identified as Jerome Cretes, John Pace and Robert Farrell (another account names Robert McCoy and not Farrell), all having come to Kansas City from St. Louis, and known associates of La Capra. They were charged with attempted murder, granted bond, freed, and skipped their January 1935 trial date.

LaCapra was in a desperate situation. Two attempts had already been made on his life, and Lt. Jeff Rayen was in town waiting to take custody of him. He no doubt realized that if Rayen got a hold of him he would in all likelihood suffer the same fate as befell his pal Jack Gregory, a "one way ride." Temporary salvation came in the form of two FBI Agents arriving in Anthony, Kansas, to interview LaCapra about the Union Station Massacre. In a twist of fate, the outfit's attempts to murder LaCapra led to the unraveling of the massacre plot.

Relying on information gleaned from FBI reports, obtained under the Freedom of Information Act, Robert Unger, in his book, *The Union Station Massacre*, tells of LaCapra's role in the apparent solution of the Union Station Massacre. The two FBI Agents appearing in Anthony, Kansas, sat down with LaCapra on August 31, 1933, and he talked freely about anything and everything he knew except for the murder of John Lazia.

According to LaCapra, on the night of June 16, 1933, Vern Miller sought out John Lazia and laid out his plan to free Frank Nash before he could be returned to Leavenworth Penitentiary. Lazia refused to offer any of his men, however, he alerted Miller that "Pretty Boy" Floyd and Adam Richetti, two wanted desperados, were in the city. Lazia instructed LaCapra's brother-in-law, Sam Scola, to escort Miller to a drug store at Missouri and Grand Avenues where Floyd was hiding out. Miller, Floyd and Richetti put their heads together and worked out a plan to free Nash. The plan called for them to be armed with a machine gun and one was provided.

On the night the massacre took place, Miller is said to have openly roamed downtown looking for Lazia, apparently to secure his help in getting his confederates out of town. Ironically he is said to have found Lazia at a Union Station restaurant, a favorite spot of the mob boss. After meeting privately with Lazia, Miller fled the city.

The next night, Lazia, Charlie Gargotta, Tano Lococo, Tony Gizzo, Sam Scola and Dominic Binaggio, all gathered at the drug store where a wounded Floyd and Adam Richetti were holed up. The plan was to use a stolen car Jack Gregory and Edwin Wilhite had brought to the city from St. Louis several months before, and had stashed away. Lazia wanted Jack Gregory to escort Floyd and Richetti out of town. Gregory refused to get involved, but agreed to give up the car for Floyd and Richetti's escape.

The intervention of the FBI prevented Lt. Rayen from getting his hands on LaCapra. The local county attorney refused to turn him over, and the FBI Agents arranged for LaCapra to be transported to the Jackson County Jail where Sheriff Tom Bash, no friend of the outfit, was in control. It was a temporary reprieve for, without question, had Rayen taken custody of him he would have disappeared as did Jack Gregory. After testifying before a Federal Grand Jury in October 1934, he was returned to the Sumner Kansas County jail as a material witness against the three who had attempted to kill him. In January 1935 he was released and left the area.

Taking into consideration LaCapra's animosity toward Lazia, and the attempts on his life orchestrated by the outfit, one would have to question his credibility. On top of that, his story implicating so many ranking crime "family" members, describing their personal involvement with non 'family" members, fly's in the face of outfit protocol. Two key people who were in a position to back LaCapra's story, if they would have, were dead. Jack Gregory and LaCapra's brother-in-law, Sam Scola, the alleged source of much of LaCapra's information, killed by Sheriff Tom Bash in the shootout at the Ferris Anthon murder scene.

LaCapra was on the run making it to the east coast and traveling constantly. His luck ran out when on August 26, 1935, his body was found dumped along side the Clintondale-Highland highway near Plattskill, New York. He had been shot at the base of the skull.

The roundup of suspects continued. Al O'Brien was one of those imported from Chicago by Lazia to join his crew of labor thugs. He had linked up with Gregory and LaCapra in a small bookmaking operation authorized by Lazia, and was bought into their plan to "muscle in" on Lazia's labor racketeering operations.

After Lazia's murder O'Brien was said to have left Kansas City traveling to Colorado Springs, Colorado. At Florence, Colorado, the murder team of Cretes, Pace and Farrell caught up with him. A shootout ensued and John Pace was killed. O'Brien escaped the attempt on his life, moving on to Seattle, Washington, where he became involved in labor racketeering operations under Dave Beck, a powerful political and labor leader, later elected President of the International Brotherhood of Teamsters.

As for Lieutenant Jeff Rayen, another of the role players, he had been a leading figure in the North Side Democratic Club, and by reason of this connection had been sponsored, appointed, and promoted in the police department. On November 3, 1934, a Federal grand jury indicted Rayen on charges of perjury based in part on the grand jury testimony of two county prosecutors from Kansas. They testified that upon Rayen's arriving in Anthony, Kansas, to take custody of LaCapra he had made the following statement to them, a statement Rayen under oath denied making:

> "I don't know what political affiliation you two gentlemen have. We have got to work for the good of the Democratic party. I am in the employ of Kansas City Missouri. Nevertheless, I owe a greater duty to the organization there which is headed by Mr. Pendergast. This man, LaCapra, is wanted very badly in Kansas City and that is what those boys were down here to do, wipe him out."

Besides Rayen, former Kansas City Chief of Police Eugene Reppert, and then Chief of Detectives Thomas Higgins were also indicted for perjury based on their testimony before the federal grand jury investigating the Union Station Massacre. The intertwining story of the Union Station Massacre and John Lazia was further advanced by testimony heard during a perjury trial in federal court in March 1935.

Reppert was the first to go to trial and he was acquitted of the perjury charges on March 12, 1935. Testifying at the trial, Kansas City Missouri ballistics expert Merle Gill from the witness stand identified one of the shotguns used in the Union Station Massacre as being the same shotgun used in the murder of John Lazia. Mr. Gill also testified that in his expert opinion an automatic revolver found on the body of Charles "Pretty Boy" Floyd, shot dead by authorities in an Ohio cornfield, was used in the Union Station Massacre.

Following the acquittal the government dismissed the charges against Higgins and Rayen, explaining they were forced to do so when Reppert was acquitted since the evidence in the Reppert case was virtually the same as that against Higgins and Rayen.

An Ill Wind Blows

With prohibition ending in January 1934, coupled with the bloody 1934 election and the murder of John Lazia, ill winds were blowing through the underworld. Those who had been living off the huge profits of liquor found themselves seeking new horizons. In the quest there would be opposition and with opposition comes conflict. Outrage over the events of the 1934 election caused upheaval in the political sphere resulting in some abandonment by ward and precinct workers on the north side.

Joe Lusco severed his ties with the Welch faction after the 1934 election and was said to have re-joined John Lazia, their differences set aside. However, Lazia at the time had all he could handle seeing to the needs of the "family." Lusco turned his attention to his night-club operation, Dante's Inferno at Independence and Troost Streets, spending practically all his time there while keeping his hand in things. He was reported to have "fronted" for his followers whose activities included tire thefts, car theft and other lower profile crimes. In January 1935 he was arrested and charged with selling liquor in violation of a federal law prohibiting the shipment of liquor from "wet" into "dry" states.

On the night of March 10, 1935 around 11:00 p.m. Lusco called it a night at his club and drove over to a garage at 2526 Independence Avenue where he stored his car overnight. He picked up the garage owner, Fred Klotz. Klotz, who would accompany Lusco home, and then return the car to the garage for overnight storage. Arriving at his 413 Olive Street residence Lusco got out of the car and Klotz slipped over to the driver's side and drove off. Lusco had failed to take note of a small dark sedan occupied by three men that pulled up to the curb. He started up the steps to his home and as he reached the top step he was hit with five shots fired from a shotgun by one of the occupants of the sedan. The police did not find any shotgun shells at the scene confirming the shots had in fact come from within the assailant's car.

At the hospital doctors initially believed a wound to the stomach was the most severe injury Lusco sustained, however x-rays revealed a shotgun slug was lodged in his brain causing complete paralysis of his left side. Lusco hovered between life and death at St. Mary's Hospital eventually surviving but was left permanently disabled.

Police investigators believed Lusco had been in the process of withdrawing from the underworld scene, tired of having to obtain lawyers, post bond and otherwise assist his followers as they came in conflict with the law. They saw no connection to the Lazia murder. In the time leading up to the assault Lusco had displayed no concerns or expectation of trouble for if he had he would have been traveling with his men and not a garage owner.

The shooting was never solved and Lusco passed away at the age of 51 on August 17, 1945 at the residence where he had been ambushed.

Chapter VII
Charles Carrollo Steps In

NOT LONG AFTER Lazia's murder Boss Tom summoned Charlie Carrollo down to 1908 Main Street. Carrollo was given the job as collector for the organization's take from gambling, the lion's share of which went to Pendergast. It was commonly known as the "lug." All gambling operators were required to kick in a percentage to the machine for protection, and collections had previously been John Lazia's responsibility. As Lazia's constant companion Carrollo was intimately familiar with the process and therefore the logical man to take over. At the same time Carrollo became collector of the "lug" he was tapped by the crime "family" powers to replace Lazia as the out front crime Boss.

Carrollo was born August 25, 1902 in Santa Ristino, Sicily, and at age 3 came to the United States, his family settling first in New Orleans. The next year the Carrollo family moved to Kansas City locating in the North End in a home at 410 Campbell Street, next door to the Lazia family. He attended the Karnes school and St John Catholic school dropping out after the 4th or 5th grade to go to work and help support the family. By the age of 21 he had acquired the swaggering bravado of the street hoodlums he hung around with. In reality he had no standing, his brother Pete being better known within police circles.

Charlie Carrollo entered the business realm in what was then called a car rental garage, and the operation soon came under the scrutiny of law enforcement. A tailor shop robbery led to unsubstantiated allegations that Carrollo had rented the car to the culprits, a practice it was believed he engaged in on a regular basis.

What brought some standing to Carrollo was the sugar business. As previously described, with the outbreak of World War I sugar was in short supply leading to widespread black market dealings in the product. Carrollo built up the business to the point he was considered near the top of the heap when the prohibition era began. With sugar representing an essential ingredient in producing bootleg booze Carrollo was in a strategic position when the scramble came to capitalize on the opportunities presented by the illegal liquor business. In turn this led to his becoming a founding member of a Sugar House Syndicate that seized control of the bootlegging racket in the north end and beyond.

Carrollo and his boyhood friend John Lazia were to become a team. Carrollo was a Lazia intimate at the time Lazia wrested control of the North Side political apparatus in 1928, a first person witness to the melding of Boss Tom's political machine with the North End criminal organization that followed. The bond between the two was cemented when he took the rap for Lazia in the 1931 when the government closed in on their illegal liquor operation. He was Lazia's constant companion, advisor, driver, and bodyguard. He was there when Lazia was ambushed, and he was the logical man to take over.

Carrollo was quick to capitalize on his newfound prominence muscling into a gambling operation at the Fortune Club, a lush bingo hall on the 2nd floor of 2 West 30th Street where many a housewife lost their grocery money. In June 1934 two men from Los Angeles, Joe Zemansky and Barney Morris got the operation off the ground. Six months later Carrollo showed up demanding a 50% interest for the value of his name. The way Carrollo put it to them, the value of his name meant if he had an interest in the operation the police wouldn't bother it, and that was worth a 50% interest. It was an offer they couldn't refuse, and they now had Carrollo for a partner.

Less than 4 years later, to their complete surprise, the two Los Angeles gamblers received a bill of sale for their signature. The terms of sale called for them to receive ten thousand dollars for their half of the business. If that was a surprise, imagine the shock when the $10,000 sale price was later scaled down to $1.00. The club was bringing in $60,000 a month.

A more detailed picture of the Fortune Club operation came to light as the result of the investigative efforts of Internal Revenue Service agents hot on Carrollo's trail. Carollo had been targeted as part of a 1939 clean up campaign directed at racket activity in the city. Scrutinizing the Fortune Club operation, it was discovered that in the year 1937 Carrollo had taken in over $64,000 as his share of the profits, and had taken steps to hide the income. He ordered the checks from the Fortune Club made payable in other individual's names, including his brother Frank. They established the checks made out to Frank Carrollo had been cashed at the Merchants Bank, endorsed in his name, but the handwriting was neither Frank Carrollo's nor his brother Charlie's.

The revenue agents pressed the bank teller cashing the checks, and finally an admission was dragged out of him. The checks had been presented to him without endorsement. A bank vice-president authorized the cashing of the checks for Charlie Carrollo, and it was the vice-president who had endorsed the checks with Frank Carrollo's name. With these admissions in hand, the agents were successful in getting the vice-president to fess up to his part in the scheme allowing Carrollo to hide income. That he could manipulate the Merchants Bank was a given, as Carrollo had to be aware of how his deceased pal John Lazia had used the bank years earlier in concealing his take from the Cuban Gardens gambling operation.

In speaking with the Federal Agents Carrollo actually boasted about the size of his take from the Fortune Club. In later years he would pay a price for his bravado, as his connection with the club led to charges by the State of Missouri of felony gambling. The felony charge was later reduced to a misdemeanor, and Carrollo got off with just a fine.

The take-over racket came easily to Charlie, and the Cowboy Inn, another gambling establishment, represented another conquest for him. The operator of the Inn, W.E. Hutchins, had been taken ill and hospitalized. The very next day Charlie Carrollo, Charlie Gargotta, and several other individuals, visited the business seizing control of the gambling devices. They dispatched employees of the Inn to pay a visit to Hutchins at the hospital to inform him he owed $12,000 to Charlie Gargotta. To pay the phantom loan, Hutchins instructed his wife to cash in sufficient government bonds to cover the $12,000, and obtain a cashier's check payable to him.

An unidentified individual appeared at the hospital to pick up the cashier's check endorsed by Hutchins, and in return was handed a made up I.O.U. Employees of the Inn corroborated this entire story for the investigators.

Internal Revenue Agents recovered the cashier's check payable to Hutchins and found it endorsed by Hutchins and a "John Smith." Once again the trail led to the Merchants Bank where the check had been cashed. The "John Smith" endorsement was determined to be the handwriting of Charlie Carrollo. The teller cashing the check admitted Carrollo had appeared at his window, and in front of him had endorsed the check "John Smith." Before paying Carrollo, who he knew was not "John Smith", the teller first checked with a vice-president, and only upon getting his authority for the endorsement did Carrollo get the money.

The historical pattern guiding political-criminal alliances held up, for it was during the period of Carrollo's reign the mob took complete control of the criminal-political machine. Tom Pendergast had succumbed completely to his gambling addiction. Estimates were he had wagered between $5-6 million on horses from 1933 to 1938, $2 million in 1935 alone, forcing him to demand ever-increasing shares of the "lug" money. His addiction had severely weakened his position, putting him at the mercy of the crime family since they, as collectors of the "lug", held the purse strings. Within the criminal-political sphere the roles had reversed, and Pengergast no longer held the upper hand.

During the period of the Lazia/Carrollo reign in Kansas City extending from 1928 to the late 1930s Kansas City reached the heights as an open city.

Open City

Kansas City came to be a true sin city, described by some as one of the worst in the entire country, gaining national recognition as a place of gangland violence, official corruption and sanctioned vice. From

1928 to 1934 John Lazia, assisted by his trusty companion Charlie Carrolla, joined at the hip with Boss Tom, rode the wave.

Lazia and Carrollo were welcomed at City Hall, visited the city manager regularly, the Police Chief daily, and at least once a week visited Pendergast headquarters at 1908 Main Street to bring him his cut of the 'lug" money. As leaders of the North Side political faction they were responsible for securing and dispensing patronage for the district's residents, enhancing their position as the "governors" of the north end and beyond.

The prohibition laws had no impact on the city as evidenced by the throngs of speakeasies operating without interference. Likewise the great depression did not impact the city as harshly as other parts of the nation. As was common in many cities, houses of prostitution abounded in so called red light districts. Numerous houses of prostitution operated openly in Kansas City, with 14th street, just east of downtown, lined with these establishments, the scantily dressed prostitutes posing in the windows.

Blatantly open gambling of all types flourished. Card games, dice, roulette, bingo, policy, slots, horse racing books, chuck-a-luck, skill-ball (also called tango) all available. One New York writer describing the city reported all one had to do to locate a gambling game was to "...ask a patrolman on the Kansas City streets. He'll guide you. It's perfectly open. You just walk in." At the height of the era it was estimated there were 2000 dealers and housemen employed in gambling operations in the city.

Gambling was estimated to have an annual take of $20 million. Its tentacles moved across 31st Street, once considered forbidden territory so as not to offend the social elite of the city.

Milton Morris, a long time liquor establishment owner and active participant during this raucous era of the 1930s, tells of establishments called drug stores that were divided into three different parts.

The front third was the soda fountain and sundries, the middle part craps and card games, and the back part dispensed bootleg liquor.

Nightclubs offering whatever vice one would desire operated openly. The Chesterfied Club, 320 East 9th Street, located one block from the Federal Court, was particularly notorious. One of the operators was gangster Charlie Gargotta's brother, Gus "Skinny" Gargotta, no slouch himself when it came to the rackets. Gambling tables were located in the entrance to the establishment. Shills would be planted at dining room tables keeping them occupied so that waiting patrons could pass the time gambling. Prostitutes were on the premises, some working as waitresses wearing nothing but high heels and a change belt, their phone numbers readily available. Strip teases came with the meal, and machine big shots held weekly sex parties at the club.

The Chesterfield Club and the Winnie Winkle Club, a like establishment, were labeled by authorities as encouraging "lewd and lascivious shows by female entertainers", and selling liquor after legal closing hours. However, it wouldn't be until a clean up campaign in 1939 that the clubs ceased operations. At that time the Missouri Attorney General obtained court injunctions against them, and eight other similar establishments.

During this incredible period Kansas City would be the base for several narcotics operations having national implications outlined in a subsequent chapter of the book.

Sports had long been part of the scene in Kansas City. As far back as 1884 the city had some form of pro baseball, and in the 1920s Boss Tom organized a city league with a team in every ward. The National Negro League was founded in 1920, and the Kansas City Monarchs were packing them in on Sunday afternoons to the point the churches had to alter their hours of service. During the period 1927 to 1933 the Kansas City Pla-Mors professional hockey team was competing as part of the American Hockey Association. On January 28, 1928 the Pla-Mors whipped the Maroons 2 to 1 in front of 4000 fans at the Pla-Mor arena.

Black businesses were doing well along 12th, and 18th & Vine Streets, especially those in the entertainment realm. Prohibition was a major factor facilitating the mob's entry into the entertainment field flourishing during the 1930s. When liquor was outlawed cabarets and jazz joint operators needed the product, and bootleggers were the only reliable source available. The situation was ready made for the bootleggers to infiltrate the nightlife industry, and at the same time increase their client base for illegal liquor. Starting modestly, they bankrolled dives, joints, small speakeasies, typically places employing only a piano player and a singer for entertainment. Cops and other authorities were paid off to avoid raids, and "reasonably clean people" were brought in as managers by the mob.

As prohibition progressed more people saw fit to defy the law, drinking was tolerated, and it was fashionable to frequent mob-controlled speakeasies. The point came where the criminal element considered itself in the entertainment business, not just servicing it. It wasn't long before the majority of club operators were offering a more upscale form of live music in their establishments. As the entertainment scene continued to escalate so did competition, and the operators were forced to upgrade their establishments. The trend was toward fancier nightclubs with plush interiors, full orchestras and elaborate floor shows. With their foot already firmly planted in the door, the mob element was the only source of ready cash for investment in such establishments, and had the clout and muscle to insure protection. The mob came to dominate the industry.

In most cities during the prohibition era the celebrated nightspots, more or less, were openly associated with gangsters. A myriad of name entertainers got their start in these establishments. Comedic star Milton Berle provided his take on this era stating, "A part of me salutes the old time New York gangster. More than any other force, and for reasons of his own, the gangster built the huge nightclubs in which many of us cut our comedy teeth. The gangster, again for private reasons that had nothing to do with the general welfare, backed the shows that lit up Broadway. Needless to say the illicit presence in our gambling resorts is measurable, but without it, Las Vegas and Atlantic City, and other resort cities, would be tiny hamlets still."

It was at this time that Kansas City Jazz came into its own earning national recognition. Black jazz musicians working in gangster owned club melded two cultures at a time when blacks and whites had little contact with each other. The gangsters and jazz men understood each other sharing common ground, to wit, nightlife habits, flashy clothes, a code of silence, things to hide, disapproval by the straight world, and the company of loose women. Jazz men first played in whorehouses and gambling joints, and were considered to be society's riff raft. Various testimonials of jazz figures described musicians back in New Orleans as all wanting to be pimps. Jelly Roll Morton was identified as one those who played the piano only as a sideline, because back then if you didn't have some kind of employment, and playing the piano wasn't considered employment, you went to jail. Being a musician was akin to being a criminal.

The main centers of jazz, New Orleans, Kansas City and Chicago, were all "mob towns", with protected sections where after-hours clubs and shady dives offered steady work for jazz men beyond the reach of moral guardians.

By 1930 the hottest jazz scene shifted to Kansas City under the protection of Boss Tom and John Lazia. Black gambling figure Felix Payne and jazz man Benny Moten controlled three clubs along 12th and 18th Streets, dictating who worked where and when. Payne's association with Tom Pendergast was the connection allowing him to wield that power, and the ability to help wayward musicians who landed in jail.

Milton Morris described Kansas City jazz as a totally different jazz from all others. It wasn't Dixieland, it wasn't New Orleans and it wasn't Chicago. It was a new blend of jazz, free flowing, with the jazz musicians' individuality and feeling coming through. One of the greatest proponents of Kansas City jazz, Charlie "Bird" Parker, got his start in the city's clubs.

Benny Moten's Ochestra included any number of musicians with big futures in store, including one by the name of William "Count" Basie. Basie would later form a band of his own playing the Reno Club at 12th & Cherry Streets, managed by Papa Sol Epstein for the Pendergast machine. It was here that he was discovered by a big city record mogul, and the rest is history. Looking back at his days in Kansas City Count Basie recalled, "For 25 blocks there used to be joints, sometimes three or four doors apart, some times every other block. There was an awful lot of good music, and it was like everything happened there. It was the first place I really heard the blues played, and sung as they should be." Recalling the Reno Club he described it as a long narrow room with a divider down the middle separating the black patrons from the white. Out in back loitered two-dollar whores and marijuana sellers looking for deals. On the bandstand marijuana joints were passed around. The band members shunned regular black people heading straight for the pimps and prostitutes who hung out with them.

Basie described a Kansas City ritual observed by club owners called "throwing-away-the-key." "In those days when they opened a club they took the key to the door and handed it with a five dollar bill to a cab driver and told him, ride as far as that'll take you and then throw the key away." The doors never closed.

Many musicians after finishing their gig in the early morning hours headed on over to the many brothels operating at the time picking up some extra money playing jazz for the customers

A prime player in the 18th and Vine Streets jazz center scene was black gangster Ivory "Seldom Seen" Johnson. His nickname came about by reason of the fact whenever the authorities were looking for Johnson he was seldom seen. Born in Oklahoma in 1883, his father a coal miner and bootlegger, he left home at 14. Some years after serving a prison sentence for murder he showed up in Kansas City arriving in the early 1920s. He was reported to have become an associate of mob bigwig Big Jim Balestrere and others involved in the city's vice activities. Johnson operated a gambling and prostitution joint on 12th Street, eventually closed down by the police. He ran a crap game at 18th and Forest Streets and was involved with several other gambling clubs.

Johnson was described as a classic depression era gangster, and one of the leading gambling operators during the wide-open 1930s. Johnson was a tall, lanky man, dapper, smooth, always armed, whose passion was gambling. He stood out, generally recognized up and down the streets he wandered. He was said to be a regular at another of the city's rituals known as the "Blue Monday" event. A day long party each week for prostitutes on their day off, hustlers, and musicians who would dress up and hit the clubs by 7:00 am. In 1951 he was charged with the murder of man scheduled to testify in a jury tampering case against a local lawyer. Johnson served 14 years in prison for the murder. He died in 1985 at the age of 102.

Of all of that which characterized the period - bootlegging, prostitution, corruption, rigged elections, kidnappings, gangland murders, protected desperados - in the end it was gambling that brought the house down.

Post Prohibition - The Beat Goes On

Prohibition was a bonanza for organized crime but it was not to be a forever thing. By the late l920s signs were surfacing that repeal was on the horizon. The 1928 Atlantic City meeting of racketeers was in part a response to a portent of things to come. In planning for that day emphasis was placed on producing quantities of liquor by means of huge but illegal distilleries. In this manner when prohibition ended there would be in place a means to supply liquor in competition with legitimate liquor distributors sure to spring up. As always the gangsters would have an edge in that they would not be paying any taxes on their liquor. The law might change but hustling illegal liquor was still on the agenda.

Cleveland syndicate members by 1930 had been involved with large-scale alcohol production but soon realized the type of operation required was too large for one syndicate to handle. The answer was a joint venture including associates in the Eastern crime syndicates.

Molaska Corporation officially came into being in Ohio in November 1933 just ten days before repeal of prohibition. It was incorporated mainly in the names of individuals fronting for gangsters such as Charles A. Polizzi, Sam Tucker and Mo Dalitz of Cleveland, and Meyer Lansky, of New York City. Others having unofficial interests in Molaska included Al Polizzi, Peter Licavoli and Charles Baron, of Cleveland; Louis Buchalter, Joe Adonis, Lucky Luciano, Frank Costello, all from New York City; and Abner "Longie" Zwillman from New Jersey. All were heavy weight members of the national crime syndicate, and some like Adonis, Luciano and Costello were Cosa Nostra leaders.

The purpose of Molaska was to build and operate large distilleries, how many will never be known. Huge operations were uncovered in Zanesville, Ohio, and Elizabeth, New Jersey. For example, the Zanesville distillery could produce 5000 gallons of 190 proof alcohol every 24 hours, in addition to equipment capable of producing 35,506 gallons of beer daily.

Investigation by the authorities centered on locating these distilleries. Information surfaced in December 1935 indicating Lou Rothkoph, a principal in Molaska operations, had arrived in Kansas City. From his hotel room he made frequent calls to David Finkelstein and Ralph Messina, two Kansas City bootleggers of some note, and numerous visitors made their way to his suite. After a two week stay an arrangement had been hammered out. Shortly after Rothkoph left Kansas City the first of several shipments of alcohol arrived from Cleveland. Two years after the repeal of prohibition the Molaska cartel had opened a new territory for illicit liquor.

At the same time illicit alcohol was being produced in mass, those who knew the most about the liquor business, the racketeer bootleggers, turned their attention to the legitimate side. Those who were far sighted, anticipating the end of prohibition, entered into agreements with legitimate distilleries to serve as their distributors. Other individuals, who had played no part in the bootlegging racket, upon being awarded distributorships became competition for the gangsters. However, they were at a distinct disadvantage. The racketeer knew the business intimately, had established contacts and outlets, and when necessary was ready, able and willing to turn to violence.

In most cities around the nation Seagram and Schenley distributorships were the two main prizes, normally held by separate, and very competitive distributors. This was not to be the case in Kansas City.

Joe and Pete DiGiovanni, and Joe Spallo, formed Midwest Distributing Company, 1109 Cherry Street in 1934, soon after the repeal of prohibition. They had the exclusive franchise to distribute Seagram products in Kansas City and Western Missouri.

Superior Wine & Liquor, 2035 Main Street formed by Vincent DiGiovanni, John Blando, a nephew of Jim Balestrere, and Vincent Chiapetta, were awarded the franchise for Schenley products. This meant individuals identified as part of the Crime "family" had control of the two most sought after distributorships.

Although now operating as legitimate distributors the operational tactics employed did not seem far different. They saw to it their products were sold exclusively in various taverns and liquor stores. Crime figures appeared as salesman for these companies, and the big shots, Jim Balestrere, Charles Binaggio, Charles Gargotta, Tony Gizzo, and, before his murder, John Lazia were strongly suspected as sharing in the profits.

Boss Tom Pendergast had extensive interests in the liquor field. He held stock in, among others T.J. Wholesale Liquors and City Beverage Company distributor of all Anheuser-Busch products in the Kansas City area, a firm Tom Pendergast Jr. was a partner in.

Prohibition may have passed into history, but when it came to the liquor business certain things stayed the same, and for one competition was not looked on favorably.

Wolf Rimann

Wolf Rimann was a case in point. For a number of years in the 1940s this widely known gambler, coin machine operator, and golf pro was considered the kingpin in Jackson County outside the city limits. Rimann was also known as a person not afraid to stand up to the north end syndicate.

Born in Waterloo, Iowa, in 1906 he moved with his parents to Johnson County, Kansas while still a small boy. He attended Antioch Grade School and Shawnee Mission Rural High School. While still in high school he became interested in the game of golf and excelled at it. He got a job as caddy master at the Milburn Country Club and not too long after graduating high school was promoted to assistant pro. A short period as golf pro at South Ridge Golf Course near Grandview, Missouri followed, and then a stint as the pro at the former Wood Hill Golf Club in Clay County, Missouri. Along the way he gained recognition as one of the best young golfers in the area.

By 1934 he was manager of the Hillcrest Country Club, eventually becoming a major stockholder there. Rimann started the Western Specialty Company dealing in jukeboxes, pinball machines, and the like. A close friendship with J.A. Purdome developed, and when Purdome became Jackson County Sheriff in 1945 Rimann benefited by reason of what the Kefauver Committee described as Purdome's lax enforcement of vice activities. Purdome handed Rimann a special deputy's commission, authorizing Rimann to equip his car with red light and siren, "In case I would need him in an emergency..", a quote Purdome later denied.

Dirty tricks and predatory tactics used in developing customers characterized the liquor, vending machine and jukebox industry. One basic, well-tested method was the use of strong-arm intimidation. Rimann was viewed as a person ready and willing to use force. However, he was far more successful in placing his machines in bars, taverns, clubs, etc, by lending money, both to individuals seeking to get into business or those already in business, but in financial trouble. The money was loaned on the condition Rimann's machines were placed in the business. He would then take 100% of the income generated by the machines until the loan was paid off, and thereafter work out a customary percentage arrangement with the owner. In this manner he not only established locations for his machines, but, as landlord, it afforded him a level of control.

Harry W. Hundley, a former police officer employed by Rimann, upon testifying before the Kefauver Committee in 1950, revealed that deputy sheriffs were on the payroll of Western Specialty Company, and described how helpful they were in placing the company's machines in taverns. According to Hundley, on one occasion Rimann stalked into a tavern, threw his special deputy badge down on the bar demanding the tavern operator change jukeboxes and pinball machines to the brand Rimann distributed

Rimann built the company up to the point it was recognized as the largest of its kind in this part of the United States. He was reported to hold an interest, by way of mortgages securing loans, in 120 of the city's 1200 liquor establishments. Rimann's attorney, John S. Cannon, put the total figure of locations where Rimann had machines at well in excess of 200.

Among his myriad of interests, he operated until 1948 the Artic Refrigerator Company, retailers of home refrigerators. He was also one of six incorporators of Mark's Music Inc., a firm employing songwriters and promoting songs, owned real estate, mainly small business buildings in Kansas City, Kansas, and was a bondsman.

By 1949 Rimann was a wealthy man, and although he had done very well he still was not satisfied, wanting even more. In a fateful decision, he opted for the wholesale liquor business as the vehicle to the added wealth he was seeking. He formed Western Wholesale Liquors setting his sights on obtaining a Schenley distributorship. He aggressively made his move bypassing the established procedure of filing the initial application locally, and went directly to Schenley's headquarters in New York City. This course of action brought him in direct conflict with the DiGiovannis, and John Blando, whose Superior Wine and Liquors had the Schenley agency.

Attorney Cannon was quoted as saying Rimann had received a telephone call from an individual identifying himself as Charlie

Binaggio, outfit Boss, warning him he could not have the distributorship, and political pressure would be brought to bear to block Rimann. Despite the fact the quote was printed in a Kansas City newspaper article, Cannon denied he made the statement. He would explain later Rimann had told him of a meeting with Binaggio concerning the Schenley deal, characterizing the session as businesslike, without any threats made or friction between the two. Binaggio allegedly indicated his interests were in support of a friend, John B. Blando, President of Superior Wines and Liquors. From what he was told Cannon described Binaggio's involvement as strictly a political matter, "Blando was a political friend of Binaggio's and it simply was a case of helping out your friends."

On March 18, 1949 Rimann received a telephone call from an unknown person who threatened his life and wanted to meet privately, warning Rimann he would be sorry if he didn't comply. The same person called a second time. Three days later the caller made a third contact instructing Rimann to meet him at the southwest corner of 7th and Garfield Streets. The caller said he would be recognizable by the grey plaid suit he would be wearing. Harry Hundley, friend and employee, convinced Rimann to let him make the meet, and when no one showed he abandoned the effort after waiting at the designated corner for some 40 minutes.

On that same Monday evening, after dinner downtown, Rimann and his wife were in their car when a black Ford closed in, remaining on their tail. Rimann pulled over to let the car go by, but the Ford remained behind continuing to follow as Rimann made two turns. At Truman Road and Troost Avenue he ran a red light and the black Ford followed suit, convincing him he was indeed being followed. Rimann then pulled into a service station at Truman Road and the Paseo, and watched as the black car proceeded on by. Rimann laughed it off, reassuring his wife that it was probably nothing to be concerned about.

Three days later, Thursday March 24, 1949, around noon Rimann was driving south on Broadway when he spotted Harry Hundley proceeding in the opposite direction. Flashing his lights he got Hundley to stop, and the two men had a brief meeting. Hundley recalled Rimann told him he had information concerning the identity of the mysterious caller who had been threatening him. Rimann stated, "I want to see you because I have some information. I had another call, and I've learned something about it". Hundley asked if Rimann knew who it was, and Rimann responded, "I know plenty now."

Rimann's next stop was a business meeting with two men at the City Hall. The meeting ended at 1:30 p.m. and Rimann proceeded to his car where a woman, never identified, was observed seated inside. He then made his way to the A.J. Stephens & Co. offices located at 2800 E.14th Street where he met with the company vice-president to discuss the upholstering of some chairs for the Hillcrest County Club. As Rimann left the building, the vice president stopped by President A.J. Stephens' office thinking Mr. Stephens might care to say hello to Rimann. Stephens readily agreed. The Vice President went to the door, observed Rimann in his car, but was in time to call him back. Rimann returned to chat with Mr. Stephens.

Rimann returned to his car, a 1948 Pontiac 2 door sedan, parked on Chestnut Street. It was 2:45 p.m., and there were any number of people out and about. As he opened his car door two men approached him, and in front of some 15 witnesses, making no effort to shield their faces, fired revolvers into Rimann's body. He slumped to the street, part of his torso lying on the front seat. Rimann, aged 43, was hit 6 times. After examination of the slugs by the police laboratory it was determined that two revolvers had been fired at Rimann.

The gunmen made their get-a-way in a 1948 black Ford, the driver having remained in the car to insure a fast escape. The Ford was recovered at 2607 Smart Street, and upon examination was found to have a siren, and a hidden gun compartment. It was determined the Ford had been purchased in St. Louis a year prior to the murder. Detectives were dispatched to St. Louis to delve into the circumstances of the sale.

The customer walking into Bison Motor Sales in St. Louis spoke broken English, leading the salesman to believe he was Italian. He was very clear that he was looking to buy a 1948 Ford, and it had to be black. The dealership did not have such a car in their inventory, however the salesman recalled having seen one at the St. Louis Auto Auction sales barn. The customer and the salesman visited the auto auction to have a look. Sure enough they located a black 1948 Ford priced at $2225, and the customer agreed to buy it paying cash. The salesman had very little background information to provide the detectives about the man, recalling only a comment that he would be taking the car to Denver. The mysterious buyer had provided a name and little else. The car purchase proved to be a dead end.

Attorney John Cannon stated it was his belief Rimann was murdered because of the "liquor deal", meaning the Schenley distributorship. The police theorized the killers had come from out of town pointing out the murder followed the pattern of other gangland killings with the one large exception. The crime was carried out in broad daylight, and these men made no attempt to hide or obscure their faces, apparently unconcerned about being seen by witnesses. Looking to a motive, the police revealed they had received reports of widespread terroristic tactics in the placing of coin operated devices

Boss man Charlie Binaggio voluntarily appeared at police headquarters in response to a request by detectives to do so. Described in newspaper as a "North Side politician", Binaggio told police he did not known Rimann, and wouldn't recognize him if seen walking on the street. He had no knowledge concerning the murder, and was not involved in liquor dealings with Rimann or anyone else. Binaggio informed the detectives, "From what I have read, it (the murder) may have been the liquor business that got him killed". Binaggio denied any effort on his part to get into the liquor business, explaining he had many friends in the industry and he would not want to be in competition with them. He had all the business he could handle, pointing to his Canadian Ace beer distributorship, and had no interest in the coin operated machine business. "I have been approached by many whiskey dealers, particularly the Seagram line, but I have declined them all", the police quoted Binaggio as telling them.

The Kansas City Star, in an article dated October 1, 1950 captioned, "Rip Purdome Laxity", set out the questioning of Sheriff Purdome by the Kefauver Committee on September 30, 1950. Purdome was pressed for answers as to why gambling, illegal whiskey sales, and "other situations" had persisted in rural Jackson County since he took office in 1945.

Purdome admitted Wolf Rimann was a very good friend. Asked if he had ever raided the Hillcrest Country Club, reported to have run slot machines, he responded he had not received any information to that effect, and there have been no slots there since 1948. He was asked to explain why he had been visiting Western Specialty Company two to three times a week in the recent past. Purdome answered he went to the company to visit Rimann's widow, Esther, as "She and I are very good friends and I often go by there in the evenings to pick her up." Purdome would latter marry Rimann's widow.

That some of his Deputies had been paid by Rimann to assist in placing machines, Purdome stated it was a situation he had only learned of a month before Rimann's murder. On the other hand, he admitted Rimann had previously told him the Deputies had been in his employ for two years. And yes, they were still employed by the department.

Mike Manzella, operator of the Playhouse Tavern, 2240 Blue Ridge, testified he had paid two deputy sheriffs $15-20 a week to help keep order, "or for any other reason." He stated it was common knowledge that Purdome let certain people sell whiskey in the county. Manzella described a meeting he attended in 1949 at the Hillcrest Country Club at which time Rimann pushed for the formation of a county tavern owners association. Sheriff Purdome was in attendance, and also made a speech at this meeting. Manzella refused to join the group, and three weeks later his tavern was raided, and he was charged with selling a half-pint of whiskey. He knew of no other tavern owners who were arrested for selling whiskey at that time.

As part of their inquiry into the Rimann murder, and liquor industry abuses, the committee explored these topics on the occasion of Joe DiGiovanni's appearance. DiGiovanni faced tough questions about his Black Hand activities and arrest record, and when the Rimann murder was raised he admitted he was aware that shortly before his death Rimann had sought the Schenley distributorship. Hadn't there been quite a contest between his brother Vincent (Part Owner of Superior Wines & Liquors, a Schenley distributorship) and Wolf Rimann, DiGiovanni was asked. "I don't know. I don't know if my brother had anything to do with the Schenley line", he answered.

The committee was interested in DiGiovanni's take on the premise that in any city whoever had the Schenley and the Seagrams distributorships had control of the liquor business in that city. As DiGiovanni saw it the business was open to everybody, denying they were especially important distributorships representing the largest part of the liquor business. If that were the case, DiGiovanni was asked, would he then be willing to give up his (Seagrams) distributorship. "No, why should I", he answered. Question: "Then it is important isn't it?" Answer: "Sure."

The DiGiovanni's Liquor Woes

In 1941 Alcohol Tax Agents uncovered a large-scale operation dealing in high priced whiskey sold at black market prices above O.P.A. ceilings (Government's Office of Price Administration). The ensuing investigation led to charges being filed against Joe and Pete DiGiovanni and their nephew Sam, operators of Midwest Distributing Company at 226 Independence Avenue. The charges were they had violated Federal tax laws by means of falsifying reports and records as to the receipt of 10,032 cases of whiskey between June 1, 1943, and November 15, 1943.

A separate complaint was filed against Midwest Distributors for submitting false reports and entries, on or about April 1, 1943, regarding the receipt of 1,192 cases of Gilberts Deluxe whiskey from Hercules Products of Brooklyn. Named in the complaint were Joe & Pete DiGiovanni along with Pete's son Sam, operators of Midwest Distributors. Implicated in the scheme were Max Ducov, operator of Independence Sales Company; and Charles Binaggio, Maurice L. Salwinsky and Logan A. Imhoff, all associated with the Wiggle Inn tavern.

Although federal agents were on record claiming they had a good case, on January 19, 1944 all charges were dismissed by Assistant U.S. Attorney David A. Thompson on the grounds the evidence was insufficient.

Ironically the individual who provided the black market liquor to Midwest Distributors, Jacob Fried, was convicted in New York on liquor charges, and testifying in the case from Kansas City were Max Ducov, Sam DiGiovanni, Jack Hoffman and Wolf Rimann.

That was not the end of the DiGiovanis troubles. In January 1950 the Missouri Attorney General brought an anti-trust case against Joe and Pete DiGiovanni charging price fixing in the distribution and sale of Seagrams products. They waived issuance of writs and consented to entry of judgment against them without trial. On January 13, 1950, fines of $1250 each were imposed, and 17 days later the fines were paid.

In the same year the Kansas City Liquor Control Director revoked Midwest Distributors wholesale liquor license. The revocation was based on Joe DiGiovanni's appearance before the Kefauver Committee at which time the issue of his arrest record was raised, a fact he had not disclosed when filing an application for a wholesale liquor license. At a license revocation hearing a long list of individuals identified to the Kefauver Committee as 'Mafia "members" was read to DiGiovanni, and he affirmed they were all "close personal friends.

Representing the DiGiovannis in both of these cases was Richard K. Phelps, former Assistant United States Attorney in Kansas City. Phelps had been the prosecutor in a major narcotics case involving multiple defendants from Kansas City, St. Louis, Missouri, and Tampa, Florida, outlined later in this book. At the license revocation hearing Mr. Phelps, in defense of Joe DiGiovanni, proposed the errors made in filling out the liquor license application was the result of DiGiovanni's lack of understanding the English language. Fred R. Johnson, Liquor Control Director, responded, "Joseph DiGiovanni is a discerning businessman who admittedly made $80,000 in one year. If, knowing that, I could decide that he was an aimless man who did not understand the contents of documents he signs, I would suspect myself of getting soft in the head."

Capone Beer

Following repeal of prohibition there was a scramble to be the first to get liquor and/or beer distributorships, either those previously held or new ones, but as always it was the mobsters who had the edge.

When prohibition became the law of the land the Leo Thoma Brewery in Kansas City converted from beer to handling carbonated beverages, becoming the Leo Thoma Bottling Works. When prohibition was repealed Thoma was one of the first to be awarded a Schlitz beer distributorship for Kansas City. According to Thoma's son, within weeks of the company beginning distribution of the Schlitz product John Lazia paid his father a visit. Lazia had come with an offer to purchase the distributorship rights, and Thoma turned it down. Lazia accepted the rejection politely. However, not to be deterred, Lazia followed up by contacting associates in Chicago who were able to persuade the Schiltz Company to rescind the Thoma company distributorship. Lazia subsequently ended up handling Schlitz beer.

The saga of Glendale Sales and Duke Sales is one of many instances where the outfit capitalized on their contacts, reputations and influence to gain a foothold in the business sphere. It is also another example of the close relationship the Kansas City outfit maintained with the Chicago mob.

A good deal of the story surfaced from testimony before the Kefauver Committee in 1950. Tony Gizzo, during a lengthy session before the committee, was pressed for details concerning Glendale and Duke Sales. He told the committee Glendale Sales was started by John Lazia (in the 1930s), and James Balestrere, Tano Lococo and Charles Carrollo also had a piece of the company. He claimed no knowledge of how Balestrere came to be a partner, nor did he believe Charles Binaggio was part of the firm. He identified William Duke as president of the company. Initially soda was the product sold, and later the company branched out to handle Schlitz beer.

It is generally futile to extract a straight story from outfit members, and it was no different when it came to the question of who did and who did not have an interest in the company. Contradicting Gizzo's version, Gaetano "Tano" Lococo admitted to the committee he was a partner with John Lazia and proceeded to name Charles Binaggio as another of the partners. On the other hand, Lococo was not aware that James Balestrere and Tony Gizzo had any interests in the company.

Big Jim Balestrere had yet another version to offer the committee, testifying he had been a partner with John Lazia in Glendale Sales Company in the 1930s, but could not name any other partners. He claimed to have lost money in the deal, receiving only 20 cents on the dollar. This should not have been a surprise, as he had also told the committee he didn't make any real money from prohibition.

Getting back to Gizzo's story, he was not involved in selling beer until 1940, although he had Glendale Sales stock before that time. By 1940 the company handled 5 or 6 different beers, including Schlitz, Manhattan and Canadian Ace. He denied that Manhattan beer was known in Chicago as "Capone beer", stating he knew it as "Mr. Greenberg beer". He explained that both Manhattan and Canadian Ace beers were produced at the same Chicago brewery.

The origin of Manhattan and Canadian Ace beer is a story of the mob moving into the legitimate business sphere. Preparing for prohibition Johnny Torrio, in the spring of 1919, bought the Malt-Maid Company installing Louis Greenberg as manager. When prohibition took effect a year later Torrio changed the company name to the Manhattan Brewing Company with Frank Nitti, prominent Chicago mob figure, owning a piece of the business. At some point New York mobster, Joe Adonis, a lieutenant in Frank Costello's Cosa Nostra "family" was cut in for a part of the business. Greenberg reported on brewery operations directly to Al Capone and John Torrio. By 1922 Capone allowed Greenberg to buy 15% of the company stock.

In 1925 the Manhattan Brewing Company name was changed to Fort Dearborn Products Co. With the repeal of prohibition the name was changed once more to Canadian Ace Brewing Company.

Continuing with Tony Gizzo's testimony, he related how the Schlitz Company revoked Glendale Sales agency to sell their beer. Gizzo traveled to Chicago to visit with Louis Greenberg, a long time acquaintance, asking if it were possible to have Canadian Ace beer put in kegs, inasmuch as Glendale customers in Kansas City were used to buying Schlitz beer in keg form. A deal was consummated, and Glendale began distributing Canadian Ace, a product Gizzo denied was an inferior beer. Despite information to the contrary, he also denied the use of strong-arm tactics in selling this beer.

Gizzo went on to explain, in 1939 he traveled to Chicago to alert Greenberg that a number of stockholders in Glendale Sales wanted to sell out, and if Greenberg wanted to keep his beer in Kansas City he had better send someone to buy the company. Gizzo had sold his stock, making a good profit, and claimed thereafter he was relegated to the position of salesman. He denied any knowledge of what happened to Glendale after that, nor did he know what happened to Jim Balestrere's stock, although Gizzo was known to handle much of Balestrere's affairs. He did identify a man by the name of Feigenbusch as the person dispatched to Kansas City to buy out William Duke who held the Canadian Ace agency.

As Gizzo understood it, Duke Sales Company was formed as the vehicle to obtain a liquor license allowing for the continued sale of Canadian Ace beer inasmuch as Mr. Feigenbusch, an out of state resident, could not obtain one. Once Duke Sales was established, and properly licensed, Feigenbusch sold out the Canadian Ace agency formerly held by Glendale Sales to the new company. Low and behold, Gizzo and Charlie Binaggio ended up with interests in Duke Sales while Max Ducov was listed as the owner of record. Ducov continued to sell beer for Duke Sales into 1949.

The story continued to unfold when Max Ducov and his brother-in-law, Nathan Basin, were called to testify before a federal grand jury in October 1949, and once again the facts didn't quite mesh.

Both Ducov and Basin were cited by the grand jury for contempt, charging they had given evasive answers during their testimony concerning Duke Sales. U.S. District Court Judge Duncan found them guilty, and committed them to jail until they purged the contempt charges by testifying truthfully. All it took was one night in jail before the brother-in-laws agreed to testify truthfully.

Ducov outlined how he had started Duke Sales at 107 W. 22nd Street in 1940 selling Edelwiess beer, and other "lousy" beers he would not recommend. In 1947 Charles Binaggio approached him with a proposition that he buy the Canadian Ace beer agency from Tony Gizzo. In Ducov 's opinion the proposition wasn't viable inasmuch as Canadian Ace was not a national beer. However, he told Binaggio, if "you fellows" represent me, will work with me, act as salesmen, then he would accept the offer.

A deal was consummated with Ducov taking 50% of the business and Gizzo and Binaggio 50%. Gizzo and Binaggio each received $7500 as their share of the business for the year 1947, and $5700 for 1948.

The arrangement proved out, and the company became a lucrative enterprise. Despite its success Ducov sold Duke Sales in July 1948 to his brother-in-law Nathan Basin for the grand sum of $2500, remaining on as sales manager. In reality the sale was a sham, simply a way for Ducov to remove himself as an owner of record, in light of the fact he had revealed his criminal record to the Federal Grand

Jury, including a prior federal conviction on liquor charges, and a 1924 narcotics conviction he had conveniently omitted when obtaining a liquor license. He estimated in the 6 months after the sale the firm's profits were between $18,000 and $20,000.

When Nathan Basin testified he informed the federal grand jury he was the sole owner of Duke Sales, and yes, Gizzo and Binaggio did each receive 25% of the profits. In return the two men were supposed to contact customers in behalf of the company. However, he could not recall the last time they contacted anybody. Basin explained, "It is their influence that holds customers for me, their contacts and influence, and with their cooperation and help I'm successful in the business" Furthermore, he explained Max Ducov had advised him that continuing the arrangement with Gizzo and Binaggio would mean success, otherwise he would fail.

Basin explained, in view of the fact Duke Sales sold beers for which there was no great demand, not nationally known brands, without individuals on board who had influence with the tavern owners these products would be most difficult to sell. .

Basin confirmed he employed Nick Penna, a Binaggio lieutenant, as a salesman at $225 a week plus an expense account. Asked to inform the grand jury how many beer sales Penna had racked up for the firm, Basin responded he had been thinking of firing Penna.

On May 3, 1950 Ducov was indicted by the grand jury for causing Basin to make a false and fraudulent statement to agents of the U.S. Treasury Department. The charge was based on the fact that when Basin applied for a wholesale basic permit for malt beverages he falsely claimed the funds invested in the business were his own. On May 22, 1950 Ducov pled guilty to the charge.

As a final note to the "Capone Beer" story, on December 8, 1954 Louis Greenberg, accompanied by his 2nd wife, had dinner at a B-B-Q restaurant not far from the Chicago brewery. It was early evening and as they walked across the street to their parked car two men stepped out from the shadows and shot Greenberg to death. He had been holding out payment on a large sum of money owed to the family of prominent Chicago mobster Frank Nitti.

Liquor Trafficking

Obviously the repeal of prohibition did nothing to diminish the lure of the liquor business for the criminal element. On the one hand they manipulated, cheated, used strong-arm tactics in the conduct of legitimate liquor businesses. On the other hand they continued to traffic in illegal alcohol products just as they did during prohibition. By this time bootleggers had substantially improved their product, as evidenced by the Molaska venture, and were motivated to compete with legal manufactures. The major difference between the two was the racketeers' product did not carry the required tax stamps, greatly enhancing the bottom line profit. In addition to outright illegal production of alcohol other schemes were in play to cash in on the liquor trade.

After having served a prison term and being released from Federal prison in May 1943, Charlie Carrollo was back on the scene casting around for sources of income. He had lost the standing he once had as political and criminal boss. He happened upon a flourishing illegal liquor operation set up at 519 Tracy, the home of his son-in-law, Mike Arnone. In that he was most familiar with the art of the takeover, Carrollo simply dealt himself in for a piece of the business. One day he walked into Arnone's house, plopped his sizeable frame into a chair announcing, "You need a cashier. From now on I'll handle all the money." There was no opposition.

Anthony "Stringbean" Marcella had built the operation up to the point it was grossing annually $500,000, surpassing the combined gross of several legitimate wholesale liquor companies. Top quality brand named liquor was being shipped to dry Oklahoma without benefit of federal tax being paid.

On April 14, 1950 Federal Alcohol Tax Agents raided the house and found Carrollo sitting quietly at the kitchen table. They seized 1053 cases of whiskey stored in the basement and an additional 40-50 cases at a nearby residence, 521 Tracy, identified by the agents as also connected to the overall operation. Carrollo, Marcella, Sam Tortorice and Mike Arone were all taken into custody.

All four subjects were indicted federally on tax charges, the government alleging liquor was distributed to Oklahoma, Kansas and the cities of Sedalia and St. Louis in Missouri. Financial figures cited indicated sales of $148,477 in December 1949; $111,920 in January 1950; $95,724 in February 1950; $107,563 in March 1950; and $56,022 for the first part of April 1950.

Among the many Carrollo-Marcella clients in this extensive network identified by government agents were Bill & Martin Edwards, two of the biggest bootleggers in Northeast Oklahoma; S.G "Curly" Evans of Oklahoma City, a lieutenant of Kenneth Sleeper, overlord of bootlegging and gambling in Oklahoma City and neighboring Cleveland & Pottawatomie counties; Fred Carlson, Enid, Oklahoma, whiskey runner associated with Sleeper; Francis Dunn, Junction City, Kansas; and Leonard Steele, Salina, Kansas.

Martin Edwards had a reputation as one of the toughest hombres in Tulsa, Oklahoma. It seems his bravado had little effect when it came time to face a Federal Grand Jury in Kansas City Missouri, and his reputation may have been somewhat tarnished. Upon appearing before the grand jury investigating the illegal liquor operation, Martin Edwards refused to answer questions, was belligerent, and at one point, upon being instructed to stay quiet and just answer the questions, told Special Prosecutor Max H. Goldschein, "I'll talk any time I have a notion." He followed that up by daring either of the Special Prosecutors to try and whip him, springing from his chair, causing some jurors to believe Edwards was actually going to swing at them. All this accomplished was a trip before no nonsense Federal Judge Richard M. Duncan.

On April 21, 1950, Judge Duncan held a hearing, and made two findings. First, Edwards was guilty of obstructing the work of the Grand Jury, and second, that Edwards was drunk. Edwards was given a 2-day jail sentence. Having learned nothing from his boorish behavior, his antics during the hearing were found disrespectful to Judge Duncan and the court, earning him a $750 fine in addition to the jail sentence. Edwards then told federal agents he had been warned not to talk, and feared for his life, but refused to identify who had threatened him. In the agents opinion his tough guy act was just that, a show to convince the "underworld" he had not cooperated.

The four Edwards brothers certainly cut a wide swath. Tough guy Martin was the second youngest, and had, four months earlier, been released from county jail in Tulsa after serving a year for assault with intent to kill one of his own brothers. The youngest brother, Jack "Cadillac" Edwards was sentenced in April 1950 in Federal court at Springfield, Missouri, to five years on counterfeiting charges. The eldest brother, Gordon Edwards, an ex-convict, was under charges of murdering J.T. "Boxy" Allison, another bootlegger, allegedly for stealing whiskey from the Edwards' brothers. Bill Edwards, said to be the brains of the family, was Martin's partner in what was alleged to be the largest bootlegging operation in Northeast Oklahoma.

On April 24, 1950 Martin Edwards, his bravado gone, was not only ready to testify, but offered an apology to the grand jury. There was still the matter of his unpaid fine now reduced to $500. In spite of a second apology, this to Judge Duncan, he was remanded back to jail until it was paid. He remained jailed for two more days when finally his wife came up with $500 cash and sprung Edwards.

Carrollo, Tortorice, Marcella and Arnone entered pleas of guilty on June 26, 1950. Carrollo was sentenced to two years incarceration on July 7, 1950. The following year, while Carrollo was still in prison, efforts got underway to deport him. Three years later Carrollo was deported to Italy.

AFTERMATH

The pervasive underworld influence in the liquor and beer industry, exposed by the Kefauver Committee and Federal Grand Jury, had broad based repercussions. The matter involving Max Ducov, and Nathan L. Bassin, operators of Duke Sales, particularly drew the interest of the Kansas City Liquor Control Director and city officials.

In November 1949, Fred R. Johnson, Liquor Control Director, pointed to the testimony of Ducov and Bassin as justifying an investigation of their activities that could well lead to formal hearings thereafter. Johnson, Mayor Kemp and City Manager L.P. Cookingham met and agreed that in light of the insufficiency of current city licensing controls steps had to be taken to correct the situation, with the aim of divorcing the industry from racketeers and political pressure.

As a result of the meeting, a plan was developed wherein the liquor control department would conduct thorough investigations into the operation and ownership of every wholesale and retail liquor license. The stated purpose was to determine true ownership, ferreting out any blind control or "false faces" (hidden ownership), and determine if pressure was being exerted on operators forcing them to handle particular brands of product. A recommendation was made that the existing liquor code, establishing licenses as valid until revoked for cause, be amended to require a yearly reissue of licenses.

An overview of the city's liquor situation disclosed that Kansas City had far more licensed locations than the national average. Back in February 1949 a restriction on the issuance of new licenses had been imposed leading to a reduction in the number of licensed operations from 1,404 to 1,290. The restriction was due to expire January 1, 1950, however, it was agreed the restriction should remain in effect.

On a national scale, Senator Estes Kefauver took action in October 1950 focusing the spotlight on those in the liquor and beer industry dependent on the underworld to distribute their products, and called for them to change their ways. His challenge to the industry was based in part on information his Senate committee developed that neither the industry, nor the federal alcohol tax unit, nor authorities in various states were very discerning in their approval of individuals seeking liquor licenses.

The Kansas City Star quoted "industry sources" confirming that breweries and distillers had received questionnaires from the Kefauver Committee requesting information on the practices employed in selecting their distributors. Information requested by Kefauver included whether consideration is given to the general character, background and reputation of the distributor; is any effort made to determine if a prior criminal record exists, and if so, would it impact on the decision to grant a distributorship; have distributorships been granted where there was prior knowledge of a criminal background; and, if information was developed that a owner or manager of a distributorship had a long criminal record, would any action be taken to terminate that franchise?

Senator Kefauver signaled out Joe DiGiovanni of Kansas City, holder of a Seagrams distributorship, and "another member of the DiGiovanni family (Vincent) having a Schenley franchise", as examples of underworld figures infesting the industry. He also named Wolf Rimann, who had sought a Schenley franchise before being murdered; Tony Gizzo, who distributed Canadian Ace beer; and Joe Fusco of Chicago's Capone mob, an officer of the Gold Seal agency, a Schenley distributor, who earned $120,000 a year.

Chapter VIII

The Downfall

A CASE COULD be made the government's assault directed at Boss Tom Pendergast was traceable in part to the role he played in the Democratic National Convention held in the windy city, Chicago, Illinois, June 27, 1932.

The two principal candidates for the Democrat nomination for President were Al Smith and Franklin D. Roosevelt, both from New York State. Smith had made an unsuccessful run for the presidency in 1928 losing out to Herbert Hoover. New York's powerful, corrupt, Tammany Hall political machine was lined up behind Smith, while the city's west side political Boss, Jimmy Hines, supported Roosevelt. The national crime syndicate was well represented with

New York City's two most powerful Bosses, Frank Costello, sharing a suite at the Drake Hotel with Hines, and Charles "Lucky" Luciano, sharing another suite with Tammany Hall's delegation leader, Albert C. Marinelli. Freelancing around the convention was Meyer Lansky. They had all the bases covered.

Also playing roles were powerful politicos such as Louisiana's Huey Long, Boston's James Curley, and Kansas City's own Tom Pendergast, all exerting what influence they could.

Roosevelt won the nomination with the help of Jimmy Hines, Huey Long, James Curley and Pendergast, but as a result he was saddled with the tag of "machine candidate." To combat the charge, after winning the presidency Roosevelt disappointed these machine forces deciding it was in his best political interests to go after and break the very big city bosses who had helped elect him, and Pendergast was one of them.

Roosevelt's turnaround had far reaching consequences. Pendergast and other machine bosses were left with no one to protect their backs when the heat was turned up. The crackdown on entrenched machine bosses weakened them and strengthened mob elements, providing an opportunity to gain the upper hand, reversing the roles of earlier times when the gangsters were at the mercy of the politician. Boss Tom had the additional handicap of a gambling addiction, and thus the loss of protection from the Nation's capitol represented a double whammy for him. Pendergast would be forced to relinquish his dominant role allowing the crime family control of gambling and vice activities, and the millions of dollars it generated.

Associates of Boss Tom's estimated his betting losses over a 10-year period amounted to some $ 6 million. Official court proceedings set Pendergast's horse-race wagers in 1935 alone at two millions dollars, with net losses of $600,000. This level of betting required income outside even Boss Tom's normal sources to finance his ever-increasing gambling fever, plus support the life style he had become accustomed to. The fever was interfering with his business interests and political affairs. Afternoons found him shut in, refusing all callers, while he listened to horse race results. There is strong reason to believe the escalating need for more and more money was the motivation behind his involvement in an insurance fund kickback scam that provided government probers just what they needed.

The Fire Insurance Scam

The genesis of the scheme came about in 1929 when fire insurance companies notified the State of Missouri they would be increasing their 16-2/3% premium rate. An immediate outcry went up on the part of policyholders and the State of Missouri. The insurance companies took their case to Federal court seeking an injunction barring State interference with the proposed rate increase. Pending a final decision of the matter all monies generated from the rate increase were impounded. By 1935 the federal fund of impounded monies amounted to more than $9 million, with another $2 million impounded as the result of State court actions. The insurance companies were anxious to get their hands on this substantial pot of money, and Missouri Superintendent of Insurance R. Emmet O'Malley was just the man to get things moving. O'Malley, a long time close friend of Tom Pendergast, had been appointed to the top state insurance job in 1933 by Missouri Governor Park.

His first step was to arrange a meeting between Tom Pendergast and Charles R. Street, Vice President of the Great American Insurance Company, and this he accomplished working through St. Louis, Missouri, insurance man and President of the Missouri Insurance Agents Association, A.L. McCormick.

On January 22, 1935, Boss Tom and Street met privately at a Chicago hotel. Street, representing all of the interested insurance companies, asked Pendergast to exert his considerable influence in getting the State of Missouri to abandon its opposition to the proposed premium increase, thus freeing up the impounded monies, and offered Boss Tom $200,000 for his efforts.

Boss Tom wasn't pleased with the amount offered, so Street raised it to $500,000, a sum Pendergast felt was appropriate. However, Boss Tom wasn't moving quickly enough to satisfy the interested parties prompting Street, at the end of March 1935, to sweeten the pot, upping the ante to $750,000.

Street passed the first $50,000 installment on to A.L. McCormick, who in turn delivered it to Boss Tom on May 9, 1935. Six days later at a meeting at Kansas City's Muelbach Hotel a compromise agreement was reached, and committed to writing by all the interested parties. O'Malley personally ran a copy down to 19th and Main Streets for Boss Tom to approve before the official signing.

The second payment of $50,500 was handled the same as the first, only this time Boss Tom took $5000 and ordered the rest to be split between McCormick and O'Malley.

For the schemers, the good news came on February 1, 1936 when a Federal Court in Kansas City ordered the impounded funds distributed in accordance with the signed compromise agreement, to wit, 80% to the insurance companies, and 20% to policy holders, with the costs of the action coming out of the companies' share. In the fine print was an unexplained 5% item, its real purpose was to cover the amount of the kickback payments still due. Fourteen insurance companies issued checks to Street amounting to $330,000. McCormick delivered this money to Boss Tom on April 1, 1936. The Boss kept $250,000, instructing that both McCormick and O'Malley receive $40,000. One last smaller installment was paid and that was it.

Three hundred thousand dollars of the originally agreed on kickback was never paid.

Not long after Boss Tom accepted what was to be the last installment the scheme began to unravel. In April 1936 Internal Revenue Agents were conducting a routine inquiry relative to the taxes of Ernest H. Hicks, a Chicago lawyer in the firm of Hicks and Felonie. Hicks had passed away in October 1935. His partner, Felonie, had been chief counsel for the fire insurance companies. The agents uncovered a $100,500 item on the partnership books identified as a transaction with Charles R. Street. They may not have realized it at first, but they had stumbled on to the insurance compromise kickback scheme.

Street stonewalled the IRS Agents but gave up enough to alert them they were on to something big. The investigation picked up steam, the trail leading to A.L.McCormick. McCormick was persuaded to cooperate, and laid it all out for the United States Attorney who would be presenting evidence to a grand jury tasked with ferreting out political corruption and organized crime activity. Time was running out for Boss Tom.

The Ghost Vote Election Of 1936

While the federal grand jury was hard at work another election scandal was in the wind. The raucous election of November 1936 came be known as the ghost vote scandal. Two days before the election the Kansas City Star, targeting machine and ghost voters, summed up the results of a two month vote fraud investigation declaring, "An honest election here Tuesday is absolutely impossible." The prediction was based on their findings that in numerous precincts, and probably one entire ward, ghosts outnumbered the legitimate voters. Indeed the election results proved an overwhelming victory for the Democrats.

Taken in conjunction with the vote frauds of the 1934 municipal election, this new scandal proved more than enough to generate investigative interest.

U.S. Attorney Milligan and U.S. Judge Albert L. Reeves' grand juries both went after the vote fraud matter. FBI agents were sent in from Washington to conduct the largest election fraud investigation ever. Thirty indictments were returned as part of the first federal grand jury report, but it was only the beginning. It would take two years before the last case was disposed of.

Estimates were between 50,000 and 60,000 illegal votes were cast in the 1936 election. In the aftermath of federal prosecutions and election law reforms, a new permanent registration law was enacted. As a result, for a period extending from the 1936 election to a city election in 1938 voter registrations fell from 270,000 to 216,033

The machine did not need the ghosts to win the election, so why do it? It was useful in boosting Boss Tom's reputation as the premier vote producer in Missouri. This in turn helped him overwhelm the opposition within his own party, override and intimidate out-state factional opposition, and keep his prestige soaring. Those caught in the net were not the higher-up machine operatives, but rather the rank and file workers. Many of these people, including many women, were individuals from modest homes who supported themselves in little jobs, and were regarded as good citizens before their participation in vote fraud. Mixed in, however, were some tough customers.

Machine workers are in large part office seekers, expected to produce results and in exchange they obtain jobs. The better showing they make the higher their standing over rival precinct, ward or district workers. In this competitive atmosphere they are pretty much forced to do the bidding of the machine higher-ups. Further illustrating the machine's command of the entire well-orchestrated scheme was the manner in which it came to the defense of those caught up in the net. The machine provided money for bail, legal staff and anything else that could be done in the worker's behalf. Judge Reeves at one point challenged those in command, pulling the strings, to surrender themselves, stating "so long as the higher-ups remain in the background, the only thing for the judge to do is impose sentence on those who have followed their orders."

Voices rang out in defense of the machine rank and file, attacking the forces of Government, especially Judge Reeves, a Republican, charging excessive action and persecution. Senator Harry S. Truman chimed in with a direct attack on U.S. Attorney Milligan, Judge Reeves and Judge Merill E. Ottis, who joined Reeves in pursuing these cases. Truman on the Senate floor proclaimed, "The Federal court at Kansas City is presided over by two as violently partisan judges as ever sat on a Federal bench since the Federalist judges of Jefferson's administration. Convictions of Democrats are what they want. A Jackson County democrat has as much chance of a fair trial in Federal District court as a Jew would have in a Hitler court or a Trotsky follower before Stalin." Judge Reeves responded to Truman's speech by commenting,"...was a speech of a man nominated by ghost votes, elected with ghost votes, whose speeches are probably written by ghost writers."

Truman's tirade succeeded only in alienating President Roosevelt who now opposed him in his bid for re-election to the Senate. His opponent, Missouri Governor Lloyd Stark, labeled Truman a "fraudulent U.S. Senator."

There was a history of bad blood between Truman and Milligan, who himself was up for re-nomination to the post of U.S. Attorney. When first nominated for the post Milligan had been opposed by both Truman and Pendergast. The infamous bloody 1934 election faced Truman off against Milligan's brother for the senate seat nomination, won by Truman aided by the tainted machine controlled vote in Jackson County. President Roosevelt stepped into the Milligan re-nomination fray requesting Truman, who had returned to Kansas City to confer with Pendergast, to abandon his fight against Milligan. Truman agreed to do so, but still cast a dissenting vote when confirmation came to a vote on the Senate floor.

Despite Senator Truman, and other defenders, the machine was up against an efficient prosecutor, two uncommonly energetic judges, aggressive FBI agents, and juries from counties outside of Kansas City, beyond local influence. The Government's response to the 1936 election came in the form of 278 defendants, 259 of whom were convicted upon pleas or trials by jury, the remainder discharged. Thirteen jury trials involving 63 defendants resulted in convictions, with no acquittals. Of 13 appeals filed only one resulted in a reversal of conviction. Total fines exceeded $60,000, and numerous defendants, including women, went to jail for terms ranging up to 4 years.

The cost to the machine was enormous. The expense of defending and supporting those charged ran into the hundreds of thousands of dollars, forcing the political/criminal organization to up the gambling "lug" to 45 % and even more in some cases. To meet the increased protection fees gambling operators engaged in phenomenal activity, provoking unfavorable public reaction, and resulting in a call for expanded investigation of crime conditions in the city. That is exactly what transpired.

The Cleanup Campaign

The new year of 1939 marked the beginning of the end for Pendergast and the machine. Boss Tom's own man, Governor Lloyd Stark, turned on him ordering his Attorney General to proceed to Kansas City on January 1 for the start of what he labeled a "cleanup year." In conjunction with the Governor's action Jackson County Judge Allen C. Southern spearheaded a cleanup push of his own, commencing with raids conducted by the Jackson County Sheriff on two principal syndicate controlled gambling operations — Charlie Carrollo's bingo operation at the Fortune Club, and the Snooker Club.

Judge Southern then empaneled a grand jury, forced to operate in secrecy in order to protect the members from intimidation, a distinct danger at the time. The Judge excluded Jackson County District Attorney W.W. Graves from any participation, and kept Attorney General McKittrick at arms length, stating neither exhibited an awareness of crime conditions in Kansas City. An apparent diplomatic way of saying they were not to be trusted. At Governor Stark's insistence three special aides were appointed, including a staff of investigators to assist the Grand Jury. It was made clear the focus of the Grand Jury inquiry was mobster Charlie Carrollo, District Attorney Graves, and the gambling syndicate.

Judge Southern received threats and was warned of the consequences he faced if he did not call off the grand jury investigation. Southern was not a man subject to intimidation.

District Attorney Graves filed an application before the Missouri Supreme Court for a writ of prohibition disbanding the grand jury, contending it was an irregular proceeding because he, as the District Attorney, had been barred. The application was rejected.

The grand jury moved against Graves returning a three-count indictment. In Count I of the indictment Graves was charged with failing to prosecute Charles Gargotta for the attempted murder of Sheriff Tom Bash in August 1933. Counts II and III charged Graves with having been present at the Oriental Club when liquor was sold on a Sunday, without a license, and failing to take any action. On the heels of the indictment, proceedings were initiated by the Missouri Attorney General to oust Graves from office.

Six years after the shootout with Sheriff Bash, charges against Charlie Gargotta were filed for attempted murder of the Sheriff. After a plea of guilty he was sent to prison serving only 7 months. In a report of its findings the Grand Jury revealed that a 12 million dollar gambling industry had grown in Kansas City. Judge Southern saw it a bit differently, putting the figure at $20 million.

Joining in the cleanup campaign Federal Judge Reeves commented, while in the process of empaneling a new federal grand jury, "Kansas City today is a seething caldron of crime, licensed and protected." Judge Reeves based his charge on a report prepared by federal rackets investigators outlining their findings, including records of large daily payoffs, hints of murder, and the frequent mention of the "Big Man" who ruled the underworld. Describing this unnamed racketeer Judge Reeves quoted from a statement by a government agent to the effect, "I never saw one individual, in all the years I have been connected with the United States Government, who seemingly had so much power as the subject."

Contained in the investigative report was a description of how the "lug" worked. When a gambling location was first established the payoff (to the criminal-political machine) was 20% of the gambling operator's take, but the percentage immediately began to climb. It amounted to 40%, more in some instances, at the time of the vote fraud cases of 1936 when the machine was in need of more income. Fear of violence and death kept people from informing, creating a wall of silence surrounding the "Big Man."

Charlie Carrollo may have been the outfit Boss for public consumption, however the investigator's report disclosed Carrollo was but a front man representing an even bigger man, another Italian named in the report, but not made public. In the one investigator's opinion Carrollo's actual authority in the underworld was over stated. His chief function was that of a collector of the "lug" and liaison man with city officials and politicians.

Judge Southern's grand jury made its final report on March 11, 1939 listing 167 indictments. In addition to the charges leveled against Graves and Charlie Gargotta, indictments were returned against Charlie Carrollo, charging him with gambling, and against the presiding judge of the county court and a former court judge for corruptly approving payment for the remodel and repair of Gil P.Bourk's Jeffersonian Democratic Club. Also indicted was a cleaners and dyers union business-agent for two bombings. A number of individuals involved in illegal liquor and gambling operations were also charged. That the grand jury's actions were effective was confirmed when the police department ordered a lid placed on vice activities in the city.

Boss Tom obviously heard the footsteps as the authorities closed in. He faced attack from the Federal Government, the criminal court of Jackson County, from Governor Stark, and local political opposition. Envoys to Washington on his behalf included Police Chief Otto P. Higgins who spent a week trying to see President Roosevelt, and James Pendergast, Boss Tom's nephew and heir apparent. The only news was bad news. President Roosevelt was 100% behind the cleanup efforts in Kansas City.

On April 4, 1939 U.S. Attorney General Frank Murphy and FBI Director J. Edgar Hoover flew to Kansas City to confer with U.S. Attorney Milligan. Three days after the visit the axe fell. A federal grand jury returned an indictment against Pendergast and R. Emmet O'Malley charging violation of income tax laws based on the $300,000 plus Boss Tom had received in insurance fund kickbacks. Later in the month Pendergast was indicted a second time on additional income tax evasion charges based on extensive evidence of various Pendergast schemes, including falsified books of eight companies in which he had an interest.

Pendergast's City Manager Henry McElroy, and Police Chief Higgins both resigned. Not long after tendering his resignation Higgins was indicted on charges of evading $65,170 in taxes. He was subsequently sentenced to prison for two years. One might say McElroy escaped indictment the hard way. He passed away September 15 at the age of 74. Numerous city officials retired. The presiding judge of the County Circuit Court resigned, and the Sheriff and County prosecutor were removed. A subsequent audit of city accounts managed by McElroy showed the city in debt some 20 million dollars.

May 22, 1939 was the day Boss Tom had to face the music. He appeared in Federal Court entering a plea of guilty to charges of hiding $1.2 million from his tax liability. Total taxes owed, including penalties, amounted to $830,494.73. The government was agreeable to a settlement reducing the amount of taxes owed to $350,000. Boss Tom's health was poor. He had suffered a heart attack in New York in 1936, and had undergone three operations for correction of intestinal obstructions. All of these facts were made known to the court in the hopes of avoiding prison time.

Federal Judge Otis sentenced Boss Tom to the penitentiary for 15 months and fined him $10,000 on one count of the indictment, and three years suspended sentence with five years probation on the second count. The terms of probation were strict. Pendergast was prohibited from engaging in any form of political activity, even discussing politics or granting interviews, until May 1945. O'Malley pled guilty five days later, and was sentenced to one year and a day, and a $5000 fine

Pendergast and O'Malley, partners in the insurance scam, joined up once again reporting together on the same day, May 29, 1930, to the Leavenworth Federal Penitentiary. Pendergast was now prisoner number 55295.

On July 21, 1939 the Federal Grand Jury indicted Charlie Carrollo on four counts of tax evasion for the years 1935 to 1938. He was also charged with violating postal laws and committing perjury. Carrollo opted to take his chances with a jury and his perjury case went to trial on October 17, 1939. The government paraded before the jury a string of witnesses to testify how they had been forced to pay Carrollo for protection. Carrollo took the stand admitting he indeed had collected monies from gamblers but claimed he had not kept any of it, passing it on to Boss Tom Pendergast. Unbelievably Carrollo admitted he actually received more money in one year than the $462,007.94 attributed to him for the four-year period covered in the indictment. He explained his annual collections were well over $500,000.

Twenty-five minutes after the perjury case went to the jury they were back with a guilty verdict. The following day Carrollo changed his not guilty pleas to two other tax counts, and to one postal charge, to guilty. Big Charlie Carrollo drew sentences totaling 8 years.

Sitting in Leavenworth Penitentiary Boss Tom was outraged by Carrollo's testimony setting annual collections at a half million dollars, and claiming it was all handed over to him. Boss Tom chimed in with his own unbelievable denial, claiming he had not received any money from Carrollo except on one occasion when he was given $60,000. All in all we are left with the protestations of a corrupt political boss on the one hand, and on the other hand, a crime "family" figure, as to who got the money.

Apparently an eight-year sentence wasn't sufficient for Charlie Carrollo. After arriving at Leavenworth Penitentiary to serve his sentence, he became involved in a conspiracy to smuggle contraband into the prison, earning him a transfer to "the rock", Alcatraz Penitentiary.

Governor Stark went a step further mounting a push in the Missouri General Assembly for a new bill that would end Home Rule in Kansas City, restoring control of the police department to the State. This was accomplished in July 1939 over the resistance of "organization" die-hards who were overwhelmed.

Boss Tom was released from prison in May 1940 having served a year and a day. His wife moved out of the mansion taking an apartment. He lived alone, his friends having deserted him. He died the night of January 26, 1945. He was laid to rest at the Quirk-Tobin Funeral Chapel. The lineup to pay their respects stretched out the door beyond Linwood and Main Streets.

On January 29, 1945, Pendergast's funeral was held at Visitation Church, 52nd & Main Streets. Among the thousand or so mourners were prominent citizens and former public officials. Vice President of the United States Harry S. Truman flew in on an army bomber from Washington D.C., causing the 10:00 am scheduled start to be delayed awaiting his arrival. Truman could have easily found reason not to attend, but he came and stated, "He was always my friend, and I have always been his".

Boss Tom's nephew James M. Pendergast took over the political reins at 1908 Main Street where he hung a large photo of his friend Harry Truman. Truman had once said he owed his political life to the Pendergast organization, and had always remained loyal.

Harry S. Truman would become President of the United States. Saddled with the legacy of his association with the Pendergast machine, and his undying and outspoken loyalty to it, has led to a debate as to the true character of the man. On the one side he is viewed as the honest public servant, able to rise above the cesspool that surrounded him, unaware of the crimes taking place. On the other side he is considered no better than those who put him in office, an honest front man protecting the power of thieves, racketeers and murderers.

Interestingly, Truman himself in his recorded private notes provides some insight into his thinking on these weighty matters.

Concerning a time when he was a Jackson County Administrative Judge he wrote of having acceded to Pendergast's request that he grant road contracts to crooked contractors. "I had to compromise with him. I had to let a former saloon keeper and murderer, a friend of the Big Boss, steal about $10,000 from the general revenues of the County to satisfy my ideal associate and keep the crooks from getting a million or more out of the bond issue. Was I right or did I compromise a felony? I don't know."

At other times during Truman's watch monies stolen were in the millions. Truman wrote, "I was able to expend $7,000,000 for the taxpayers benefit...At the same time I gave away about a million in general revenue to satisfy the politicians. But if I hadn't done that the crooks would have had half the seven million... I wonder if I did right to put a lot of no account sons of bitches on the payroll and pay other sons of bitches more money for supplies than they were worth in order to satisfy the political powers and save three and one half million. I believe I did do right." Truman even questioned whether he should have stolen himself. "I could have had $1,500,000. I haven't $150. Am I a fool or an ethical giant? I don't know." His private admissions concerning his knowledge of such corruption were in stark contrast to his public statements. As time passed he became even more rigid denying anything untoward occurred on his watch.

If Truman was aware of the corruption then he also had to be aware the machine was aligned with mobsters, meaning a fair share of the beatings, bombings, kidnappings, intimidation, vote frauds and even murder that occurred could be laid at the doorstep of the machine. On this point Truman wrote he had been doing "some deep and conscientious thinking", and further, "I think that maybe that machines are not so good for the country."

Good Government & The Reformers

In 1938, a year prior to the downfall, in what could be described as a "clean election", machine candidates were once again success-ful in winning eight of nine city council seats. Despite the victory the climate had been altered. Following the conviction and jailing of Boss Tom and Charlie Carrollo disparate reform groups were en-ergized, precipitating unification and an organized push against the machine.

After the fall of Boss Tom, the Good Government Association de-vised a plan to unseat the current city council, and further clean the city up. Prior recall petitions had routinely been buried by the city clerk beholden to Pendergast. The new plan bypassed the use of the recall petition requiring submission to the city clerk. Instead they sought a city charter amendment calling for a reduction in the terms of elected officials from 4 years to 2 years. Proposed charter amend-ments were not submitted to the city clerk, but rather went to the Board of Election Commissioners appointed by the Governor. The reformers' charter amendment was put to a vote of the public, and it passed. The next city election was moved up from 1942 to 1940. The plan worked to perfection when in 1940 the voters tossed out mayor Bryce Smith and most the city council

The 1940 campaign was hard fought and John B. Gage was elected mayor heading up a non- partisan city council. Gage's father, John C. Gage, was a pioneer civic leader and a lawyer who practiced law from 1859 until his death in 1915. Gage had worked in his father's firm while attending night law school. After graduation he established his own firm in 1930, now known as Lathrop & Gage.

As Mayor, Gage inherited a city in fiscal chaos, and faced a new breed of politician bent on establishing a patronage system of their own. Gage would have none of that, and installed a system of merit examinations for all city employees, cut the city budget, and established an orderly, businesslike way of conducting city affairs. Gage had not wanted the Mayor's job, running only when others had turned it down. However, it is universally agreed he was the right man for the job, described as one of the great mayors of modern American cities. He served three two-year terms from 1940 to 1946.

In an interview with the Kansas City Star in 1990, Gage's widow, Marjorie Hires Gage, recalled those years when she and her husband did battle with the Pendergast machine. In the months preceding the mayoral election the Gage family suffered threats and harassment. Garbage collection at their home was cut off, threatening phone calls day and night, their taxes were hiked, and some friendships faded away. "That's just the way things were in those days. If the people in government didn't like you, they could do whatever they wanted, such as taking out your water meter. It cost $100 to put in a new one", Mrs. Gage explained.

This was a time when anyone opposing the machine could expect reprisals and inducements to cease and desist. The husband of Eloise Comer, a leader in the women's movement, owner of an advertising agency with some clients connected to the machine, was offered a new Cadillac if he would get his wife to quit her political activism. Where he had previously been opposed to political involvement, the bribe offer so angered him that he joined his wife in the crusade.

Mrs. Gage was one of throngs of women who became active in the fight to oust the Pendergast machine. In 1940 women were a political force taking over from their husbands, sons, brothers, fathers, uncles, who earned their living from the machine, afraid to actively oppose it and its candidates. They supported John Gage for the position of mayor and won. The headline in the Colorado Springs Gazette read, "Women Defeat Machine Rule In Kansas City." The symbol of their fight was the broom, representing the goal of a clean sweep.

At rallies the women came armed with real brooms in addition to sporting broom pins. Estimates put the number of the women involved between 5000 and 7000.

L.P. Cookingham, a professional city manger, was chosen for the post in Kansas City charged with directing the cleanup. Cookingham's career as a city manager started with a job as city manager of a Detroit suburban city in 1927. In 1936 he was hired as city manager of Saginaw, Michigan, and was serving in this capacity when he got the call from Kansas City. The challenge he faced was a city hall marred by two decades of Pendergast influence, including wasteful spending, padded payrolls, vote fraud, patronage, corruption, and the "cut and lug" system. The "cut" was a kickback from city hall salaries to the machine. The "lug" was a mandatory campaign contribution city employees had to make. Reports set the cost to city and Jackson County employees over a ten-year period at more than 10 million dollars.

There was little doubt as to Cookingham's qualification for the job, however there was a sticking point. He balked at the prospect of having to be the one to implement wholesale firings. To solve the problem an interim city manager was appointed, a lawyer named Kenneth Midgley. His sole job was to remove just about every department head owing his job to the Pendergast machine. After one month Midgley had accomplished the task and Cookingham took over on June 10, 1940. Twelve hundred of some thirty-eight-hundred city employees had been fired or had resigned.

Similar to Mayor Gage, Cookingham was indeed the right man for the job, and is recognized for his role in restoring honest government to a city that was nationally known as wide open, criminally infested, and corrupt to the core. He resigned in 1959 leaving a lasting legacy on the city.

Mrs. Marjorie Gage, never one to sit on the sidelines, returned to the fray in the fight against the machine in 1946 when it reared its ugly head. She took to the radio to rally the public, particularly women to vote Republican. She railed against the return to power of "the clique who nearly destroyed it", referring to the city itself. "The same group of men with the aid of those whom they drop the crumbs from their table to, who reaped such gigantic graft at the expense of the masses in years gone by, has again made a definite and open bid for return to power. The attempted comeback hinges on the election of the presiding judge of the county court and the prosecuting attorney."

The Outfit After Pendergast

With the onslaught of Federal, State and County investigations culminating in the indictments and jailing of Boss Tom Pendergast and Charlie Carrollo, the members of the ruling council of the criminal organization, except for Tony Gizzo, were conveniently absent from the city. Big Jim Balestrere traveled to Milwaukee, while Gaetano Lococco, complaining of an arthritic ailment, sought the sun in Arizona and Nogales, Mexico, where he purchased a 10-unit motel called the El Reposo. Charlie Gargotta was in the penitentiary and Charlie Binaggo was out of the city.

With Boss Tom out of the picture, Charlie Carrollo in jail, John Lazia dead, the machine in tatters, reformers in office, conditions were, to say the least, tight. But demand was still there, the taste of the wide-open days still lingered, and the crime family, as one must understand, is in it for the long run. An inherent characteristic of Cosa Nostra is the leaders and members anticipate and plan for a continuous, indefinite lifespan of operations. The ability to adjust and meet changing conditions was one of Cosa Nostra's greatest strengths. Combined with its unique criminal history and culture Cosa Nostra outlasted the field, and became the dominant organized crime force.

During this period, from approximately January 1939 to October 1939, it appeared Tony Gizzo assumed the reigns as the out front mob boss. Gizzo, along with Tano Lococco, Charlie Gargotta, and Charlie Binaggio were among the group of younger toughs brought along by Boss John Lazia in the 1920s. By the 1930s these men had graduated to the upper ranks of the crime "family", and shared in the profits from racket activities. They would have a large say in ongoing operations regardless who was put out front as Boss. They were beholden to Big Jim Balestrere and Joe DiGiovanni operating behind the scenes, and whose advice and consent was essential. Gizzo was especially tied to Balestrere acting as his personal representative in Balestrere's many and varied interests.

Over a period of time Gizzo had developed a wide range of acquaintances among racket figures all around the nation, prompting Senator Estes Kefauver to remark that Gizzo had wider personal acquaintance with gangsters around the country than any racketeer the committee had come across to date. Gizzo was in fact believed to be the Kansas City outfits' traveling contact man with mobsters in numerous other cities.

Gizzo claimed he was born in New York City in 1901 both of his parents having come to America from Italy. He stood 5'7" tall, weighed over 200 pounds, and dressed expensively. His public face was that of an affable, pleasant sort disguising what he really was. He loved to eat well, was a womanizer, and known for his grand entrances upon visits to his favorite nightspots, restaurants and taverns. He served a two- year sentence in 1924 on a conviction for possession of a large quantity of narcotics, his one and only prison stay.

Gizzo, a gambler at heart, sought to put gambling operations on a business basis, and to do this he elevated a Jewish gambling whiz named Morris "Snag" Klein. Gizzo's flamboyant style belied the fact he was anything but an astute businessman or organizer. He was seen as a weak leader, too weak to hold things together. Unrest and considerable dissension rippled through the ranks representing a challenge to his leadership position.

By the mid 1940s the situation shifted to the point Gizzo stepped aside, and Charlie Binaggio, who had accumulated substantial political clout, assumed the out front leadership post. His reign would be one big roller coaster ride.

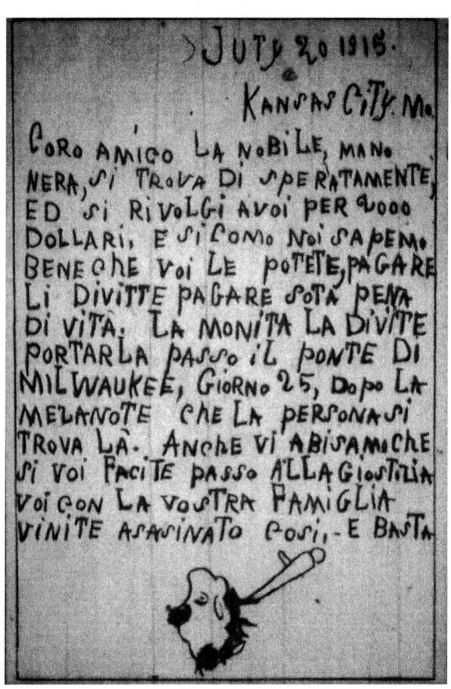

1915 Black Hand letter demanding $2000
on the threat of death.

Black Hand members rounded up July 1915.
L-R: John Cirricione, Antonio Maniscalo, Mariano Alonzi,
Salvatore Tripiraro, Dominic Carrollo, Paul Cantanzaro.

Kansas City Police Officer,
Joe Raimo, murdered
March 28, 1911.

Kansas City Police Detective,
Louis Olivero, murdered
November 28, 1930.

Big Jim Balestrere.

Pete DiGiovanni, right, and brother Joe, left.

Chicago Boss, Al Capone.

*Chicago racket figure
Charles Fiscetti.*

Charles Carrollo.

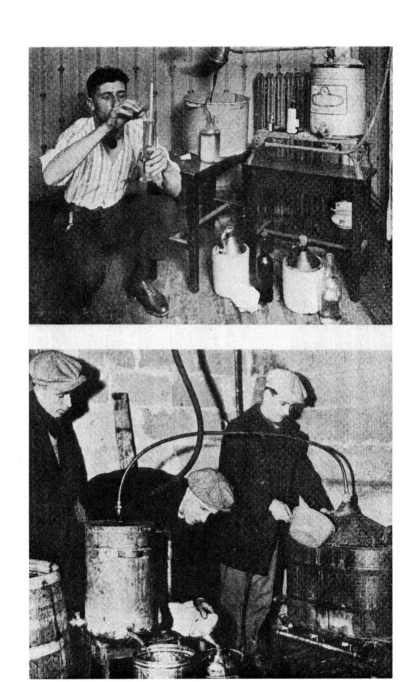

A prohibition era home alcohol still.

After Sheriff
Bash arrested
a Pendergast
man, Truman
cut the
sheriff's
budget.

Sheriff Bash
(right);
dergast man
les Gargotta
(above).

Jackson County Sheriff Thomas Bash and Charles Gargotta (inset).

Gaetano "Tano" Lococo   Tony Gizzo, circa 1939.

COUNTY COURT
JACKSON COUNTY, MISSOURI

EUGENE I. PURCELL
ASSOCIATE JUDGE
EASTERN DISTRICT

HARRY S. TRUMAN
PRESIDING JUDGE

BATTLE McCARDLE
ASSOCIATE JUDGE
WESTERN DISTRICT

KANSAS CITY, MO.

ROBERT LEE NIVENS
LICENSE INSPECTOR

Oct. 16, 1933

Mr. James M. Pendergast,
1908 Main Street,
Kansas City, Missouri

Dear Mr. Pendergast:

The bearer Mr. R. R. Cramer, 3722 Wabash Ave.,
has lived in the 13th. Ward for about two years, and has the
recommendation of Mr. C. H. Phillips, his Precinct Captain.

I know this boy's father, who is connected with
the Jenkins Music Co. now located in Wichita, Kansas.

If possible I would appreciate the favor if you
could place this young man somewhere. Thanking you you for
past favors, I am,

Yours truly,

R. L. Nivens.
13th. WARD.

Letter signed by John Lazia and James Pendergast approving request for a Kansas City Missouri Police Department hire.

217

John Lazia.

Joe Lusco (seated).

File photo

The State Line Tavern, later the Last Chance, sat on the state line (arrow) at 3205 Southwest Blvd. The building, with Goulding's Saloon in the front, was divided by a line painted on the floor. Gamblers moved to the west side if Missouri officers visited, and to the east if the police were from Kansas.

State Line Tavern/Last Chance Saloon S.W. Blvd. and State Line.

THE INTERIOR OF THE FIRST DISTRICT DEMOCRATIC club at 716-18 Truman road, scene of the fatal shooting of Charles Binaggio and Cha gotta, is shown here in a cutaway sketch drawn by Frank Miller, an artist for The Star, who went to the location shortly after the bodies were di The office in the rear of the clubroom at the left generally was used by Henry McKissick and Binaggio occupied the one at the right. Binaggio's found in a chair by one of two desks located in an outer office enclosed only by a wooden guard railing. Less than two feet from the front door at

Murder scene, June 1950, assassination of Charles Binaggio and Charles Gargotta,
First Democatic Club, 716-18 Truman Road.

219

The Two Charlies - Binaggio and Gargotta.

Teamster Union powers, Roy L. Williams, right and James R Hoffa, left.

Eddie "Spitz" Osadchey (left), Tony Gizzo (right),
at Kefauver Committee hearing.

Landmark Tower, Las Vegas, Nevada.

Chapter IX

The Kansas City Narcotics Syndicate

NARCOTICS WERE ANOTHER vice made illegal early in the 19th century prompting thousands of addicts hooked on opiates and cocaine found in hundreds of health elixirs and patent medicines to seek drugs illegally. Following the normal pattern, racketeers and criminals capitalized on the drug prohibition, just as they did with alcohol, entering the field and filling the demand. What had previously been a client base of hard drug users, such as pimps, whores, thieves, and the like, now expanded to the middle and upper class, elixir addicted housewives craving their 'fix." Where drug trafficking had been a modest sideline it would now experience extraordinary growth. Kansas City soon would gain recognition as a locale where during the 1930s and 1940s the outfit came to dominate the field of narcotics trafficking.

Jewish racketeers had dominated the narcotics field until the mid 1930s. To a far lesser extent Italian gangs had been trafficking in drugs since the early 1900s. Enhancing their position as they consolidated nationally, the organization began taking over the narcotics trade, a shift law enforcement authorities had not immediately noticed. Henry J. Anslinger, of the Federal Bureua of Narcotics, tells of debriefing an informant of Sicilian extraction in the late 1930s, and learning of the Mafia's heavy involvement in narcotics. Although aware of the existence of powerful Italian gangs, having extraordinary cohesion, their true significance was as yet unrecognized.

By 1940 Anslinger and his Bureau of Narcotics had a handle on what by then had developed into a national cartel, they labeled the "Maifa", recognizing it as far more than just another criminal grouping. At this time the concept of an organized crime entity this significant seemed so unreal, so foreign, that it was dismissed by most other law enforcement agencies as a myth. Despite resistance, the Bureau of Narcotics stood its ground, warning any and all of the existence of such an organization, and the threat it represented. Time would prove the Bureau of Narcotics correct.

Support for the Bureau of Narcotics' findings, and their warnings, came in the form of a major narcotics operation unearthed in Kansas City in 1940. Serving as a backdrop, leading up to that case, the following events and individuals composed a mosaic that was the Kansas City narcotics scene.

Drugs In The City

Men who would become prominent in the Kansas City crime "family", and their associates, had at one time or another been involved with narcotics trafficking, as evidenced by arrest and conviction records. To name a few, Joe Lascuola was arrested in April 1919 for investigation as a "dope peddler." He was indicted in August 1921 for possession of morphine and cocaine, convicted and received a 6-month sentence. His brother Michael Lascoula was arrested in December 1929 for sale and possession of narcotics. Angelo "Bossie" Nigro was charged federally with narcotics violations in May 1924, convicted and received a four-year sentence. Anthony Mangiaracina was convicted in 1939, receiving a two-year sentence, and Max Ducov had a 1924 narcotics conviction. Carl "Cork" Civella was convicted on narcotics charges. How many others had similar involvement may never be known as police records were cleaned out during the home rule heyday.

In September 1923 two well-dressed young men speeding wildly up and down the streets in a high-powered car caught the attention of the police. An investigation followed and surveillance of the two men led to a house at 2822 Bales Avenue. On September 27, 1923, at a time the residence was unoccupied, the police made entry. They discovered a door to the basement behind which bricks had been piled. Once the door was forced, the police located four new car tires fitting the description of tires stolen the night of September 6th at 13th and Lydia from Mr. C.J. Allis of Independence, Mo.

The tires were taken to Police Headquarters and the officers returned to the Bales Avenue residence to conduct a complete search. They were just about to wrap things up when a dilapidated suitcase was found containing a large quantity of morphine, cocaine and opium, having a wholesale value of $3500. While the police were still inside the house the two men showed up in a new Ford Sedan, one going to the front door, the other to the rear of the house. The man at the front door had a key and was about to open the door when he was arrested. His name was Anthony "Tony" Gizzo, and his associate was a William E. Clifford.

According to the police one of the men offered a bribe of $1500 crying out, "For God's sake we want to do business with you officers. You've got the goods on us. We've got $1500 in cash here between us. We'll give it to you, and also the Ford sedan, and the Apperson car out in the front yard." The officers' rejected the bribe whereupon the offer was raised to $10,000, also turned down.

At Police Headquarters the two men were uncooperative, claiming no knowledge of the drugs. Four memo books were found in their possession contained what police described as 110 listed sales of narcotics ranging from $20 to $100. The owners of the Bales Avenue residence informed the police Gizzo and Clifford had been rooming there for some 3 weeks.

On January 24, 1924 Gizzo and Clifford appeared in Federal District Court entering pleas of guilty to charges of possession of narcotics. Each received a prison sentence of one year and one day. Better days were in store for Gizzo who became one of John Lazia's principle operatives, and in later years rose to the position of outward leader of the crime 'family."

On the night of March 14 and the morning of March 15, 1935 federal narcotics agents and local police conducted simultaneous raids as part of a nationwide sweep of drug dealers and users. Fifty-one subjects were taken into custody, and a quantity of narcotics seized. In all 96 arrests were made within the Bureau of Narcotics Kansas City District, including eleven in St. Joseph, Missouri.

A raiding party, on the morning of March 15, 1935, hit a 5th floor room of the Midwest Hotel, 1925 Main Street, breaking in when they were refused entrance. Charles Bolen, 44, and his wife Virginia, 30 were found inside the room, and were arrested. Officers could hear others in an adjoining room making a get-away. Looking out an open window the officers spotted a tobacco pouch, and upon recovering it found 200 ounces of morphine inside. Caught after fleeing the hotel was Betty Harvey, 35, Alice Johnson 21, and John Keys aged 44. During their attempt to escape they discarded a box which the police recovered. It contained 150 grains of morphine.

Joe Russo, another subject targeted by the drug agents, made his drug sales under the ruse of running a taxicab service. Customers, mainly women, would call asking for a cab when in fact they were ordering drugs. At his apartment at 6th and Holmes Streets the officers nabbed Russo and seized a list with the names of thirty-six women, undoubtedly drug customers. Ted Ellis was arrested at his apartment in the process of weighing out morphine. William Rogers, when arrested, swallowed a quantity of morphine, and not surprisingly became violently ill while held at police headquarters.

Rose Affronti was yet another caught up in the net. She was the wife of Lonnie Affronti an ex-convict, known drug trafficker, and fugitive from justice, having narcotics and first-degree murder charges pending against him.

The nation wide round up involved thousands of law enforcement personnel coming from the Narcotics Bureau, Coast Guard, Customs Service, Alcohol Tax Unit, I.R.S. Intelligence Division, and local police. Besides Kansas City, arrests and seizures were made in Washington D.C, New York, New Jersey, Chicago, San Francisco, and Los Angeles.

A front-page story in the Kansas City Star in April 1939 reported on the arrests of a group of men, referred to as the "Angelo Donnici Ring", involved in a twelve million dollar a year interstate drug operation specializing in heroin.

For years Angelo Donnici operated as a professional bondsman, and in 1939 was the proprietor of the Buffet Tavern. His exterior demeanor belied the fact in his earlier years he had been connected with the infamous "Black Hand."

An analysis of the heroin recovered in the case established it had come from the Japanese concession in Tientsin, China. The ring also obtained small amounts of narcotics from the Balkan states. The China heroin came through the Suez Canal to France, then to New York, arriving in Kansas City packed in many different ways, for one, toys addressed to women. From Kansas City the drugs were distributed to the Pacific coast, Wyoming, Colorado, Oklahoma, New Orleans and Minneapolis.

Some eleven subjects were arrested and implicated in the operation of this drug network, a number of whom had ties to the Joe Lusco faction. Among those arrested was Angelo "Bossie" Nigro, described as an executive in the operation, and his cousin, James Nigro. Also rounded up were James Abbott, brother-in-law of Joe Lusco, free on bond from a narcotics arrest the prior month, and Tony Mangiaracina, both described as runners for the ring. If he had not been murdered, labor thug Tony "Shirt" Cammisa reportedly would have been charged as a member of the ring.

Nine years later, in April 1948, Mike Licausi, one of those involved with the ring, was murdered two weeks after opening a gambling establishment.

The Outfit - Narcotics Branch

The Federal Bureau of Narcotics cited the end of prohibition as the time the Kansas City outfit formed what they labeled the "Narcotics Branch" of the criminal organization. The entire operation was laid out for the Kefauver Committee by then Federal Narcotics Agent Claude Follmer. Joseph DeLuca was identified as heading up the operation, while the outfit's top men, James Balestrere, Joe DiGiovanni, Pete DiGiovanni and Tony Gizzo profited from it. The Narcotics Bureau identified eight others including Joe DeLuca's brother Frank, as principles, describing the entire group as "Mafia members."

Joe DeLuca was born April 17, 1893, in Giardinello, Sicily, arriving in the United States April 10, 1910. Upon his arrival he is believed to have first gone to St. Louis, Missouri, before moving on to Kansas City. Once in Kansas City he sent for his brother Frank, also born in Sicily. The two brothers got their start in the bootleg liquor business, building it up to the point they were considered among the most prominent operators in the field. They were among the founders of the original Sugar House Syndicate in the late 1920s. After repeal of prohibition the DeLucas, supported by the outfit, entered the narcotics trade establishing narcotics contacts throughout the country.

Frank DeLuca was known to travel extensively to locales such as Miami, Florida, New York City, Chicago, Memphis, California, and St. Louis. A particularly close associate was St. Louis racketeer Tony Lopiparo. On June 13, 1943, while the Second World War was raging, Frank was arrested as an enemy alien, and for a period of time interred in a government camp.

Nick Impastato held the position of second in command to Joe DeLuca, acting as the general manager of the ring. Impastato was born June 1, 1900 in Cinisi, Sicily and reportedly fled Sicily in 1927 to escape Dictator Musolini's purge of Mafia members. A Kansas City newspaper in recounting Impastato's illegal entry into the country described him making it to our shores in a rowboat, coming from a ship in the waters outside New Orleans, Louisiana.

Federal narcotics agent Claude Follmer was involved in the investigation and described for the Kefauver Committee how Nick

Impastato first came to the attention of narcotics officers. In 1929 the agents were given the name "Nicoline" and a lead that this person had come to Kansas City from Chicago, Illinois, back in 1924 to serve as an enforcer for John Lazia. That was all they had to go on at the time.

Then investigation of Nicolo Gentile, and his partner, Charles "Big Nose" LaGaipa, according to a knowledgeable law enforcement source, determined that in 1937 they were engaged as narcotics distributors traveling throughout the United States. On one such trip the two men visited Kansas City, an old stomping ground for Gentile, where they attempted to convince Nicolo Impastato and Joe DeLuca to purchase narcotics through them. However, Impastato explained they were already set up with a source, a Turkish contact that shipped the drugs via a Cuban intermediary. Instead of selling any drugs, Gentile and La Gaipa agreed they would purchase any narcotics Impastato and DeLuca were unable to dispose of.

In 1937, Bureau of Narcotics agents in New Orleans, LA arrested Gentile in connection with a nation-wide narcotics ring involving 88 individuals strung out around the country and in Europe. By this time Gentile, as documented in earlier chapters, was recognized as a traveling delegate, arbitrator and conciliator for the Mafia-like clans around the country, both feared and respected. In his possession were address books representing a veritable who's who of Mafia drug traffickers, including the name of Kansas City outfit figure Nick Impostato. These events established Impastato as a person of great interest to the narcotics agents in Kansas City.

Under DeLuca and Impastato's direction narcotics trafficking was put on a business basis, employing managers, supervisors, a legal advisor, bookkeeper, traveling representatives and a sales force. Contacts were developed with major sources of narcotics outside the city, and the ring was soon supplying markets outside of Kansas City, in Texas, Oklahoma, Iowa, Nebraska, Arkansas, Kansas, Colorado, and Illinois.

The first crack in the foundation came about in early 1940 when Louis & Patsy Ventola were arrested by federal narcotics agents and Kansas City police detectives after numerous small narcotics purchases had been made by a Federal undercover agent. Heroin having a wholesale value of $3000 was seized. The drugs were found in a briefcase the officers established was owned by Pete DiGiovanni, Patsy Ventola's father-in-law.

Charles Bengimina and the Ventolas were subsequently charged with drug trafficking, pled guilty, and received minor prison sentences.

Narcotics agents were systematically unearthing details of the operation and plotting the organizational setup of the ring. The two Ventolas acted as salesmen working for Charles "Red Brick" Bengimina, who in turn was a distributor for Carl Caramusa. Caramusa, a fringe outfit figure, was associated with Joe DeLuca in the operation of a nightclub, and the front man for the drug syndicate's partners who remained in the background.

The investigation pushed on and expanded during the years 1941 and 1942 with the agents continuing to make undercover buys, and conducting surveillances. For one, they shadowed Carl Caramusa and he led them to a large cache of drugs ingeniously concealed behind a secret panel in the wall of an apartment belonging to Samuel and Fellipo Pernice. Caramusa and Charles Taibi, aka Ryan, were arrested along with both Pernices in February 1942. The wholesale value of the heroin seized was placed at $40,000, and when "cut" and retailed it would have brought approximately one quarter million dollars.

At each stage of the investigation, as arrests and seizures were made, further details surfaced as to the nature and scope of the drug ring's operation. Raw opium was obtained from legitimate producers in countries such as Persia (Now Iran), India, Turkey, and others, then processed into heroin in clandestine labs. The heroin was then delivered to members of the Sicilian Mafia and the French underworld to be smuggled out from French and Italian ports to New York City and Cuba. The Cuban contact in the network was identified as a politician and internationally known drug smuggler, Juan Manuel Alfonso. Narcotics were then smuggled from Havana, Cuba, to the Antinori brothers in Tampa, Florida, and this represented a source of supply for the Kansas City ring.

James DiSimone, representing the Kansas City narcotics syndicate, acted as a courier transporting the drugs from Tampa to Kansas City. In the spring of 1939 DeSimone introduced Caramusa to Paul Antinori in Tampa, and Caramusa transported a quantity of narcotics back to Kansas City. Thereafter, Caramusa obtained drugs from the Antinori's in August 1939, February 1940, and June 1940.

Upon Impastato's instructions, Caramusa took the drugs he brought in from Florida to the Pernice residence where they were concealed. The Pernices were being paid $35.00 a month for the use of their residence as a drop off point for the drugs.

Drug traffickers Paul & Joseph Antinori assumed command of the Tampa operation upon the murder of their father Ignacio on October 18, 1940 in Miami, Florida. Government agents believed Antinori was murdered in retaliation for a spot killing the prior year of a Tampa rival in the narcotics business.

Sebastino Nani, one time Brooklyn, New York mob member, had relocated to California where he represented another drug contact for the Kansas City ring, furnishing several large shipments to them. In later years Nani was a person of interest for the Kefauver Committee during hearings held in San Francisco. The committee heard testimony concerning Nani's "acquaintanceship and contacts" with Joe

DiGiovanni and Jim Balestrere of Kansas City.

Heroin was supplied by the Kansas City ring to a St. Louis branch of the operation managed by racket figure John Vitale who in turn worked for Tom Buffa and Tony Lopiparo, the leaders of the St. Louis crime syndicate.

The first round of charges came on April 1, 1942 when a federal grand jury indicted 11 individuals for conspiracy to violate Federal narcotics laws. This indictment was followed by a superseding 155 count indictment, returned December 18, 1942, expanding the case with the addition of two defendants, Thomas Buffa and Tony Lopiparo of St. Louis.

Eight members of the ring were convicted and received prison sentences. Of those playing major roles, Joe DeLuca received a 3 years prison sentence; Nicolo Impastato a 2 years sentence; James DiSimone a 6-year sentence; Paul and Joseph Antinori 5-year sentences; and Carl Caramusa a 4-year sentence.

The charges against the Ventolas and Charles Bengimina were dismissed in light of their prior conviction and sentence. Charges against Buffa and Lopiparo of St. Louis were subsequently dismissed for lack of evidence.

Caught up in the quagmire, Joe DeLuca's girlfriend was convicted of perjury. In 1940 DeLuca and Frances Perry resided in adjoining units at the Ricardo Apartments. Telephone records for Perry's apartment, obtained by investigators, revealed three calls to Tampa, two of which were to Paul Antinori. Ms. Perry, called to testify before a federal grand jury, was not truthful in her responses to questions asked about the calls, and other related matters. As a result she was charged with perjury, and convicted. In December 1942 she and DeLuca married.

Thomas Buffa, a member of the St. Louis branch of the ring, opted to cooperate, and appeared as a witness for the government in the perjury trial of Perry. Not surprisingly, upon his return to St. Louis an unsuccessful attempt was made to assassinate him. Buffa wisely fled to California. As the saying goes, you can run but you can't hide, and on March 27, 1947, in Lodi, California, he was shotgunned to death.

In what was considered a startling breakthrough, the narcotics agents were able to get Carl Caramusa to cooperate, and in a large measure insured a successful prosecution of the case. In testifying in open court for the government, something no other insider had ever done, Caramusa had violated the sacred code of omerta. There is strong reason to believe his motivation stemmed from the fact his 11 year-old-brother was slain by the Black Hand. Frank Caramusa Jr was shot to death in 1919 in front of a crowd of witnesses none of whom were willing to testify, allowing the alleged killer, Paul Cantanzaro, to walk free.

In a page right out of the Sicilian Mafia's handbook, Cantanzao was called on to perform a very special service, one having a distinct old world flavor. In March 1943 Cantanzaro was conspicuously present in federal court while Caramusa was on the witness stand testifying. Caramusa couldn't miss his brother's killer as Cantanzaro was seated in the very front row. Staring down the witness while making subtle and threatening gestures, Cantanzaro did his very best to intimidate the witness until he was finally ejected from the courtroom.

At the time of his testimony Caramusa was serving in the US Army. In consideration of his invaluable cooperation the court first reduced his 4-year prison term, and then further altered the sentence, placing him on probation. Upon completing his tour of duty he took the only real option left for him. He went into hiding, changing his name, beginning a new life with his wife and family in Chicago, Ill. where he became a part owner of a furniture factory.

As he no doubt realized, one day he would face the long arm of the outfit. In June 1945 the 37-year old Caramusa was shotgunned to death. A car, with three men inside, had followed him home, murdering him in front of his 16-year old daughter and several of her friends. His family told the police Caramusa was never without the revolver they found on his body.

Although Caramusa was aware death was near it did him no good. Several days before he was killed, desperate for help, he had telephoned Narcotics Agent Claude Follmer telling him, "They're after me. I am being followed and watched." Caramusa explained he had spotted one of his "enemies" watching him from a car with Florida plates, the driver ducking low to avoid recognition. Follmer couldn't get help to Caramusa in time.

Suspicion centered on James Lumia of Tampa, Florida, an associate of the Antinori brothers, and Leonard Calamea, believed to be the driver of the murder car. Calamea had a prior connection to Kansas City, having been arrested there in a narcotics case. Chicago police picked up Calamea and questioned him about the murder. Of course he had nothing to say, and with evidence lacking the police had to release him.

Five years after the Caramusa murder, in June 1950, Lumia was murdered in Tampa, Florida. Some three and one half years after that, in November 1953, Joe Antinori of Tampa was murdered. Counting Tom Buffa and Caramusa, four individuals connected in one way or the other with the narcotics syndicate were murdered.

Murder was not the only threat some members of the ring had to face inasmuch as the government was seeking to deport them. First, James DiSimone, the ring's drug courier, was deported in 1953. Nicolo Impastato, who in the interim years had been provided employment at Joe Filardo's Roma Bakery and in the DiGiovanni liquor businesses, also faced government efforts to deport him, as did Joe DeLuca.

Ironically Inmpostato and DeLuca were aided in their fight to avoid deportation by the very Assistant United States Attorney who had been assigned to prosecute the narcotics ring, Richard K. Phelps. After Phelps left the United States Attorney's Office in Kansas City he represented a number of organized crime subjects, several of whom he had previously prosecuted on behalf of the Government. He had represented Joe and Pete DiGiovanni, charged by the State of Missouri with liquor price fixing in the conduct of their liquor distributorship. He also represented them in a liquor license revocation hearing held by the Kansas City Liquor Control Director.

In 1953 Phelps testified as a witness for Joe DeLuca in a hearing held in response to a government order of deportation. At the time of his testimony Phelps was the Jackson County District Attorney.

Other forces were also at work in Impastato's behalf. U.S. Senator Olin D. Johnson of South Carolina introduced a bill calling for Impastato to be declared a legal citizen despite the fact his appeal of a formal order of deportation had been turned down, having gone all the way to the Supreme Court.

In May 1955 attorney Phelps had dropped a letter to Senator Johnson on behalf of Impastato advising that as the prosecuting Assistant United States Attorney in the Kansas City "Narcotics Branch" case he "gave Impastato to understand" that if he pleaded guilty there would be a no deportation recommendation made to the presiding judge. Based on Phelp's representations Senator Johnson was prompted to introduce the bill on Impastato's behalf.

On June 16, 1955 Senator Langer of North Dakota, co-sponsor of the bill, made a speech from the Senate floor defending Impastato. As Senator Langer saw it Impastato's record since coming to America thirty-one years ago was "apparently good aside from this one matter in which he became involved." Senator Langer added, "It may be that Mr. Impastato has married an American girl. It may be that he has a large family, and that these innocent people would be vitally affected by the deportation of the husband and the father to a foreign country...." What Senator Langer either was unaware of, did not bother to check, or chose to ignore, Impastato had never married.

Senator Alexander Wiley of Wisconsin, a member of the Kefauver Committee, attacked the bill describing Impastato's crime, "Of all the low, filthy crimes in the United States, there is nothing lower or filthier than peddling dope." Senator Wiley made public a letter from Harry Anslinger, Commissioner of the Federal Bureau of Narcotics, describing Impastato as a "professional killer."

In response to the exchange between the two Senators, Senator Johnson in part stated, "I have not become excited over it. (The proposed bill) I do not intend to become excited over it." Concerning the question of why the bill was introduced, and who was behind it, Senator Johnson explained, "I introduced the bill at the request of several people, and I have no apologies to make to any man or group of men."

Late in the year 1955 Impastato was finally deported to Italy. On the other hand, Joe DeLuca, one of the main cogs in the narcotics ring, escaped deportation. DeLuca had appealed the order of deportation pending against him, and the Eight Circuit U.S. Court of Appeals in St. Louis upheld his appeal. In its decision the court ruled the no deportation promise by the Assistant United States Attorney was a valid defense. This raises the question how was it that the same ruling didn't apply to Impastato? The explanation provided had to do with Impastato's illegal entry into the country after 1923, a cutoff date applicable to what was then a new immigration law.

Postscripts

There are many other stories adding color to the mosaic of the life and times of drug traffickers and drug rings, and the fact for a time Kansas City's was as a hub for drug distribution. The following are but a few them.

Mendy Weiss was a hulking killer, member of the infamous "Murder Incorporated" hit squad, and numero uno under mob luminary Louis "Lepke" Bukhalter. Weiss was also a narcotics trafficker. In 1940 he was indicted in New York City along with Bukhalter and 4 others for the September 13, 1936 murder of Brooklyn candy store owner Joseph Rosen. The case was broken when Abe Reles, another member of Murder Incorporated, turned informer naming the 6 men as Rosen's killers. By the time the indictments were handed down Weiss and Bukhalter had disappeared, leading to a nationwide manhunt. Reles was killed when he mysteriously fell, or was pushed, from the window of a hotel room while in protective custody, guarded by a number of New York City police detectives.

On the night of April 6, 1941, Federal Bureau of Narcotics Agent Albert Aman, assigned to Kansas City, spotted the new car Weiss was known to be driving. Weiss had put on weight, sported a reddish mustache and wore eyeglasses, but the change in appearance was not sufficient to fool Agent Aman. Weiss was in the company of his wife and the girlfriend of an unnamed big time Missouri gambler. When agents closed in Weiss became indignant claiming he was James W. Bell and they had made a big mistake. His protests went for naught, and he soon gave up the ghost, ending the charade. Besides the new car, Weiss had $1000 in a local bank account, and was carrying $2713. He had hid out between Kansas City and Colorado for some 14 months.

Living in Kansas City for six months prior to his arrest, Weiss had been able to gather under the Bell alias a social security card, and a draft registration from the 7th ward, ostensibly signed by some official. During this period Weiss was one of the most wanted men in America, his photo in every police station house, but despite that he was released on each of the 15 occasions he was stopped and/or arrested for traffic violations. Weiss casually explained he had talked his way of it on each occasion. Or could it have been Weiss had friends in the right places?

Yet another narcotics trafficker, named Joe Pici, found his way to the city to deal drugs. Charles Siragusa, of the Federal Bureau of Narcotics, testifying before a Senate crime committee identified Pici as a chief lieutenant in 1951 of the infamous Charles "Lucky" Luciano, both having been deported to Sicily in 1946. Pici was described as having a criminal career in Pittsburgh, Pennsylvania, and prior to his deportation had traveled frequently between Pittsburgh, New York and Kansas City. Pici, according to the information provided the Senate Committee, had illegally reentered the United States from Sicily in 1948 to deliver heroin to Kansas City.

Siragusa, in his autobiography, recounts his investigative efforts in 1951 and 1952 in combating the trafficking operations of Pici. Siragusa tracked a shipment of heroin Pici handed over to a courier in Sicily to be delivered to New York City. During his investigation Siragusa developed information that pure heroin was not only being transported from Italy to East and West Coast cities, but was being pumped into Detroit, St. Louis, Kansas City, and New Orleans. Frank Coppola was the boss of this operation, and he was yet another deported gangster with excellent connections to Kansas City. Coppola was described as an arch enemy of Lucky Luciano in the drug trade, the two having clashed when Coppola laid claim to the lucrative Midwestern drug market as his exclusively.

Siragusa points out, with the end of World War II in Europe in 1945, mobsters, whose drug operation had been interrupted by the war, wasted no time getting back in business. About this same time the American Government deported to Italy more than 100 top Mafia mobsters from New York, Chicago, Kansas City, Detroit, and New Orleans. These racketeers joined with their counterparts in Italy and Sicily swelling the ranks of well-connected drug traffickers who continued to ply their trade.

Nicolo Gentile - Final Chapter

The narcotics trade would represent the final chapter in the story of the intrepid "Zio Cola" Gentile, labeled by the Federal Narcotics Bureau as "a traveling delegate for the Mafia" during his years in the United States. Zio, the Italian word for uncle, is used by Cosa Nostra members as a sign of respect in addressing another member, normally one of rank. Gentile in recounting his downfall described it as "the account of this last part of my life, of which she (a girlfriend) was unknowingly the author of my ruin."

It is the late 1930s and Gentile is living in New York City connected to the crime "family" headed by Vincent Mangano. He had been hearing the most "flattering talk" about a young lady named Maria, a person of refinement, and "holder of a nursing degree." His interest grew by the day and he finally begged a friend, Calogero Jacono, a drug dealer, to introduce him to Maria. Although Jacono had a mistress he also had eyes for Maria and was reluctant to introduce a potential rival. Finally through another friend Gentile met Maria and soon "an amorous relationship" developed.

On one Sunday afternoon he was at Mary's apartment when Jacono's mistress paid a visit accompanied by three lovely ladies, one of whom, named Dorothy, was exceptionally beautiful. Dressed all in black, the veil of her hat covering her face, Dorothy cut quite an alluring figure. Jacono's mistress arranges for the two to meet and Dorothy confides in him parts of her background, and admits she knows of Gentile's reputation. She knew he was a dangerous man, but she had made up her mind to "conquer" him, even if her love should cost her life. He visited her each day, becoming romantically involved, and as Gentile writes, their relationship "became more intimate."

While embroiled in this romantic adventure, Gentile was paid a visit by a prominent Sicilian born narcotics trafficker by the name Charles "Big Nose" LaGaipa. La Gaipa sounded him out, and satisfied with Gentile's answers proposed a joint venture in the drug trade. This came at a time when Gentile's financial situation had seriously deteriorated, and LaGaipa had in all likelihood been tipped off to this fact, leaving him confident Gentile would be receptive to the offer. He was right, as Gentile accepted the offer. LaGaipa's plan called for Gentile to travel to Texas and Louisiana and organize all the groups handling narcotics with the aim of forming a syndicate that would monopolize the drug trade in the area.

Before proceeding further protocol demanded that Gentile consult with the Boss of his crime family, Vincenzo Mangano. Gentile informed the Boss of LaGaipa's offer and that he would not have to put up any money. He would get 40% of the profits, allowing him to satisfy his debt obligations to the family. Securing the Boss's authority to proceed he now had to inform his paramour that he would be leaving.

On October 5, 1937, Federal Narcotics Agents swept up more than 80 drug subjects including Gentile who was arrested in New Orleans, Louisiana. In Gentile's version of the facts, the agents took him to his house to conduct a search, and finding no incriminating evidence they slashed up a suitcase and planted three grams of cocaine in it.

By naming him as the head of the cartel, operating nationally and internationally, his bond was set at $30,000, six times higher than the others arrested. He was eventually released after making a reduced bond of $18,000. It was at this time Gentile's address book listing the names of mob figures throughout the country, including those of Kansas City's own Vincent Chiapetta and Nick Impastato, was seized.

Looking back, Gentile writes he strongly suspected his paramour Dorothy had betrayed him. In his mind she was aware of the drug operation, and the identities of those involved, having garnered inside information from her friend, Jacono's mistress. After being released from jail, every effort to find Dorothy proved futile. She had disappeared. Gentile came to the conclusion Dorothy was a U.S. Treasury operative "who had been instructed and directed in the smallest particulars" and who was "prepared in special schools...in the most delicate operations of police work."

Gentile was well aware that his notoriety, and being named head of the cartel, meant he was looking at a long, long prison sentence, similar to the 50 years the notorious "Lucky" Luciano received. The decision as to what course he should follow was made for him by the hierarchy of the Mangano crime "family." He was instructed to jump bail and stowaway on a ship to Sicily. Following instructions he fled, arriving in Palermo in September 1937. In later years his partner LaGaipa, disappeared, his fate unknown.

The break up of the crime family's "Narcotics Branch" played a large role in the demise of drug trafficking on the part of the Kansas City outfit. A story passed down over the years identifies as another contributing factor the well publicized drug addiction leading to the death of former Boss Tony Gizzo's son Robert.

Chapter X
Gambling

G AMBLING HAS BEEN an integral part of Kansas City's history from the very earliest times, its impact extraordinary, and its connection to politics evident. It is abundantly clear, that historically, efforts to suppress gambling were uniformly unsuccessful. Reformers, adhering to principles of ethical conduct and obedience to the law, believed they could remove any offensive conduct by rendering it illegal. Prohibition was imposed on the nation only to see bootleggers get rich and organized crime prosper. Boxing and horse racing were outlawed allowing the criminal element to move in. Once these activities were once again made legal, entrenched gangster influence remains, as they are not about to relinquish their hold. Narcotics were regulated and the mob took it to new heights. It is clear repressive measures directed at gambling, although well intentioned, were ineffective, and served only to stimulate the gambling habit, playing into the hands of corrupt politicians and the criminal element dedicated to protecting and fostering it.

The Town of Kansas, as a riverboat stop and gateway to the west, developed into a gambling hub. In the mid 1860's hundreds of travelers arrived daily on their way west, many adventurous, risk taking, free wheeling types, ready made clients for the gamblers arriving along with them.

By the 1870s the town's reputation for gambling attracted characters of every stripe, including the wild west's most notable figures. The city's Market Square was said to have more gambling dens than any city in the nation. There seemed to be no limit whatsoever on the events these gamblers would bet on, from cockfights and dog fights, to which of two mosquitoes would move first.

In 1881 the State of Missouri outlawed gambling, a development that would have no real impact. The tone for the city had been set, and the wide open, freewheeling, anything goes atmosphere would characterize Kansas City for decades to come.

Political boss Big Jim Pendergast's philosophy was to oppose any and all anti-gambling efforts and laws. He paid no attention to them, running gambling games at both of his saloons in the late 1890s, and didn't expect anyone else to pay them heed. His ties with all gambling interests were strong, and he unabashedly used his growing political influence in their behalf. In turn the gambling element employed all their "special talents" working in his behalf on the political front. By 1895 Pendergast allies were in office, politically dominant, and in a position to insure the police department would protect gambling. Beyond protection, Pendergast wielding his political hammer, used the authorities to force any independent operators to join his sponsored gambling combine, or get out of business.

Upon taking over the machine Boss Tom Pendergast not only followed in his brother's footsteps, but as an addicted bettor himself took gambling to new heights. In fact Tom Pendergast has been described as the political and spiritual leader of Kansas City's gambling fraternity.

Boss Tom hyped interest in horse racing, not only as a regular visitor to race tracks in other parts of the country, and owning a stable of race horses, but by bringing racing back to Kansas City. Horse racing had been banished for some 20 years when in 1928 a group of men organized the Riverside Park Jockey Club utilizing a former dog track facility five miles north of Kansas City. Although Pendergast was not among the named organizers, close friends and allies of his were, and the track came to be known as "Pendergast's Track." To encourage the citizenry to attend the races Pendergast is said to have ordered bookmakers in the city to shut down their operation during the hours the track was in session.

The fact gambling was illegal proved to be a minor hindrance as patrons were said to have made "contributions" on the races, and received "refunds" on winning selections. The track was not only very successful in its own right, but it heightened interest in horse racing generally to the benefit of the horse books operating in the city. The track was in business until 1927 when another reform movement succeeded in closing it down.

The dark side of gambling was pretty much ignored, except for the voices of various reform groups that for the most part went unheard. An exception was the well publicized, but quickly forgotten, story of Harry Smart.

A front-page headline of the March 4, 1920 edition of the Kansas City Star read, "Took Money & Husband - Protected Gamblers Crush Happiness of the Smart Family." A tragic story, one of thousands like it that normally never saw the light of day.

On the afternoon of March 3, 1920, the body of Harry Smart, 25 years old, traveling salesman, was found in a room of the Hotel Glennon. He had taken his own life by ingesting poison. In three notes left by Smart he explained he was taking his own life having lost all his money at a notorious gambling game at 1112 Wyandotte Street. Conscience struck by the thought that a thousand dollar insurance polity was all he could leave for his family, he penned a farewell note to his wife:

> I am sorry for what I am about to do, but hope you will forgive me as you are in no way to blame for anything I have done. I hate to do this and leave you and Betty (a baby daughter) alone, but I can't stand this mental strain any longer. I hope you can use my insurance to the best advantage for yours and Betty's future. Don't spend any more than you can help for my expenses as you must keep the money for yourself and Betty. You know my love for you and Betty has never changed and no one could hate to leave you both as I but what else is there for me to do? Now please don't worry about me. Only pray for my soul. Kiss Betty Lou for me.
>
> Your's lovingly - Harry.

His widow told of a happy married life the past five years, explaining her husband's gambling had started almost a year and half before. His visits to gambling dens became more frequent and when she asked him to quit he would say as soon as he got even he would stop. The downward spiral continued as he got in deeper and deeper, causing them to fall further and further behind with their bills. Harry often told her he was visiting a game on Wyandotte Street as it was a protected operation and would not be bothered by the police.

In the widow's eyes the police were to blame. "It seems the police could have closed that place if they had wanted to" she told the newspaper reporter. The Chief of Police stated he had no knowledge of the game at 1112 Wyandotte despite the fact the street was monitored by his vice squad, and anyone looking couldn't miss the stream of patrons entering the place nightly.

The Police Chief may have claimed no knowledge, but the newspaper seemingly was able to learn plenty. It printed a full account of what they labeled a "gambling resort" at 1112 Wyandotte, including a diagram of the layout of the gambling rooms on the second floor of the building. In one news report the "gambling resort" was described as operating unmolested for several months, and a follow-up story reported the game had been ongoing for "several years." That the "same crowd" previously operating a game at the Mansion Hotel were now running it at the Wyandotte Street location. "Red" Anderson was identified as presiding over the games. Customers were offered a choice of black jack, dice, poker and roulette.

According to these reports, after the Mansion Hotel game closed it was moved to the Jefferson Hotel where just as the game was developing substantial play, W.F. Cain, "one of the lookouts", killed a deputy county marshal, shooting him in the back of the head. That was enough to end the gambling at the Jefferson Hotel. When things quieted down the operation was re opened at the 1112 Wyandotte location. This gaming establishment was one commonly referred to as a "steer joint" where players are fleeced with crooked dice.

The roulette wheel operation at this "gambling resort" is an interesting sidelight to the story. Described as the only roulette wheel in Kansas City, it was a popular feature with the gambling crowd. As a courtesy extended by the city's gambling fraternity, the operators at 1112 Wyandotte enjoyed an exclusive on this form of wagering. Therefore, during those times the Mansion Hotel and Jefferson

Hotel games were closed there was nowhere else to go for roulette gambling. No other "gambling resorts" would infringe on the privilege, forcing players to mark time until the new location was opened on Wyandotte Street.

The newspaper seized on Smart's suicide to delve into the overall status of gambling in the city, pointing out that on the same night Harry drank poison in a room at the Hotel Glennon right across the street, at the Hotel Baltimore, Missouri Governor Frederick D. Gardner was proclaiming his satisfaction with the manner in which the police board was conducting police affairs in Kansas City. This in spite of many complaints of unmolested gambling made to the Police Commissioners, and several letters to the Governor from different local organizations alerting him to the situation. The Governor failed to answer any of the complaints, and not only refused to order an investigation but stated he had no intention of looking into police conditions in the city.

Gambler's Code and Big Solly

Centered at 12th & Baltimore Streets colorful gambling figures plied their trade. Harry Brewer, a blind bookmaker; "Gold Tooth" Maxie, a crap shooter; Johnnie Johnston, friendly fat man; Jake Feinberg, and Tom Finnigan, the unofficial mayor of 12th Street, were all gamblers who followed a code of fair play and ethical conduct in their gambling operations.

One larger than life gambling figure of the early 1920s didn't much abide by the high standards of the 12th Street crowd. Big Solly Weissman, also known as "Cutcher-Head-Off" Weissman, a 300 pound bootlegger, career criminal, cutthroat, strong-arm man for Pendergast politicians and John Lazia, who is said to have brought him to Kansas City from Chicago. Although Weissman was never known to have actually cut anyone's head off, his moniker derived from the fact this was his favorite threat to any who would cross him. He did carry a long bladed knife with him, and more than one revolver.

He set up shop at 13th & Baltimore Streets, readily engaging in a variety of gambling ventures, his goal was acceptance as a big time operator. As success came, Big Solly known as an airy type fellow with a gift of gab, upgraded his image driving a fancy sports car, dressing in expensive business suits, wearing glasses, and projecting a business-like, even scholarly, appearance.

Weissman became involved in wrestling matches, generally recognized as fixed contests, and dance marathons, a craze of the era, even fixing them. Operating as a bootlegger he had established ties with gangsters in various other cities, including Chicago, St. Louis, and St. Paul. It was a big step up for him when he joined in with rackets boss John Lazia in the operation of a dog track near North Kansas City, an association that lasted until 1929.

His ambitions for the big time still unfulfilled, he formulated a plan he felt would cement his position as a man of prominence in the rackets. He would tap into a race wire from one of the national race wire syndicates, and by learning the results before they were posted at the horse books he would have the betting edge needed to make a bundle of money. Big Solly approached Charlie Haughton, operator of General News Bureau, a wire service providing bookmakers with race results, and proposed a joint venture in this scam. Haughton, a quiet white haired, unimpressive man in his 60s, was just the sort of person Solly was sure he could intimidate. He was wrong. Despite Big Solly's bluster, threats, and reputation, Haughton rejected the plan. What Weissman apparently had not understood, Haughton belonged to that fraternity of principled gambling operators, believing in fair play and ethical conduct.

Weissman is said to have left town right after his session with Haughton due to the fact federal authorities were breathing down his back, and some believed he might not ever return, but return he did. On October 28, 1930, Solly was back in the city. His first order of business was to settle a Federal prohibition law case pending against him. He was comfortable in returning as he had disposed of the key witness in the case, forcing the government to dismiss the charges for lack of evidence.

His second order of business was a visit to Charlie Haughton. Solly was not accustomed to being turned down, and had to set things straight. He found Haughton in his second floor office above Rayens Turf Betting Agency, 1211 Baltimore Avenue. As Haughton tells it, Big Solly came into his office and "cursed and abused" him. Well aware of Solly's reputation, when Haughton saw Solly reach for his pocket he pulled a revolver and fired. Big Solly was felled by the .45 caliber bullet that hit him in the throat. Still alive, Solly was taken to Research Hospital where he was questioned by authorities. He admitted to the police he had sure underestimated Charlie Haughton, believing Haughton didn't have the guts to shoot him. Well, he was wrong about that. A police officer commiserating with Solly called it a "tough break", to which Solly responded, "No such thing as a tough break." He lapsed into a coma, and early on the morning of October 29, 1930 he died. Big Solly was 35 years, old and never did achieve the recognition he so baby craved as a big time operator.

No charges were pressed against Haughton, and on 12th Street the gambling society celebrated the death of Big Solly as a victory of the good guy gamblers over criminals.

The Carpet Joints

The same year "Pendergast's Track" opened in 1928, Jack Feinberg, a member of the 12ᵗʰ Street gambling society, put together a group of like-minded backers who agreed with Feinberg's concept that the wealthy would be willing to risk their money in a upscale, plush, gambling establishment. The result was the opening of the Green Hills Club in Platte County Missouri ushering in a trend toward what were commonly called "carpet joints." These elegant type gaming emporiums gained popularity around the country and added a level of refinement to the gambling industry. After a short run the Green Hills Club was forced to close due to religious based resistance, coupled with the high cost of protection required to fend off the threat of the criminal element "muscling in." The club would see far better days in the future when the outfit became involved.

The Green Hills club reopened and ran intermittently from 1941 to 1949. The cost of protection was no longer an issue as prominent outfit member Tony Gizzo, and his associate Fred Wedow were the backers. Between 1942 and 1945, additional backers became involved to include Charlie Binaggio, Tim Moran, Abe Freelander, Solly McLeroy, Charlie Gargotta, Morris Klein, Tano Lococo and Big Jim Balestrere.

It seems Big Jim Balestrere was a person others simply could not resist lending a helping hand. The manner in which he became associated with the Green Hills is a case in point. In his own words Balestrere described how he came to have an interest in the gaming club without putting up any of his own money. Testifying before the Kefauver Committee in 1950 he told of taking a cut from the Green Hills, but was unable to recall at what point he no longer was involved. Under questioning by Chief Counsel Rudolph Halley, Balestrere told the story.

A. I went downtown, 12th Street, to go to a picture show. I see Charlie Binaggio. I know him since he was baby. He lived in the same building I did on Harrison. He said, 'What you doing?' I said, I ain't doing nothing. He said I got a piece out at Green Hills. He said, 'You want some of it?' I said, 'I'm not much on gambling.' He said, 'Well, that's all right.' I didn't see him no more. About 30 days later Binaggio came around and gave me money. I said, 'What is this?' and he said, 'We win, and here is your end.' Okay, I took the money.

Q: Binaggo never told you who your partners were?

A: No sir.

Q: He never told you what your percentage of the take was?

A: No sir.

Q: You never asked him who your partners were just in case of trouble?

A: I didn't ask him nothing at all.

Q: You made no investment?

A: Charlie just came around every month and brought money.

Q: How much money did he bring you?

A: I don't remember how much it was, Mr. Halley, but in the period it was open I got $5000.

Mr. Halley, tongue in cheek, asked what would have happened if Binaggio had come to him and told him he had lost $500. Very seriously Balestrere responded, "With the kid, I used to know him so well, I don't think he would tell me anything out of the way."

Several years prior to the Green Hills windfall, Balestrere was the beneficiary of more good fortune. Big Jim explained how just after prohibition he had left the business of selling sugar to bootleggers and needed a job.

> A: I went to see Boss politician, Mr. Tom Pendergast. I asked if he had anything to do for me. He said I come back. I come back in a week. He said, 'You want to work or go some place you can make a little money?' He said, 'I'll put you building a sewer, $8, $9 a day'. Then he spoke of Keno (a gambling game). He said, 'You go see the Eddy boys' and I did and said who sent me. From then on I just went up every month and they give me a check. That's all I had to do.
>
> Q: Did you pay any money to get into the keno?
>
> A: No, no, Mr. Halley, no he said it was already up.
>
> Q: Did you do any work in the keno or did you just get paid...
>
> A: I just went up there every month and check up there and they give me a check, and I walk right out - all by checks.
>
> Q: You made no investment and you didn't have to do anything? Mr. Pendergast just giving you a gift?
>
> A: Give me something to live. Mr. Tom Pendergast did that for everybody not just me.

The next in a line of the lush casinos was the Havana Club in Clay County, Missouri, opening in 1928. The club was housed in a white colonial mansion, and became known as "Little Monte Carlo." Attendants wore tuxedos, the layout was sumptuous, and the gambling volume was high.

The Cuban Gardens was an even more elaborate operation, a nightclub and gambling casino on private grounds near the Riverside Horse Race Track in Clay County. John Lazia was the prime mover in establishing the club with start up monies provided by a Pendergast associate. This was a high dollar operation where on a good night the take was $8000, and reportedly netted Lazia over $2 million a year. It was the income from this operation IRS Agents discovered was being laundered by Lazia through the Merchants Bank.

The religious community in Liberty, Mo, county seat of Clay County, raised its voice against this establishment, however after five unsuccessful raids the Clay County Sheriff was at a loss. The club was too well guarded, an outbuilding at the entrance driveway manned by armed guards who scrutinized all arriving patrons. Upon entering the club patrons had to pass muster, as armed employees in evening dress checked them out before gaining admission to the casino gambling area.

The State Line Tavern - Last Chance Saloon

With a long and sordid history, the State Line Tavern and Last Chance Saloon, located on Southwest Boulevard where the State line intersects, were looked on as especially infamous and unique gambling operations during the 1930s and 1940s. The building housing the State Line Tavern and the Last Chance Saloon sat right a top the state line, and the operators capitalized on this to thwart law enforcement. As notorious as the operation was, authorities of both States, Kansas and Missouri, were stymied by a line painted on the floor demarking the State Line, and the placement of the gambling tables and machines right on that line. Upon any hint of a raid, the tables and machines would be pushed to the side of the line opposite the State from which the officers came, depriving them of jurisdictional authority to make arrests and seize the equipment. Why authorities from the two states did not coordinate their efforts apparently was never considered or explained.

John Goulding operated the The Last Chance beginning in approximately 1937, and by 1947 he was also the owner of a one-story building at 9 Southwest Boulevard. Fred Renegar, a known gambling figure, was Gouldings partner in the conduct of gambling games at both locations. The crime "family" coveted a piece of the operation, but Renegar resisted.

On the night of January 9, 1947, two Sheriff's Deputies scouting the boulevard on the lookout for gambling action spotted Renegar near the Shawnee Club, 3043 Southwest Boulevard, yet another club owned by Goulding. Upon recognizing Renegar the deputies stopped and chatted him up briefly.

A little before 8:00 a.m. the next morning a local resident, heading for the bus stop on his way to work, happened to notice blood stains on the street. His interest piqued he followed the blood trail to a light green 1946 Dodge vehicle parked on the south side of West 29th, just west of Summit Street. Looking in the car window he observed a man seated on the drivers side, his head turned toward the passenger side window. Forty-six years old Fred Renegar was that man—dead as the result of four shots to the head.

The police believed Renegar, dead about two hours, had been killed at another location, and the car, moved by the killer or killers, appearing to have stalled out at the spot where it was found abandoned. It was classified a "spot killing." On Renegar's body the police found the keys to the building at 9 Southwest Boulevard, and used them to enter and search that location They found dice and a poker tables set up, stale cigarette smoke still lingering in the air and butts littering the floor, all indicative gambling activity had been on going during the night. Based on all the circumstances the police speculated that after Renegar closed up the game early that morning he went to his car, parked in a nearby lot, where his assailant or assailants laid in wait, forcing him to take his last ride.

Following Renegar's murder the outfit moved in on the gambling operation, described by a federal grand jury as an enterprise sought after by organized gamblers. In his book, "Crime In America", Senator Estes Kefauver described the State Line Tavern take over as typical of the mob's modus operandi. Kefauver wrote, "Binaggio and company would spot a profitable gambling operation in the area and decide they ought be invited in. If the operators were not smart enough to issue such an "invitation" their places of business would be bombed, robbed or otherwise harassed until they got smarter."

Senator Kefauver's analysis of the situation was based on the testimony of a number of witnesses involved with or knowledgeable about the State Line-Last Chance gambling operation, provided during committee hearings held in Kansas City in 1950.

John Goulding admitted, after the murder of Fred Renegar he took in as partners Morris Klein and Eddie "Spitz" Osadchey upon being informed that if he did so there would be no further trouble, and ended up with a 25% interest in the operation When speaking of trouble he explained he was referring to two bombings of the club, and the murder of Renegar, his former partner.

Morris "Snag" Klein verified he had an interest in the dice operation at the State Line Tavern beginning in 1947, lasting until he went to jail in 1950. Klein identified others having an interest as

John Goulding, Abe Freelander, Solly McElroy, Tano Lococo, Charles Gargotta and Eddie "Spitz" Osadchey, and denied that Charles Binaggio had an interest.

As was generally the case, it would be difficult for the committee to get a true picture of who had what interest. Emering from the testimony was a picture of partners coming and going in an ever-changing lineup card. On one occasion the partners included Goulding, Klein and Homer Cooper. On yet another occasion it was a combination of Goulding, Abe Freelander, Tim Moran, S.O." Solly" McLeroy, Tano Lococo, Charlie Gargotta, Earl Kennedy, Morris Kelin and Eddie "Spitz" Osadchey.

From 1947 until the club closed in April 1950, Lococo, Osadchey, Gargotta and John Goulding were the mainstays each having a 25% interest, and the operation was generating a net profit reported to be $100,000 per year.

Tano Lococo admitted only to a 15% interest, identifying his partners as Charlie Binaggio, also with a 15% interest, plus Charlie Gargotta, and Eddie "Spitz' Osadchey. According to Lococo he became involved with the venture when "they" needed a bankroll, and he was approached as a potential investor, agreeing to take whatever percentage was left. What he knew about the Renegar murder was what was in the newspapers. He had never met the man, and knew nothing of any bombings of the establishment.

Playing the Numbers

"Policy" is a popular form of gambling believed to have been introduced in lottery shops in London England in the 1700s followed by its spread to other European countries. By the early 1800s policy gambling had made its way to our shores becoming a favorite of the masses, a particular lure for the poor since a wager could be made of as little as a nickel or dime. An offshoot of policy gambling is called "numbers" and can best be described as a simplification of the policy process.

Policy gambling appeared on the scene in Kansas City in the period before World War I and flourished thereafter. The basic premise is simple enough. A bettor may wager as little as little as a nickel on a number or combination of numbers of his or her choice with the hope that number, or combination, is drawn. The bettor may select any number, or combination of numbers, from 1 to 78, known as the "Little Wheel", or play the "Big Wheel" encompassing numbers from 1 to 100.

The policy wheel operator or operators employ individuals called "writers" who work the neighborhoods collecting bets and the money wagered. In turn, the writers deliver the bets and the money, less their commission, to the operator at whatever location he may be using at the time. There is little in the way of equipment needed to run the racket, so no special location is required allowing for easy relocation from place to place.

One or two times a day the operators draw eleven winning numbers for each wheel. Inasmuch as the operators have complete control, there is no guarantee the selection process will be on the up and up. Although labeled the "Little Wheel" and "Big Wheel" there is no actual wheel involved in selecting the numbers. The numbers are written on pieces of paper, rolled up and inserted in a "quill," short pieces of hollow straws. The 78 or 100 numbered quills are placed in a container of some sort, and the 11 winning number drawn.

Uncertainty as to the fairness of the drawing is only one of the disadvantages the bettor faces. In the first place it is highly unlikely one will select a winning number. On top of that, even upon picking the right number, or numbers, the payoff odds are steeply stacked in favor of the operators. As an example, the true odds of winning a three number combination bet, called a "gig", are 980 to 1, but the bettor is paid at odds of only 360 to 1. The difference in payoff odds represents profit for the wheel. .

A simplification of the process was introduced on the east coast, known as numbers betting. In the numbers system three winning numbers were determined by utilizing publications that appeared in the public realm, such as the last three numbers of a figure contained in the Federal Reserve Clearing House report. A degree of legitimacy attached on the premise Federal Reserve reporting could not be tampered with. The result was numbers betting became wildly popular.

In an effort to suppress numbers gambling authorities secured an agreement on the part of newspapers to print the Federal Reserve report in whole numbers. Gambling syndicates responded by turning to published daily reports of racetrack pari-mutual racing totals. Unlike the Federal Reserve, mobsters owned or controlled many racetracks allowing them to manipulate these pari-mutual totals to their advantage. Once again a reform effort failed to curtail its target, and ended up giving the criminal element an advantage they did not previously have.

In Kansas City the policy form of gambling was exclusively in vogue, and in 1950 a Federal Grand interim report provided the public with a glimpse of just how pervasive this form of gambling was. In describing gambling enterprises in the city, the grand jury report had this to say about policy gambling:

> The Grand Jury would further present to the court that so vast as to almost challenge the credulity of the average citizen is the volume of business done by the octopus commonly known as the policy racket. Its tentacles extract 3-1/2 million dollars a year from the

pockets, generally the poor, who make its existence possible. The "numbers" or "policy" racket, operated by a select few, employes hundreds of numbers writers. One of these enterprises grosses 1-1/2 million dollars a year and employs approximately 100 numbers writers. This is the actual testimony of witnesses before this grand jury.

A Kansas City Star news article of June 29, 1969 described the policy racket as having operated for several decades, and represented a way by which the underworld, in most large cities, is able to exploit the poor black community.

Recognizing the huge moneymaking potential of policy gambling, and using predatory tactics, the outfit moved in.

Coming into the year 1949 there were any number of active policy operations run by individuals such as John "Peck" McBride, Louis Schaeffer, "Dutch" Bandel, George "The Greek " Mehan and John Lewis, all of whom had been in the business for years.

McBride and Schaeffer were partners, and one of their policy wheels was located in the Lafayete Hotel, 1205 Troost Street. McBride had started out his career as a policy writer in 1927, later joining a similar enterprise run by Bud Tralle. McBride' partner Louis Henry Schaeffer had been in the numbers business since 1937 or 1938, and together they had interests in 8 policy wheels. McBride held a 62% interest and Schaeffer 38% in this gambling enterprise.

The two were doing very well, thank you, until an individual by the name of Max Jaben paid a visit. Jaben was born October 24, 1902 in Ribijesov, Poland, his birth name, Motel Grzebienacz, officially changed to Jaben upon his naturalization in January 1943. He came to the U.S. in 1920 settling first in Portland, Oregon, and then coming to Kansas City in 1926. Jaben at 5'8", well built, black curly hair, was described as a cocky individual, and tough. His reputation was that of a "bomber and torpedo" for the outfit, a suspect in several gangland murders, and active in gambling during the late 40s and early 50s in Colorado. He would play a large role in outfit activities for many years.

Jaben informed McBride he was about to start up some policy wheels of his own that would no doubt put McBride and Schaeffer out of the business. Jaben's ploy worked, as McBride feared Jaben had the ability to make good on his word exerting influence within in the police department. With this in his mind, McBride offered Jaben, and his partner John Mangiaracina, a 50% interest. Jaben, playing it to the hilt, said he would have to think it over, but of course the offer was accepted.

McBride had good reason to believe as he did. Looking back, his policy operation had started with C.T. "Bud" Tralle, Schaeffer's uncle, and another uncle, Ernie Tralle, later joined in. It was no secret what business C.T. was in, however, he had no problems with the police, or anyone else. That all changed after C.T.'s death. The police began raiding the policy office and arresting the writers. McBride realized that some influence had been brought to bear causing the change in police tactics, and felt that if Jaben and Mangiaracina were not made partners their operation would be vulnerable, forcing them out of business.

On October 1, 1949 Jaben and Mangiaracina were officially taken in, and in return they were to provide political protection. Under the new arrangement McBride's interest was reduced to 30%, Schaeffer's to 20%, and Jaben and Mangiaracina each took a 25% cut. For the first month of operation under the new arrangement, Schaeffer's 20% interest netted him a little over $3000, McBride made something like $4500, and Jaben and Mangiaracina each got $7500. Running the wheels for the operation were Rodney Brown, Harry Huntman, Joe Wehyman, and James Schaeffer, Louis's brother.

Despite the promised "political protection" police raids of policy operations continued on unabated. Mangiaracina's excuse was they simply couldn't do anything about it. Jaben and Mangiaracina had simply cut themselves in for a piece of the operation, making no investment, provided no protection, labor, or anything else to further the business. They put Joe Simone, brother of outfit member Thomas "Hiway" Simone, to work at $75 a week to assist Jim Schaeffer operate the wheel, and gave Charles Cacioppo the job of overseeing financial aspects as a means of protecting Jaben and Mangiaracina's interests. McBride opted to get out, selling his interest to well known gambling figure, Walter Rainey.

The 1950 federal grand jury interim report placed the total annual net profit to the policy operation at $168,000 making it the largest such operation in the city.

Another policy operator by the name of Ray Bandel would suffer the same fate on the same day. Bandel had been in the business, off and on, for 25 years coming into 1950 when his policy operation was located at 1625-27 W. 9th Street.

From February 1946 to October 1,1949 Bandel operated in partnership with Ernest Duncan under the name S.E.&D Enterprise. October 1 was the day he received word the Cammisano brothers, Joe and Willie, would be opening a policy operation. It is more than likely Bandel had no idea Max Jaben and John Mangiaracina were not far away using this same ploy on McBride and Schaeffer.

Bandel and Duncan were fearful their policy writers, who were paid 32-1/2% commission, would be lured away by a better offer from the Cammisanos. To avoid losing their writers and being pushed out of business they agreed to take the Cammisanos in as partners, and the operation was renamed Kentucky & Tennessee Enterprises. It was no surprise the new partners didn't put up a dime for their 25% each interest. Nor did they perform any other services, only once in a while sending a new writer over. For Bandel and Duncan it was a simple proposition. They had to go along if they wanted to avoid the perceived threat of the Cammisano's opening a competing business, plus they were fully cognizant of the Cammisano's stature in the underworld. On a fair month the policy operation netted $2200 to $3000 representing a return of between 8% & 10% of gross receipts.

Without question the date October 1, 1949 was indeed a black day for policy operators. In addition to McBride, Schaeffer, Bandel and Duncan, another policy operator, John Lewis would fall prey to these orchestrated takeovers. On that date Joe and Willie Cammisano walked in on John Lewis and took a 50% interest in his policy wheel operation renaming it Sunflower Enterprises, once again making no investment and performing no services.

The outfit's assault rolled on, their next target, Israel Allen Brenner, a policy operator in Kansas City for some 25 years. Brenner, coming into 1950, was grossing an estimated $300,000 a year in policy proceeds, employing some 30 writers. On January 1, 1950, his turn came around, and he was forced to take in Joe Guerra as a partner. Guerra, a gangster, provided no service, made no investment, and had absolutely no knowledge of the business.

It was not only gambling enterprises that fell to onslaught of outfit takeovers. In November 1948 the directors of Olympic Athletic Field Incorporated, doing business as the Olympic Stadium, a midget car racing track, were approached by John Mangiaracina, Max Jaben, Louie Cangelose and William Cammisano, a formidable delegation, with an offer to install 5000 additional seats in the stadium in return for a one-quarter interest in the profits of the corporation. Considering the character and reputation of these individuals the directors decided they had no real choice other than to go along with the proposal.

When federal and state authorities caught up with Mangiaracina, Cammisano and Jaben in 1950 they were forced to alter the Olympic Stadium arrangement. Mangiaracina was indicted by both federal and county grand juries, while Jaben and Cammisano were indicted by the county grand jury. They were now in need of ready cash for lawyers so they sold their one-quarter "interest." The buyers included Angelo "Bossie" Nigro, Joe Dasta, Ross Lipari and A. Romano.

Mangiaracina, Jaben, Joe Guerra and Willie and Joe Cammisano, and sixteen other individuals, were all indicted by the Jackson County Grand Jury in July 1950 on charges of running policy gambling operations.

Mangiaracina was also indicted by a federal grand jury in that same month, charged with income tax evasion. Appearing in Federal District Court on November 8, 1950 he pled guilty to two counts of income tax evasion, and nine days later was sentenced to a four-year prison term.

The disclosure by the federal grand jury of the outfit's takeover of policy gambling, along with the indictments returned by the Jackson County grand jury, in addition to publicity generated by the Kefauver Committee hearings, substantially reduced the mob's interests in the field. Policy gambling continued to be a fact of Kansas City life although on a much smaller scale, and with the passage of time black operators would emerge as the major players in the policy racket.

A Fraternity of Gamblers

The State Line Tavern-Last Chance gaming operation represents a prime example of how the outfit employed an extensive cadre of individuals in their varied gambling ventures. The same names in different combinations continually surfaced as these operations were uncovered. One the prominent members of this gambling fraternity was Walter Rainey, and his story is typical of many of his peers in the fraternity. Like the others, he benefited from his connection with the outfit, for one, much of his police record was removed from the files. From what can be pieced together, a picture emerges of Rainey's criminal background, and his progression from small time criminal to the rackets.

What may have been his first misadventure came at the age of 19 when on November 15, 1915, he, and a companion, entered pleas of guilty to charges of robbing the Rose and Ilkenberg pool hall located at 3100 Main Street. To label this small time would be an understatement. They admitted to stealing cigars and tobacco valued at $40, claiming they were drunk at the time. Small time, to be sure, however, the sentence was substantial - two years incarceration. Seven years later, in March 1922, Rainey was arrested for his part in a shooting incident at the Edgewood Chicken Dinner Farm, a roadhouse south of "Dodson." He was charged in the case but the disposition is unknown. From there he graduated to bank robbery, alleged to have held up the State Bank of Sugar Creek in 1926. A jury acquitted him in November of the next year.

With the advent of the roaring 1920s Rainey, like so many others, joined the rush to cash in on the bootlegging racket. He leased the White House Tavern, 301 W. 85th Street, from Big Jim Balestrere while, at the same time, running bootleg liquor as a sideline. In August 1944 he was arrested on bootlegging charges when Federal Alcohol & Tax Agents caught Rainey, James Samuel Weinberg, and three others, unloading 129 cases of bootleg whiskey in Clinton, Oklahoma. Charged with illegal liquor violations Rainey received a sentence of one- year probation, and a $2500 fine. His crime partner, James Samuel Weinberg, an ex-convict and former salesman in Chicago for Canadian Ace beer, was an acquaintance of Charlie Binaggio

Following the path of many gangsters and gamblers of the day, Rainey became active in the political arena. He was identified as a member of the Joe Shannon democrat faction, and with Shannon's backing he played a big part in gambling activities in the county outside the city limits.

The White House tavern, where Rainey ran a horse book and dice operation was, at the time, located outside the city limits. Rainey's operation came under the scrutiny of the Kefauver Committee's probe of vice activities in Jackson County during the administration of Binaggio backed Sheriff J.A. Purdome, commencing in 1945. Senator Kefauver viewed the manner in which Purdome handled vice activities in the count as representing "an unwholesome situation." During his appearance before the committee, Purdome was confronted with allegations of illegal liquor sales, and "other situations" persisting in rural Jackson County, labeled by other witnesses as lax enforcement.

Rainey, testifying before the committee, stated he was confident his control of 5000 to 6000 votes in the county meant his operation would not be interfered with. It may have bought him protection in the county, but it did nothing for him when in 1947 Kansas City expanded its boundaries placing Rainey's tavern within in the city limits. The police wasted no time in raiding his operation. Rainey's gambling activities at the White House Tavern was news to Sheriff Purdome, although the city police had no trouble discovering it. Purdome told the committee it was only later that he heard Rainey had been "secretly operating a horse book", something he never witnessed. Purdome, asked to explain why after being raided, Rainey moved right back out into the county, taking up shop at the Plantation Club? Again Purdome was in the dark, claiming he wasn't aware Rainey was connected with the Plantation Club.

Rainey remained a mainstay in the illegal gaming industry, his name continually surfacing as various gambling locations were identified. He was a partner along with outfit big shots Tano Lococo and Charlie Gargotta, in the Town Recreation gambling club, labeled by a federal grand jury in 1950 as the largest operation in the city during its eight-month run. Indicative of the size of this enterprise there were a total of fifteen individuals involved in running the place, and it netted almost $200,000 in that short period of time.

He expanded his gambling horizons in 1949 when he bought out "Peck" McBride's interest in a policy wheel business. His partners, Max Jaben and John Mangiaracina, had "muscled" into the operation for a half interest.

In still another venture, Rainey was involved in a gambling club at 1800A E. 32st Street started up in September 1949 at the very time a federal grand jury was conducting its inquiry into citywide gambling. Before the club could get fully operational it was railroaded by a Kansas City Star expose. The set up was elaborate with a second floor steel door installed to thwart police raids. Dice and card games had started up, and word was circulated that a horse book would soon be added. Charlie Binaggio, the criminal and political boss at the time, had an interest in the operation. After the newspaper disclosure the police raided the club, but they were too late. They found the place cleaned out. Shortly thereafter the operation restarted, a sign in the window proclaimed the location as the Fourth Ward Democratic Club. Rainey was also identified as participating in the operation of gambling games held at the Show Bar and the Cloverleaf Tavern. Despite his criminal record, Rainey was back in the bar business in 1952, one of the operators of the Boulevard Lounge at 607 Linwood Boulevard.

On May 25, 1950 a federal grand jury returned a three-count indictment charging Rainey with concealing income (gambling related) totaling $15,433 during the years 1946, 1947 and 1948. In the same month a Jackson County Grand Jury indicted him on charges of operating a policy wheel. Rainey went to trial on the federal tax charges and the jury found him guilty. Appearing in Federal District Court in November 1950, Rainey was sentenced to a two-year prison term.

Serving time had little effect on this intrepid gambler. In January 1954 Rainey's name surfaced along with that of John Mangiaracina, who had also served a jail term for tax evasion, in connection with reports of dice games taking place at the Spaghetti House on west 85th Street, owned by Jim Balestrere, the same site formerly housing the White House tavern Rainey had previously run.

The Stork Club

The criminal outfit's interests in gambling were not limited to the Kansas City area. One of its most notable forays into out of state operations involved the Stork Club in Council Bluffs, Iowa.

An integral part of the Stork Club story involved the armed robbery of Vernon's Chicken Hut restaurant located on the out skirts of Harlan, Iowa in February 1947.

Charlie Gargotta along with his brother Gus "Skinny" Gargotta had a run of bad luck, their bankroll depleted they left the dice game in the basement of Vernon's Chicken Hut. At 4:30 a.m. February 23, 1947, they returned to the game, but not to shoot craps. They cut the telephone lines, and relieved the patrons of their car keys and all their money. After five witnesses positively identified the Gargotta brothers, charges were filed against them.

On April 4, 1947 the brothers were arrested in Kansas City on Iowa robbery warrants. They were extradited and returned to Iowa on April 5, jailed in Atlantic, Iowa, neither able to make their $15,000 bond. They put out a call for held to friends in Kansas City.

Two days later, at 4:00 a.m. Easter Sunday, five owners of the Stork Club, a Council Bluffs, Iowa, nightclub, gambling casino and horse book, closed up the club and headed home. As they approached the south Omaha, Nebraska, bridge, 2 miles from the club, a warning burst of machine gun fire across the hood of their car brought them to an abrupt halt. Five men were in the car that ambushed the club owners.

The club had suffered a bombing a month earlier, a crime described by the police as part of a "softening up process" on the part of Kansas City gangsters. With this fresh in their minds, they offered no resistance when ordered back to the club. In fact, once back at the club, Ernest "Buster" Stranger, one of the owners, willingly pointed out the location of the safes and hiding places where the club money was kept. The robbers made off with $78,000.

According to a May 3, 1950 newspaper account, later on the morning of the robbery, two of the gunmen showed up in Atlantic, Iowa, and with $30,000 in crumpled up bills, made bond for the Gargotta brothers. By the time Iowa authorities were prepared to bring the Gargottas to trial none of the witnesses to the holdup could now identify them, one having left for California on an all expenses paid trip. It was rumored it cost the Gargottas $35,000 to fix the case, and take care of the witnesses. If the news report was in fact accurate, the Stork Club robbery, seemingly orchestrated by the Kansas City outfit, served two purposes. It generated the Gargottas bond money, plus some, and furthered the "softening up process" in anticipation of the takeover of the club

Following the Stork Club robbery Kansas City outfit operatives moved in. Morris "Snag" Klein, Eddie "Sptiz" Osadchey, George Beskas, and Earl Kennedy were now the operators of the club. Joining them were Omaha ex-convict, Charles "Snooks' Hutter, and bootleg-ger Charles "Gutsy" Hutter. Together the group held a 50% interest. Cy Silver, one of the former partners, sold out for a pittance, while another of the former owners, Fred Barnes, took over the remaining 50% interest having to pay $20,000 for the privilege.

A grand jury inquiry in Kansas City focused on the Stork Club af-fair, and based on testimony it heard characterized the takeover as one accomplished at gunpoint without the investment of one cent. The grand jury traced the history of the Stork Club from its opening in 1942 as a competitive venture to the well-established Chez Paree. Starting out modestly it grew into an elaborate gambling casino. After one change in ownership the club was sold in 1945 to a part-nership of Cy Silver, Max and Einer Abramson, Frey Weyerman and Fred Barnes, all owners at the time of the robbery and take over.

Max Abramson and Fred Barnes were major bookmakers in Omaha, Nebraska connected with at least four different bookmak-ing establishments in that city. The partners invested $45,000 to modernize the gambling casino that offered slot machines, blackjack tables, roulette wheels, crap tables and a horse book. According to the grand jury the Stork Club operated unmolested from its incep-tion through 1949 except for two interruptions; a raid in 1945 and a bombing in 1947.

The Chez Paree casino also operated unmolested, a situation the Sheriff of Pottawotomie County Iowa, appearing as a witness before the grand jury, explained was due to the fact public opinion has a lot to do with the enforcement of laws in certain localities.

The Kefauver Committee also found the Stork Club affair a most intriguing subject matter. During extensive questioning, Morris "Snag" Klein provided a version of the events testifying that he and Eddie "Spitz" Osadchey paid $20,000 to Charles Berman for the Stork Club. That same afternoon they sold half of their interest for

$20,000 to two Omaha men. He, of course, knew nothing of a bombing the club suffered shortly before they "bought" into it. Nor had he heard that one of the Stork Club partners, Al Abrams, had been taken for a ride by gunmen who suggested he sell the club, or that another partner, Cy Silver, had been held captive overnight. Certainly he had no knowledge of the Easter Sunday $78,000 robbery in Harlan, Iowa.

Further adding to this sordid story, in June 1947 "Buster" Stanger, the former partner who had disclosed for the robbers where the club's money was hidden, was shot and wounded on a Omaha street. He recovered, left Omaha, and was not heard from again.

The story provided the Kefauver committee did not jibe with newspaper accounts as to the source of the Gargottas bond money. Had the money come from the Stork Club robbery as reported? Not according to the outfit's version.

Tony Gizzo testified that on the Saturday before Easter 1947, a day all banks were closed, Tano Lococo was in the process of putting together $30,000 bond money to help out the Gargotta brothers. Gizzo for his part came up with $5000 in cash he had on hand. After the entire $30,000 was in hand, Lococo traveled to Iowa placing the money with the court for the Gargotta's bail. Upon dismissal of the robbery charges the court returned the $30,000 in the form a check issued to Charlie Gargotta. Gizzo put the check through at the Merchants Bank in Kansas City whereupon Lococo returned his $5000.

Although Gizzo had no information concerning the $78,000 robbery of the Stork Club, testifying he knew nothing about it, he did not think any of that money was used for Gargotta's bail. Gizzo explained he was able to help Lococo out as he always carried two to three thousand dollars in cash in his pocket.

Lococo, when it was his turn to explain his role, backed up Gizzo's story. He got involved when Charlie Gargotta's wife called him informing him of the arrest of the two brothers in Iowa, and their need for $30,000 to make bond. Mrs Gargotta was able to come up with $7500 and he was able to get $5000 from Tony Gizzo. Two other friends came up with $10, 000, and he made up the remaining $7500. He claimed he delivered $30,000 for the Gargotta brother's bail to Lou Farrell (a Chicago racketeer headquartered in Iowa) in a small Iowa town, the name of which he could not recall. Lococo informed the committee he always had ready cash on hand to meet the needs of his gambling business, and kept a box at his home that at times had as much as $20,000.

Following the party line, Lococo had no knowledge of the $78,000 robbery of the Stork Club.He had heard of the club, but had never been there, and did not even know that two of his former partners in various gambling operations, Morris Klein and Eddie "Spitz" Osadchey, had become involved in the operation of the club.

The National Wire Service

The topic of horse racing provides an appropriate lead in to the story of the national race wire service, and at the same time serves as another illustration of how moral reformers end up causing more harm than good.

In early times the upper class generally owned the horses and racetracks, and were responsible for horse racing's general recognition as a sport, in fact, "The Sport of Kings". Meanwhile the rank and file who made it all work, trainers, jockeys, stable personnel, and those handling the wagering, were at best, a fringe element, at worst downright unsavory. By the 1890s the real power passed to the ruffian element working the stables and paddocks. The type politician who considered turf morality similar to that of the political machine, along with gamblers and bookmakers were taking over. It started with ownership of horses and racetracks. Kansas City's own Boss Tom Pendergast and Tony Gizzo were prime examples of this dynamic. Both were big time gamblers and owners of racehorses. Accompanying this shift in control cheating, in every form applicable to horse racing, became commonplace.

Enter the reformers. They weighed in and gradually horse racing and betting on the races was outlawed. By 1920 only a half dozen states, mainly in the south, allowed horse racing. Following reform, as was generally the case, the criminal element seized on the opportunity and took the sport underground. Tom Pendergast, despite its illegality, was behind the opening of the Riverside Park Jockey Club, a former dog track, and racing began in 1928. Boss Tom attended regularly and the citizens followed suit filling the track. The Capone mob in Chicago was running Sportsman Park racetrack while racket figures in other cities followed suit.

The depression era witnessed the return of legal racing after 1930 as an economic necessity. The State realized no revenue from gangster owned, outlaw tracks as they were unable to tax them. However, State sanctioned operations when re instituted opened the door for much needed revenue, jobs, and tourist dollars. By 1934 pari-mutual betting tracks were operating in 17 states. Para-mutual betting is a method allowing track management to control and benefit from betting, in theory combating the bookmakers and corruption

However, once allowed to gain a foothold by operating outlaw tracks, the gangsters were not about to loosen their grip. They continued to control the racetracks, sometimes using fronts, sometimes out in the open. With gangsters came gangster tactics. Horse doping, bribed jockeys, horse substitutions, the whole bag of dirty tricks.

Once entrenched, legalization would have no substantial impact on mob involvement in the industry.

By 1939 some 80 tracks were up and running in over half the states. The moralists took the position that horse racing was all about gambling, not sport, and gambling was evil. Considering that race-tracks would never have come into existence or prospered were it not for the betting, it appears the moralists had a point.

In the years before the run away popularity of betting on all forms of sporting events, brought about largely by television, horse race betting was the only game in town. For the horse bookmaker to operate it was essential to have access to instant and immediate information from the various racetracks across the nation. They had to have last minute track and weather condition reports, names of jockeys, last minute scratches, etc. They had to have immediate news on the races, how the horses ran, and, most important, the exact time the race went off so as to know when to stop taking bets, and when to lay off wagers. A business enterprise that could provide this service would be invaluable to the bookmaker.

At the turn of the century the Western Union Telegraph Company provided just such a service. Company employees collected results at the tracks and provided them to any customer who rented a telegraph ticker. Enter the reformers. In 1905 they forced Western Union out of this $ 2 million a year part of their business. Following the well-established pattern, reform action provided a new opportunity for organized crime elements. They duplicated the wire service, and then employed their ruthless methods in the operation of the business. Whereas Western Union had no desire to control bookmaking, the gangsters did, and used the wire service as a hammer to bring into line any bookies failing to toe the line.

The development of a national race wire service is a story replete with intrigue, manipulation, colorful characters and mob infiltration.

To grasp the role the Kansas City outfit played in this saga some background and color is in order.

A Cincinnati man name Payne had a race wire service in the early 1900s. He demanded 50% of the profits of every handbook in Cincinnati in return for the use of his service. Some resisted, but a few bullets and some dynamite helped change their minds. By 1910 Mont Tennes a Chicago politico/criminal figure, recognized as the gambling king of the Chicago's North Side, had set up his own wire service called General News Bureau. Payne got a taste of his own medicine and was forced out of business, leaving Tennes as the undisputed wire service boss with control of a national wire service.

Emerging from newspaper circulation wars, raging in many cities in the early 1900s, characterized by the hiring of thugs, gunmen, and future organized crime figures, were three of the most prominent figures in the evolution of the national wire service; Moses Annenberg, James Ragen Sr.and Arthur "Mickey" McBride. Annenberg had experienced a violent Chicago newspaper circulation war in 1910, first as circulation manager for the Examiner, and then jumping ship to the rival Tribune.

In 1920 Annenberg, working for the Hurst newspaper chain in Chicago, was brought to New York City as circulation boss of the entire Hurst chain. In 1922 he branched out purchasing a horse racing publication, the Daily Racing Form, a venture so successful he quit his post with the Hurst chain. Expanding his horizons, he swallowing up competing publications. These publications provided gamblers with racing charts, tips, workout data, odds, past performances, track conditions, weights, jockey listings, and much more.

Under pressure, Mont Tennes sold half of his General News Bureau wire service to Annenberg and half to Chicago gambler Jack Lynch. The two partners both coveted sole ownership, but neither would give in. Annenberg made his move starting a rival wire service, Nationwide News Service, in effect competing with himself, but at the same time developed it into the dominant of the two wire services. Lynch gave in, selling out his interests thereby leaving the field to Annenberg. According to another version of events, Lynch was forced to sell out under pressure from the mob.

Most horse race bets placed were not made at the track but rather with illegal bookies. In turn the bookies needed hard to trace real time race results, and the wire service provided it. To obtain the necessary information the wire service employed spotters, at or near the track, who called the races as the horses left the post, at various mile poles along the way, and at the finish. These reports were communicated by telephone and telegraph, instantly and invisibly, to 15,000 bookies in 233 cities and 39 states. The system included 14 corporations, and 36 branches, and as a monopoly it charged whatever it felt like to the tune of a $50 million a year take. It was said, at the time no one in the United States could match Moses Annenberg's income.

Annenberg needed someone to run Nationwide News Service for him and he picked a tough product of Chicago street gangs and newspaper circulation wars, James M. Ragen. Ragen, as a 24 year old, had worked in Cleveland for the Daniel Hanna, Sr, owned papers, and as circulation manager solved ongoing conflict with rivals over circulation by hiring on young thugs who later became prominent organized crime figures in the city - contacts that would serve Ragen well in the future.

Under Ragen, Nationwide did business with major racket figures such as Longy Zwillman in New Jersey, Meyer Lansky and many other crime luminaries of the day. Annenberg reportedly was paying the Capone Chicago mob $1 million a year for protection and enforcement services.

Annenberg joined the ranks of those caught cheating on their taxes, and in 1939, facing sentencing in Federal court on charges of income tax fraud, disbanded his Nationwide News Service. Up until that time his wire service, working with bookmakers around the country, was the number one purveyor of racing information in the nation.

Entering the picture to fill the void created by Annenberg quitting business was the extremely prosperous Arthur "Mickey" McBride, a close associate of Ragen, and veteran in his own right of the Cleveland newspaper circulation wars. He had become a multi millionaire through ownership of a taxi-cab fleet, extensive real estate holdings, ownership of a professional football club, the Cleveland Browns, and a Miami, Florida, radio station. On November 15, 1929 McBride jumped in where Annenberg left off and Continental Press was born. McBride would insist Continental was a new venture started with $20,000, and that nothing was bought from Annenberg's defunct service. His brother-in-law, Tom Kelley, and Ragen's son, James Jr., were given the job of managing the service.

The Kefauver Committee, based on its inquiries during hearings held in Chicago, proposed a different version. The committee alluded to McBride having been brought into the picture by reason of his "powerful connections" with "the Mafia leaders of Cleveland."

Seeking to avoid legal entanglements, Continental's operational plan called for the service to be handled by regional "distributors" thereby avoiding direct dealings with the bookmaker clients. These distributors, 24 in number, were held out as being in the "publishing" business, producing racing guides, "scratch" sheets, and related information utilized by horse bettors.

Continental gathered racing news through an elaborate nationwide system, and telegraphed the information to its distributors. The distributors in turn, for a fee, passed on the information to illegal bookies all over the country. Thus buffered, Continental could deny knowledge the information was being utilized by illegal bookmakers.

The Kefauver Committee exposed the set up as a sham, uncovering the fact a good number of Continental's so-called distributors were merely fronts forwarding on the bulk of their profits to Continental. The committee also found Continental's client list to be a veritable Who's Who of the underworld.

According to "Mickey" McBride, he sold Continental in August 1942 to James Ragen Jr., and 14 months later James Sr. came on board as a partner. In a story akin to musical chairs, Ragen Sr. now looks to "Mickey" McBride asking him to once again get involved, but McBride was reluctant. Finally after a convoluted series of events, McBride returned to the business, some would say because his organized crime contacts were still needed. McBride would deny personal involvement stating he had only invested money in behalf of his son.

At this point various authors, historians, and recounters of organized crime history diverge regarding the conflict between Ragen Sr. and the Capone mob. On one hand it is proposed a lucrative venture such as the race wire service, headquartered within the Capone mob's domain, would undoubtedly attract the mob's attention. Control of a national wire service would not only provide untold wealth, and a source of thousands of jobs for Capone mobsters, but also would insure a virtual monopoly over illegal bookmaking in the United States to the benefit of Capone and his national syndicate associates.

In this version, Ragen Sr. felt the pressure, but as a strong-minded Irishman would not give in, willing to take whatever came his way. In time-honored fashion, the mob's first foray was a businesslike offer of a reasonable and mutually beneficial arrangement. However, Ragen well knew once the mob was in, and gained sufficient expertise, he would be excess baggage, and wind up dead. He also recognized the Government would never tolerate the Capone mob having control of an interstate racing service. Ragen refused the offer, hired on bodyguards, discussed the situation with the FBI, and provided the States Attorney a ninety-page affidavit setting out the whole story.

Efforts to convince Ragen to reconsider failing, the Capone mob responded by starting a rival wire service, Trans-America Publishing & News Service. The new service, begun on March 20, 1946, seemed to have a substantial edge in light of its extensive connections to various crime syndicates, and did in fact cut Continental's income by half.

Another version of events discredits stories of Ragen Sr. having been muscled by the Chicago mob. Reportedly the Chicago gambling combines were not paying for Continental's service, and Ragan Sr. put an end to that, demanding they pay like everyone else. He eventually cut off free wire service to the one bookmaker who was providing it to the gambling combine. It was at this juncture the mob formed Trans-American Publishing and News Service to compete. Ragen Sr. took the added step of informing on Patrick J. Burns, who had jumped ship, leaving Continental for Trans-America. Ragan Sr. reminded authorities that Burns was a wanted man having escaped during his trial on assault and robbery charges in 1916.

Ragen Sr. allegedly realized his mistake. He was now an informer, and there was nothing worse in he eyes of the mob than a rat. Seeking protection he went to the FBI, and unwilling to admit the real source of his fear, claimed the mob was looking to take control of Continental, and his life was in danger. This gave birth to the legend he had been muscled by Capone.

Whatever the true facts were, it is abundantly clear the Chicago mob's rival Trans-America service relied on its connections with outfits in other cities in an attempt to dominate the field. When it came to crime syndicate connections Chicago had them in spades in Kansas City. As described by Senator Kefauver, "gangster dominated" Kansas City represented one of the most clear cut examples of the manner in which the Capone organization used Trans-American in their rivalry with Continental Press.

For years Simon Partnoy had been content with his wire service operation in Kansas City, one of those seemingly independent Continental Press distributors. He operated under the name Harmony Publishing Company, located in Room 513, Columbia Bank Building 921 Walnut Street, Kansas City, Missouri. As a distributor his arrangement with Continental called for him to pass on the lion's share of profits to Continental in return for a $125 a week salary.

When Chicago's mobsters started up rival Trans-American things were about to get sticky for Partnoy. Patrick J. Burns, the man Ragen Sr. allegedly "ratted out" and now "President" of Trans-America, happened to show up in Kansas City in 1946, and happened to have a chance meeting with long time outfit associate Edward "Eddie Spitz" Osadchey. Burns just happened to mention he was looking for someone to be the Trans-America franchise holder in Kansas City.

Following the meeting, Osadchey formed Mo-Kan Publishing Company with offices in Room 212, LaSalle Building, 8 E. 9th Street, putting up a $5000 franchise deposit with Trans-America. It was said the offer from Burns included an understanding Osadchey would be in a position to pull strings to open up Kansas City for horse books.

There is little question this was all pre-arranged between the Capone mob and the Kansas City outfit, with Burns fronting for Chicago and Osadchey fronting for Kansas City. Following the script, Osadchey claimed after obtaining the franchise rights he then went about looking for investors. The fact they happened to be Tano Lococo, Charles Gargotta and Morris Klein, all connected to the crime "family", was apparently just a coincidence.

According to Osadchey the Boss Man, Charles Binaggio, had no interest in the venture, however he had courted Binaggio hoping to capitalize on his wide-ranging influence to open up the city, creating new customers for the race wire business. It was all part of a paper thin cover story. It was common knowledge Charlie Gargotta was Binaggio's numero uno and constant companion, and whatever Gargotta had, Binaggio had. And a reliable source close to the operation reported it was Charles Binaggio, along with Osadchey, who had hired a female employee at Mo-Kan strictly for show purposes, and to allay the suspicions of other tenants in the building.

With Osadchey running a rival company, Partnoy discontinued his arrangement with Continental Press agreeing to go to work for Osadchey and Trans-America. He would receive a lump sum payment of $7500 and draw a weekly salary of $200, plus receive 15% of the net profits. All the parties involved denied any force or intimidation was used in getting Partnoy to join the new venture. It was strictly a business proposition wherein Partnoy ended up with a better deal overall.

When called before the Kefauver Committee in 1950, Osadchey stated the yearly net profit from the wire service was $20,000, agreeing there had been an increase in revenue after his new service was initiated, due in part to increased business. He balked at providing an explaining of exactly how the remainder of revenue increases came about.

Tano Lococo and Morris "Snag" Klein had similar stories for the committee. They came by their quarter interest in the wire service venture when Osadchey offered the opportunity to invest in a new race wire service. They both invested $1250, which was returned to them some five or six weeks later by Osadchey. Both admitted they never performed any work, nor did they bring in any new business. Lococo stated that for the next two to two and a half years he drew money from the company, labeling his partnership position a good deal, earning him a substantial sum of money.

Klein told the committee he knew nothing of Patrick Burns of Chicago, or was he aware of any publicity that the Capone mob was linked to Trans-America. He was aware of Simon Portnoy's prior arrangement with Continental Press calling for him to funnel all proceeds to Continental in return for a $125 a week salary. Portnoy's joining Mo-Kan Publishing was a simple business proposition whereby he was bought out, and retained to run the new business with Osadchey. For two and a half years Klein received steady income, and his take from the business was in the range of $15,000. He subsequently sold out his interest, simply taking $3200 from the bank account, and no new partner took his place.

Despite assertions there had been no violence or intimidation connected with the wire service business, one witness provided the Kefauver Committee with a somewhat different picture. Kansas City attorney. Michael D. Konomos, testifying in 1950, advised he had been retained several years back as an attorney for two men who were representatives of Continental Press, the national race wire service based in Chicago. He was asked to assist the two men inasmuch as the Chicago Capone Trans-America, was muscling into the wire service arena. After agreeing to represent the two men, on two occasions he was stopped on the street, at night, by armed men who threatened him. On one occasion it was three men in a car, and on another occasion it was two men, none of whom he recognized.

Under the new arrangement Harmony Publishing, which remained in business, received Trans-America's wire service through Mo-Kan for a fee of $1080.00 a month. Portnoy, who kept the books for both Harmony and Mo-Kan, was responsible for paying all expenses, including Western Union facilities, "employees salaries", etc. If reported figures can be believed, after subtracting expenses, plus his $200 salary and 15% commission, the remainder, an average of $750 a week, was sent on to Mo-Kan. In effect Mo-Kan Publishing was a shell operation with Harmony Publishing its sole customer, serving as a standby location in the event of any troubles or difficulties Harmony might encounter.

The wire service operated in the following manner. Each customer had one of ten unlisted phone numbers as his to call. Once a customer called in, usually at 11:00 am, his telephone line remained open until the last race of the day. Inside the wire service office there was a "horse board", a loud speaker box, and a rack on which each of the telephones, with an open line, is hung so the customer could hear the race results as they came in.

In 1946, Harmony Publishing was operating with the ten unlisted phone lines, a Western Union ticker line from Chicago, and a Western Union teleprinter with tie lines to customers in Council Bluffs, Iowa; Des Moines, Iowa; Lincoln, Nebraska; Omaha, Nebraska; Oklahoma City, Oklahoma; Leavenworth, Kansas; Tulsa, Oklahoma; Wichita, Kansas; St. Joseph, Missouri; and Sioux City, Iowa. By February 1947 service was discontinued to Des Moines, Tulsa and Oklahoma City due to an official crackdown on gambling in those cities.

A knowledgeable source familiar with the operation reported that as of February 1947 there were only 2-4 bookmaking operations in the city, the rest being in the metro area, and only one tie line outside the city, that to the Paddock Club in St. Joseph, Missouri, operated by Bennie Sembler. One of the local customers was the ever-familiar gambling figure Walt Rainey, operating out of the Plantation Club off East 40 Highway, outside the city limits, and within the purview of friendly Jackson County Sheriff Purdome.

In early 1947 the climate turned stormy across Missouri for race wire services, putting a crimp in their operations. The Missouri Attorney General ordered the telephone company to discontinue service to Pioneer Publishing, a St. Louis, Missouri operation with a client list of 130 bookmaker subscribers, obtaining its wire service from Chicago. Pioneer fought back and succeeded in getting telephone company service restored, but by that time they had lost half of their client base.

Bad news travels fast, and in Kansas City Simon Partnoy, anticipating similar problems, engaged an attorney, and had his ducks in order when on, March 10, 1947, Missouri Attorney General J.E. Taylor ordered the telephone company to refuse service to Harmony Publishing. The very next day Portnoy was in court, legal documents in hand, obtaining a temporary restraining order successfully reducing the time he was without service to only some 8 hours.

Twelve day later the State was back in court appearing before Jackson County Circuit Court Judge John F. Cook. The court action attracted a host of interested spectators including a number of police officials, politicians and Charles Binaggio, accompanied by his driver Nick Penna. The same Charles Binaggio who according to Eddie Osadchey had no interest in the wire service business.

Once again Partnoy prevailed. Judge Cook ruled in his favor, issuing a temporary injunction directing the telephone company to continue phone service to Harmony. The Judge concluded that even if Partnoy knew his customers were engaged in illegal gambling, evidence was lacking that Partnoy personally participated in illegal gambling. The judge went on to explain that the telephone company was in favor of the issue being tried before the Public Service Commission, and he agreed it was the proper venue to resolve the matter. He ruled the injunction would remain in force until that body made a decision.

Partnoy's legal victories ended when in July, 1947 the Public Service Commission made its ruling denying telephone service to Harmony and Mo-Kan. Their decision was appealed to the Missouri Supreme Court, and pending the appeal Partnoy continued operating, but had lost all of his out of state customers.

The race wire service business next came under the scrutiny of a United States Senate Sub Committee holding hearings aimed at formulating new legislation regulating the dissemination of gambling information in interstate commerce. Kansas City's own Eddie Osadchey and Tano Lococo were subpoenaed to testify before the sub committee. Spitz told the committee at the time of his deal with Partnoy, Harmony received its information from Trans-America. Later it switched to Mid West Service of Chicago, Illinois, and switched again in January 1949 to General News Service, also of Chicago, Ill.

Osadchey informed the committee that Standard News Service succeeded Harmony with Simon Partnoy continuing on as manager, assisted by an auditor, Abe "Ginger" Rosenbaum. He explained the name change was occasioned by the fact an injunction was pending against Harmony, and it was in this same time frame that Mid West Service of Chicago gave notice they were discontinuing service. General News Service then stepped in as the supplier for Standard News. According to Osadchey the business was now closed as they were without any customers. He provided gross revenues figures of $40,000 a year, with a net of $20,000. When asked to identify the number of customers they had, and their names, Osadchey declined to give up that information.

A Kansas City newspaper article dated May 4, 1950 reported that at the time Lococo and Osadchey were testifying in Washington D.C. a police officer checked the offices of Standard News Services located on the 5th Floor of the Railway Exchange Building, and found them locked and silent.

United States Senator McFarland, Chairman of the Senate Sub Committee, voiced special interest in testimony of J.E. Taylor, Missouri Attorney General, that Osadchey's wire served had operated for 2-3 years while under an injunction restraining the telephone company from refusing him service. Taylor appeared reluctant to name the Kansas City judge issuing the restraining order. Responding to the question of why the injunction had not been dissolved, Taylor explained there was no reason, except the judge's own. He had asked the judge, named only as Cook, on at least three occasions for an answer and had never got one. Stating he did not intend any criticism of the court, Taylor felt he had been fighting a losing battle against the bookmaking racket, citing the fact that Partnoy was still operating.

Back in Chicago, time ran out for James Ragen Sr. On June 24, 1946 he was ambushed on a Chicago street, and shotgunned to death. For nearly a year afterward the two wire services continued to do battle, neither making any money. Just when it appeared Continental would be unable to continue, Mickey McBride reappeared on the scene in May 1947 buying Continental back from Ragen interests for $370,000, payable over ten years. The plan was for the business to be the sole property of young Eddie McBride, Mickey's son, who had returned to Chicago from army service.

With the Ragens gone, the Capone mob folded Trans-America the very next month. With peace allegedly restored, the bitterness forgotten, many of the old Trans-America crowd melded into Continental. Kansas City's operation had no problem joining the new order of things, as was the case across the nation. McBride, and his Continental crowd, all vigorously denied the existence of any deals, connections or understandings with the Capone syndicate, however a Kefauver Committee report stated the evidence indicated otherwise.

It was the Kefauver Committee's contention, based on its hearings, that McBride's claim that he had no connection with Continental Press after he had sold it (August 1942), and his son Eddie was 100% owner was a sham. Mickey McBride was the real driving force behind Continental. Further, the report concluded Continental Press was in fact under the control of the gangsters constituting the Capone syndicate. The Committee rejected the "façade of legality" set up by Continental's legal counsel, and their contention that Continental was insulated from the ultimate customers, illegal bookmakers. The finding of the Committee was Continental, operating through agents and subagents, steals information from race tracks and supplies it through direct and indirect channels to bookmakers, operating in violation of the law, throughout the country. Additionally, McBride's operation deliberately makes a gift to Mafia controlled wire services by charging them less for the service than other clients.

The conclusion, Mafia elements in cities around the country are in control of the distribution of racing wire news with a resultant source of enormous profits and power over bookmaking. The Committee report placed Continental's gross income for 1949 at two million, five hundred thousand dollars.

In July 1950, Senator McFarland's Sub Committee made public a list of racing news distributors and customers across the nation. The list included more than 2000 firms and individuals who receive or distribute race news over an intricate network of telegraph and telephone lines fanning out from Chicago. The report stated that no doubt most were in the bookmaking business, however, others were legitimate users who haven't even a remote connection with illegal gambling interests. Harmony Publishing Company, Simon Partnoy manager, was named as a distributor in Kansas City, also operating as Standard Distributing Company and Standard News Company. Standard was identified as receiving race news from Continental Press in Cleveland through the General News Service of Chicago, described as dominated by the Capone syndicate.

Nineteen Kansas City customers were on the Senate Committee's list, 15 were known bookies as of May 1, 1950. The information meshed with the disclosure that investigators in Kansas City had visited the offices of Standard News Service two days after it ceased operations on May 2,1950, finding 19 telephone connections.

Noteworthy, among the 19 named, was Joseph Tigerman who melded his profession as an undertaker with an extensive bookmaking operation run out of his Tigerman & Son Funeral Home,

2738 Prospect Avenue. Tigerman was the victim of a gangland murder on October 31, 1963.

In addition to Standard News Service two other wire service distributors named were Cox Publishing Company, 3400 W. Douglas, Wichita, Kansas, and Harris Publishing Company, 233 Bartlett Building, St. Joseph, Missouri.

The Coats House Book

Holding a position in the higher echelons of the outfit Tony Gizzo had interests, often undisclosed, in most of the major gambling operations in the city. It was common knowledge that Gizzo was the prime mover in a bookmaking establishment run out of a cigar store in the Coates House Hotel building, 10th & Broadway Streets. The operation was started up in February 1947 by Charlie Binaggio, Gizzo, Mel Levitt, Sam Butler and Joe Danzo. Binaggio and Gizzo each had a 25% interest. A federal grand jury would report that in 1947 and 1948 the take from the enterprise was $100,000 a year. Gizzo and Levitt had previously been partners in a sports book at 344 W. 9th Street, accepting wagers on football, baseball and basketball.

Sam Butler was under subpoena to testify before the federal grand jury delving into gambling and other racket activities, when on October 18, 1949 he was found shot to death at the Coats House sports book, apparently a suicide. Considering his line of work, his partner's reputations, and his date with the grand jury, it would be logical to doubt a finding of suicide. However, Butler's wife, interviewed by the police, described her husband as having been "very melancholy and distraught" since receiving a grand jury subpoena, and in a phone conversation just prior to his death he talked of never seeing her again. Investigators also determined that on the day he died, immediately after having lunch, Butler drove to Kansas City, Kansas where he purchased a new revolver. He returned to the book-making office at the Coates House where he was found dead. A paraffin test showed Butler had fired a revolver - case closed.

Following Butler's death Mel Levitt sold out his interest, and the operation was reorganized as the Gizzo News Company.

On July 10, 1950 a five-count indictment was returned by a Jackson County grand jury charging Gizzo, Mel H. Levitt and Robert S. Holmes as operators of a sports book out of a cigar store at 1009 Broadway, in the lobby of the Coates House Hotel. The charges stemmed from a police raid resulting in the seizure of evidence that wagers were accepted on basketball games.

Charging these organized crime figures is one thing; getting them in jail another. The defendants filed a motion on April 30, 1951 asking the court to suppress the evidence seized by police officers, and Circuit Court Judge John F. Cook sustained the motion. The judge ruled the evidence could not be used at trial due to the fact the police did not have a search warrant when they seized the betting records.

Despite the adverse ruling the prosecutors opted to go forward, bringing the three men to trial on May 7, 1951. It was an uphill battle as each prosecution witnesses had been identified by means of the betting records ruled inadmissible. Therefore their testimony came under the fruit of the poisoned tree doctrine. The Judge sustained a defense motion for a directed verdict, and the defendants walked free.

Assault on Gambling

It is, to say the least, difficult to adequately portray the role gambling played in the historical experience of the city, and its size and scope. Periodic pushes by federal and local grand juries did much to expose the problem, however, little to suppress it.

The January 1939 "clean up" campaign, an assault by federal, state and local entities on organized crime activity in the city, successfully brought down Boss Tom Pendergast and outfit Boss Charlie Carrollo, and provided a fair idea of the scope of the gambling industry. The Jackson County grand jury made public its findings that a $12 million gambling industry had grown in the city. Judge Allen C. Southern, to whom the grand jury reported, put the figure at $20 million. Despite their efforts there would be no abatement in the expansion of gambling enterprises.

Ten years later, probably the most comprehensive effort to uncover the scope of racket and gambling activity was undertaken by a federal grand jury initially impaneled in April 1949. Commencing the probe in September 1949, hundreds of gamblers, enforcers, law enforcement officials, bookkeepers, lawyers, and others, including individuals from a number of other states, were quizzed by the grand jury. Once again the pervasiveness and scope of gambling in the city would be laid bare.

Special prosecutors were appointed by the U.S. Department of Justice to assist in conducting the probe, assisted by a host of federal investigators. The very fact of the inquiry, and the investigative activity surrounding it, put a severe crimp in gambling operations, and ongoing efforts by the crime family to expand it. In light of his promise to various crime syndicates to open up the city and State to gambling, the timing could not have been worse for outfit leader Charlie Binaggio.

In May 1950, the grand jury published their findings in an interim report titled, "Presentment of Local Crime Conditions." Although the grand jury term had not expired, the grand jury felt it was of the utmost importance to reveal they had uncovered many violations of state laws over which the jury had no jurisdiction. In view of this, the grand jury hoped their report would result in proper steps being undertaken to arrest "this terrible lawlessness, and the utter disregard for our state as well as our municipal laws."

The grand jury reported, "..racketeers in this district are largely concerned with the operation of gambling enterprises and are organized. Nearly all the large gambling operations in bookmaking (horse and sports), policy wheels, and dice or crap games, are controlled by comparatively few men. The gambling operations in the Kansas City area amount to the staggering sum of approximately 34-1/2 million dollars a year." Specifically, dice game operations were labeled as a "vast and intricate picture" with the same individuals or combinations of these individuals, a select clique of Charlie Binaggio associates, holding the top positions in virtually every gambling operation of note." Furthermore, gambling enterprises operated without the slightest danger of prosecution, and intentionally avoided violating federal laws, a situation representing a breakdown of law enforcement administered by state and local officials.

Eleven of the largest dice operations, eleven bookmaking operations and control of the national sports wire service, indispensable to bookmaking establishments, were identified in the grand jury report. Adding to the crime mosaic, the grand jury outlined out of state rackets linked to Kansas City gangsters in such locales as Colorado; Council Bluffs, Iowa; St. Joseph, Missouri; and Kansas City and Wichita, Kansas.

In all more than 50 individuals were named as partners or participants, in various combinations, in gaming operations uncovered. Of note, two men named exemplified the age-old melding of politics and gambling. Sam Hayden, an assistant Jackson County District Attorney, fired after the report was published, and Robert S. Greene, Superintendent of Jackson County buildings, were prominent among the line up of named gamblers.

Town Recreation, located at 3111 Homes Street, in operation for an eight-month period in 1948 was identified as the largest gambling operation in Kansas City. During that short period it netted almost $200,000. Partners in the venture included, Charlie Gargotta, Tano Lococo, John Goulding, S.O. "Solly" McLeroy, Tim Moran, Tince Walker, Walter Rainey, Earl Kennedy, W.F. Wedow, Francis M. Leslie, Julius "Abe" Freelander, Clyde Keeling, William Cole, and the aforementioned, Robert Green and Sam Hayden. As members of the gambling fraternity these names would appear over and over connected to the various outfit gambling enterprises uncovered.

As the grand jury pointed out in its interim report, the gambling ventures identified, and the men behind them, were not in violation of federal statutes. The only recourse left to the grand jury was to return indictments on charges of tax evasion. Nine individuals were so charged in addition to tax liens being levied.

The same week the federal grand jury issued its report the Jackson County grand jury announced the results of its inquiry into organized gambling. Indictments were returned against 26 individuals charged with bookmaking and policy wheel gambling.

Business As Usual

The lure of gambling is akin to the lure of alcohol for the alcoholic. It did not matter how many reform movements, grand jury probes, investigations, indictments, prison sentences, exposes, attempted to alter the landscape, gamblers will look to gamble, and the outfit would provide it.

Eleven years after the highly publicized actions of federal and county grand juries in 1950, a new probe would disclose the mob had hardly missed a beat in pursuing its favorite pastime. Bold headlines of the May 4, 1961 Kansas City Star trumpeted, "CRIME PLAYGROUND HERE." A Jackson County grand jury report released that day stated, based on sworn testimony it's the grand jury's belief that professional criminals in the city are highly organized and ruled by an inner circle called the syndicate, functioning like a board of directors, and probably connected to the "Mafia or Black Hand society." The report declared the syndicate has had a "criminal playground" dating back to 1953.

Quoting from the report, "Based on sworn testimony presented to this grand jury, it now seems apparent that sometime in 1953 a 'deal' was made between the syndicate and certain members of the Kansas City Missouri Police department which led to the 'syndicate' being permitted to operate a number of gambling and after hours liquor establishment, control prostitution and fence stolen merchandise in Kansas City. In return the 'syndicate' supposedly promised to commit no major robberies and burglaries within the city limits. It is the belief of this jury that it was because of this deal with the underworld that the Downtown Bridge Club located at 1425 Baltimore was permitted to operate with little or no interference from the Police Department."

Acknowledging the Bridge Club may have been raided frequently by the police the jury also found it was apparent one or more members of the Police Department was tipping off the operators of impending police action. Account books of the club revealed that on those days it was raided the gambling activity was only interrupted for a brief time.

The Bridge Club was only one of several permanent ongoing outfit gambling establishments operating. Testimony provided the grand jury also uncovered at least five ongoing commercial gambling ventures run by blacks that have run 24 hours a day, 365 day a year, for a number of years.

"Competent" experienced law enforcement officials informed the grand jury such conditions could not flourish to the extent they have without the complicity of some members of the law enforcement community. The grand jury's stated opinion was such complicity could not be secured simply in exchange for a promise major crimes would be kept out of the city, and there had to be a reward over and above a simple promise.

Chapter XI

The Labor Rackets

JOHN LAZIA RECOGNIZED the potential that lay in the labor arena, and following the path of other local labor racketeers, he moved in organizing the cleaning and dying business. He imported underworld characters, strong-arm types, from St. Louis and Chicago putting them out front to handle the dirty work. Associated with Lazia were Morris Salwinsky, aka, Morrie Sol, John Kramer, President of the Linoleum & Carpet Layers Union, and Sam Gross, a former Kansas City Police Officer who became an international representative of the Cleaners and Dyers Union. They organized by terror. Shops were blown up, employees beaten, and to make up the cost of protection payoffs businessmen were forced to raise prices for services rendered.

With control of the police department, outfit backing, and a lofty political status, Lazia was able to exert influence in other areas of the business sphere, dictating policies, practices and methods to selected labor leaders. The take from the labor rackets was enormous.

One of the many business targeted were movie theatre operators. In the late 1920s W. Lee Vaughan was just such a businessman. He was a man ahead of the curve in his field having installed a "talk-ie machine" in his Neptune Movie Theatre, located at 39th and Bell Streets, in May 1929. He had in his employ, as a motion picture operator, a member of the Motion Picture Operators Union, Local 170. However, the union was not satisfied, demanding that Vaughan hire additional union helpers he did not need, and raise the weekly salary of his onboard union man. His refusal was met with threats of retaliation "of an indefinite and indiscriminate sort."

Vaughan, in addition to the Neptune Theatre, also operated the New Center Theatre, 15th & Troost Streets, and the Art Theatre, 18th & Central Streets, Kansas City, Kansas. Upon his refusal to accede to union demands Vaughan claimed that "stench bombs" were placed in all of his theatres, union pickets intimidated theatre patrons, and literature and posters were distributed warning of dangerous fumes in the theatres. On July 3, 1929, he went to the U.S. District Court and obtained a temporary injunction against the union local, also filing suit against the union, its officers and several motion picture machine operators.

That the outfit would be involved in the shake downs of movie theatre operators was confirmed on November 29, 1931 when Tano Lococo, one of Lazia's henchmen, was arrested after being seen by the manager of the Pershing Theatre in Kansas City, Kansas, placing a stink bomb under a seat, and then leaving the theatre. In what was an all to common occurrence, on December 2, 1931 charges of malicious destruction of property and disturbing the peace filed against Lococo were discharged.

Another labor racketeer of the day was Max Dyer, a bread truck driver and salesman, who won election to the post of secretary of the Central Labor Body. In late 1927 he led the charge in organizing the Building Service Employees Union, Local 98, whose members included elevator operators, janitors, window washers and the like. Organizing efforts utilized all the usual tactics of intimidation favored by labor racketeers.

The strike against the Fidelity Building, 9th & Walnut Streets, typified Dyer's methods. An employee at the building, having no connection to the target of the organizing effort, the building operators, was beaten half to death. Joe Evola, an individual well known to the police, was arrested for the beating, while his accomplice, Tony "Tony Shirt" Cammisa, escaped. Evola pled guilty to assault charges and was sent to prison for two years. Cammisa had the distinction of carrying a label, pinned on him by authorities, as one of the very worst criminals in the entire city.

The BMA building was struck on Dyer's orders, and as soon as the pickets went up, a bomb planted in a northeast corner storeroom of the building exploded.

Dyer's next target was the Manufacturer's Trust building, 8th and Wyandotte Streets. A union negotiating session was planned between officers of the building and Dyer in anticipation of a union contract. As a prelude to the meeting a bomb exploded in the building. Tony Cammisa was believed responsible for planting the explosive device.

In addition to his strong arm and bombing talents, Tony Cammisa was also known to be involved in drug operations, reportedly due to be charged as part of the Angelo Donnici drug ring. His reputation as one of the city's worst criminals caught up with him on

March 16, 1938 when his body was found in a car at Excelsior Springs, Missouri. He had not died of natural causes.

Dyer extended his particular style of union organizing to the Jones Store, George B. Peck Dry Goods Company and Bob Jones, a wholesale cleaning establishment. Jones was victimized by imported goons from St. Louis who fired shots at him, and then bombed his shop.

Joe Arvin was yet another labor racketeer infesting the business sphere. Arvin had worked as a taxi driver and held a second job operating a notorious burlesque show on Twelfth Street, seemingly the perfect credentials for the job of labor organizer. Once he recognized there was big money to be made in the labor field he went about attempting to organize laundry workers, employing all the established tactics of terror and intimidation.

Arvin's methods were put on public display in March 1938 when he was brought to trial on State charges of malicious destruction of property. According to the prosecution, George "Frenchy" Andrea met Arvin some four year previous, at a time when Arvin was serving as a business agent for steel workers in St. Joseph, Missouri. Andrea hooked up with Arvin again in September 1937 when Arvin was business agent for the Kansas City laundry drivers and workers union. Andrea, looking to find work, was told by Arvin there was nothing in the way of employment, but he did have something he needed handled.

That night he met Arvin, and three other men Andrea did not know. Arvin had two lists of laundry establishments, handing one to Andrea and one of the three men. The second list was given to the other two men. Arvin instructed them to go forth and break the windows of the laundries listed, and any other laundry they might spot along the way advertising finished shirts for ten cents or less. They would be paid five dollars for every window they broke. Andrea and his partner carried out the assignment, smashing the window of a Chinese laundry, and the next morning he was paid five dollars.

Arvin's reputation led to a call for help from strikers in St. Joseph, Missouri, who were not having much success organizing a cab company operating in both St. Joseph and Kansas City. Arvin knew exactly what to do. He targeted a cab driver who had refused to join the union. He then arranged for the union boys to set the driver up. When the cabby arrived to pick up what he believed to be a legitimate fare, a car pulled up alongside and acid was thrown in his face. Arvin was prosecuted for the assault, receiving a 25-year sentence. For unknown reasons the sentence was set aside.

The Federal Government finally caught up with Arvin, and by 1941 he was safely off the streets, locked up in the Federal Penitentiary at Leavenworth serving a five-year sentence on a white slavery conviction. There was no setting aside the sentence this time.

The Teamsters

Was Bill Polley an honest hard working truck driver who believed in the good a union could accomplish for its members, acting in a lawful, ethical manner in organizing efforts? So said former Kansas City Police Chief Lear B. Reed in his book, Human Wolves. Or, was Polley, as described by other police officials " ...of the old school of labor organizers who believed force was the convincing weapon."

Polley's involvement as a labor representative dated to 1913. He became business agent in approximately 1933, in what was then called the Truck Drivers Local 41, and prior to that was business agent for the ironworker's union.

Polley took an active role in attempting to organize the trucking industry and was behind any number of strike actions called by the union. About the time Polley became business agent the Perky Brothers Transfer and Storage Company was bombed. Polley was implicated in the incident and indicted by a Jackson County grand jury, however the case never went to trial. In May 1934, the Chevrolet Motor Company assembly plant in Kansas City, Kansas, was experiencing labor troubles, and Polley and four other men were arrested near the plant. Polley found in possession of a blackjack was held for a short period of time and released.

Polley's best friend was Teamster Assistant Business Agent Emmett M. Eslinger, and together they attended an 8:30 p.m. meeting at the Pickwick Hotel on the night of October 11, 1935. Polley had called the meeting to discuss unionizing strategies for organizing several motor transport firms. At the conclusion of the meeting the two friends agreed to stop off for a cold one at the nearby Winnie Winkle Club, a notorious night spot on 10th Street, before going home.

They got to the club sometime after midnight, calling it a night sometime around 12:45 a.m. All indications were Polley was heading to his residence in Kansas City, Kansas. It was approximately 1:00 a.m., October 12, 1935, and Polley was proceeding west on the Sixth Street Trafficway, car windows rolled up as "a safety precaution." If he did in fact feel unsafe, the reasons for his fears were unknown.

As he was stopped at a red light at Sixth & Broadway a car pulled up alongside, sounding its horn. Possibly believing the occupants were friends, Polley lowered the window. Unfortunately they were anything but friends, as gunshots rang out from inside the car, and Bill Polley, 45, was shot dead.

Polley's wife advised the police her husband had of late appeared greatly worried, but had offered no explanation as to the reason. Inquiries made by the investigating officers turned up reports of recent conflict within the union local between Polley and several of his lieutenants who allegedly were trying to take over by "muscling" him out of his leadership position. Labor officials responded with a statement to the effect Polley had enemies all right, but they were not within the ranks of labor. They did not elaborate as to who they saw as his enemies.

Former Police Chief Lear B. Reed did not agree with the labor officials."So steadfast and forthright in his devotion to his organization was Polley that apparently some other leaders must have decided that he was in the way. He refused to become a partner to a shake-down of businessmen in the city", Reed wrote in his book.

With the murder of Bill Polley, his friend Emmett M. Eslinger, along with O.B. Enloe, President of Teamster Local 41, and Lon C. Oliver, became the dominant figures in Teamster organizing efforts. Eslinger, born in Nevada, Missouri, was characterized as "an energetic labor organizer in the 1930s and 1940s, and is generally credited with being the man who fostered (Teamster) Local 541." Friends called him "forceful" in his dealings, physically strong and fearing no man.

Strikes called by these union officials were often rough affairs with drivers beaten, property damaged or destroyed, trucks run off the road, and targeted drivers, including their innocent family members, threatened. Every form of intimidation one can imagine was put into play. In one case, Harry Lockwood, William Bailey and Francis Lacy were arrested in connection with labor racketeering activities, and confessed they had been in the employ of Enslinger, Enloe, and others, to commit acts of mayhem in their behalf. The three were charged in municipal court, however, not only were the fines minimal, $100 each, but also payment of the fines was stayed.

In an era of ramped up union organizing, Teamster Local 41 Business Agent, Floyd R. Hayes was a force to be reckoned with. In 1937 he paid a visit to his uncle, the owner of Reardon Truck Line suggesting if he signed up with the Teamsters Union he would earn their support in making Reardon Truck Line the biggest in Kansas City.

In Reardon's eyes the Teamster Union was inhabited by a bunch of crazy punks, and he had no interest in his nephew's offer.

Kinship meant little or nothing when it came to union organizing, and Reardon's truck line was targeted by the union. In about three months the company did not have one piece of equipment that had not been damaged or rendered inoperable. If nothing else, Reardon was a hardheaded sort with lots of money to fight back, and he would not given in.

Most of the other truck lines signed up, while others opted to hire strikebreakers, a tactic that did not prove out. Union goons out-muscled the strikebreakers, breaking heads, arms and legs till they decided enough was enough, and quit.

Eventually Kansas City's truck lines were in the fold, signed on with the Teamsters, and other related businesses soon followed suit. As part of the organizing arrangement Hayes demanded and received kickbacks from the companies. The totality of information available leads to the conclusion Hayes, at this time, was not allied with organized crime elements, but on the contrary, resisted mob efforts to infiltrate the union. Not that Hayes' motives were pure in this regard. Rather, he had no desire to share his ill-gotten gains with the criminal element. Eventually he would be overwhelmed by the rising tide of outfit involvement.

Moving on, Teamster organizers went after milk companies. The drivers worked on a commission basis making from $30 to $75 a week, considered excellent money in the 1930s. The job called for the drivers to start work between 3:00 am and 4:00 a.m. in order to complete their routes by about 1:00 p.m. Then they had to re-run the route making their own collections, resulting in a 10 to 14 hour workday. Should they want a day off, the route driver had to pay for someone to run their route.

There was little enthusiasm on the part of most drivers to join the union. For one, they feared joining would incur the anger of their bosses, never a good thing. The union organizers would make their approach in the morning asking the driver if he had joined the Teamster Union. Those having joined needed only to display their union card. For those who had not, it was suggested they join immediately, causing some of the drivers to become belligerent. Undeterred, the organizers would persist, attempting to convince the drivers to join. If the driver still resisted he was told he would be re-contacted in a couple of days. Continued resistance resulted in violence, starting out with a beating.

It did not take many beatings before the drivers saw the light, and joined up. The dairy companies realized just how vulnerable their equipment was to sabotage and put up little or no fight.

The bread truck drivers turned out to be even more of a challenge as they looked on themselves as bread salesmen rather than truck drivers. Numerous heads were cracked and bones broken before they finally came to the conclusion joining the Teamsters was a good idea. The bread companies themselves were still another matter, and, unlike the dairies, proved difficult to bring around.

Rather than breaking more heads, the innovative union operatives came up with other, just as effective, methods to use against the bread companies. For one, they found that mixing salt in with the sugar and flour used in baking bread did not make for a palatable product. Another more exotic technique involved spreading around the plant about a pint of skunk urine, guaranteed to render the premises off limits for about a week. The ingenuity of the labor organizer seemed to have no bounds. When one of the larger bakeries shut down temporarily to allow repairmen to work on the ovens, the bakers returning the next day discovered the repairmen had some how made a mistake. All the oven doors had been welded shut.

To circumvent the union, some of the companies began to buy modest sized bakeries in small towns outside Kansas City. Unfortunately, Teamster union officials learned of the move, and upon discovering the small town operations were employing non-union help, the fight was on again.

Organized crime elements around the nation were in the process of ramping up efforts to infiltrate the Teamster's union. To their good fortune they had the perfect man to pave the way, an up and coming Detroit Teamster Official, James Riddle Hoffa.

A source familiar with Teamster affairs, spoke of a meeting held during the 1940s indicative of the involvement by crime "families" in Teamsters' affairs. As reported by the source, "Jimmy Hoffa met in Chicago, Illinois, with Copolla, Charlie Binaggio, Tony Gizzo, Lopipari, Tony Accardo, and Hump." Binaggio and Gizzo were Kansas City's representatives, while "Copolla" is most likely Frank Copolla, a notorious national and international drug trafficker, eventually deported to Italy. "Lopipari" in all likelihood refers to St. Louis mob leader Tony Lopipero. Tony Accardo was the Chicago mob boss at the time, while "Hump" is the recognized nickname of Murrary Humpries, then a prominent Chicago labor racketeer and Accardo associate.

Around the year 1950 Lee Quisenberry, President of Kansas City Teamster Local 955 was shot and wounded by an unknown assailant. He believed the North End criminal outfit was responsible for the incident. As an insurance policy he hired Sam Ancona as an assistant business agent, but in reality his job was to look after Quisenberry's welfare. By hiring Ancona the criminal organization would be pacified.

In the early part of that same year, Orville Ring became president of Teamster Local 541, then the largest of the Teamster's locals in Kansas City. Ring was an ambitious and savvy man. He brought on board streetwise, tough guys such as Ernie Anderson, Carl "Curly" Rogers, Del Nabors, Bob Williams and Tripoli "Trip" Milone.

The Kansas City Star, in a 1972 article, identified Floyd Hayes, then Secretary-Treasurer of Local 41, and Orville Ring, then President of Local 541, as the two most powerful union leaders in Kansas City in the year 1952. Dave Beck, a west coast Teamster, serving his first year as Teamster National President, was waging a nationwide campaign to increase Teamster power and membership. During this period jurisdictional battles between the building crafts and the Teamsters unions raged, and Kansas City was a major violent battleground. In the summer of 1953 a Congressional Committee held hearings in Kansas City concerning union violence, lost man-hours in Korean War defense work, and a ten-week strike that put 22,500 men out of work.

Based on recommendations of the Congressional Committee, a federal grand jury was commissioned to scrutinize Orville Ring's activities, however, no indictments were forthcoming. A Jackson County grand jury inquiry followed, and they returned an indictment against Ring and several other union figures, but no convictions resulted.

The situation in Kansas City continued to deteriorate to the point the Teamster International placed Local 41 and Local 955 in trusteeship, ordering Sam Ancona in as President of Local 955. Following this action, Jimmy Hoffa sent Roy Lee Williams to Kansas City to run Local 41. Williams, who had been operating out of Wichita, Kansas, would be a force in Teamster affairs locally and nationally for years to come.

Born on March 22, 1915 in Ottumwa, Iowa, Williams was one of 12 children. Reared in southeast Missouri he first entered the freight industry in 1935 as a driver for C.W. Pascal Company. He joined Kansas City Local 41 in 1938. Ten years later, after distinguished World War II army service, he was asked by Jimmy Hoffa to go to Wichita, Kansas to serve as a business Agent. While still in Wichita he was elected a Trustee of Teamsters Joint Council 56 in Kansas

City, and by 1953 Williams became president of Joint Council 56, by-passing the established procedure calling for the office holder first to be president of a local. The joint council is an umbrella entity over-seeing all Teamster locals in Western Missouri and all of Kansas.

As near as can be determined, around 1952 the Kansas City crime "family" made its move on the union. The attempt on Lee Quisenberry's life may well have been the opening salvo. The enormous potential the Teamster Union represented as a source of money, jobs and influence was abundantly clear, and the crime "family" was eager to capitalize on it.

Men who owed allegiance to the outfit became well entrenched in the various locals in Kansas City. Sam Ancona, Secretary-Treasurer of Joint Council 56 and President of Local 955; Curly Rogers and Trip Milone, President and Secretary-Treasurer respectively, of Local 541; and John Balestrere, brother of Big Jim Balestrere, Assistant Business Agent of local 955, have been identified as in that category.

Ancona would become the unofficial liaison man between the outfit and the Teamsters Union, reporting directly to Nick Civella, when he took over as outfit Boss. With the passage of time Civella would have Williams in his pocket, passing on orders and instructions to Williams through Ancona.

In speaking with FBI agents in 1954, after he resigned from the Teamsters and retired to his farm, Orville Ring provided further corroboration of the outfit's infiltration. Mr. Ring informed the agents that Ernie Anderson and Del Nabors, both of whom he had hired, had become aligned with the criminal organization at a time in 1952-1953 when the outfit was seeking control of the labor movement in Kansas City. He cited as proof the fact Anderson had arranged for Ring to meet in 1952 with Tony Gizzo, described by Ring as the "leader of the North End" and a "powerful political figure"

Gizzo informed Ring he wanted all teamsters to vote for Gene Purdome for Jackson County Sheriff, and if Ring knew what was good for him he would work very hard in Purdome's behalf. This presented a problem in that Ring supported a different candidate, and he believed this was reason enough for the crime syndicate and the Pendergast political machine to be out to get him. He claimed Ernie Anderson and Del Nabors consistently supported "north-enders and ex-convicts" and were gaining control of the union local.

Ring went on to describe how in the late fall of 1953 he was approached by Nick Civella and asked to go along with Civella and his people, who Civella described as "running the town." In Civella's words, "they would make him (Ring) the biggest son-of-a-bitch" if Ring swung the labor vote for "their candidates", and also let them handle union shakedowns and payoffs. On the other hand, if Ring opted to resist, then Civella's advice was he had better resign if he wanted to continue living.

For Ring this was the last straw. Civella's threats combined with numerous others warning that he and his wife would be killed, were motivation enough to submit his resignation on March 1, 1954. Ring was still able to negotiate with Williams and Anderson, securing an agreement for a years salary in advance, plus car expenses, in return for him getting out. Two years later Ring would be dead, killed in a tractor accident at his farm.

On April 6, 1954, without any notification to the general membership, a meeting was held attended by only 136 of the 5000 members of Local 541. At this time Anderson was elected President of the local to fulfill Ring's unexpired term. A few weeks prior to the election Anderson, interviewed by a Kansas City Star reporter, displayed confidence he had the inside track for the job, but said he wouldn't know for sure until Roy Williams received word from "higher officials." So much for union elections.

Shortly after this election, Jimmy Hoffa visited Kansas City to attend a meeting of Local 41 at which time Roy Williams was elected president of the local. Williams was on his way to becoming the most powerful Teamster Official in Kansas City and beyond.

Re-entering the scene was former Assistant Business Agent Emmett Eslinger. He had retired from his post with Local 541 and following a stint as part owner of a tavern hired on, in approximately 1952, at the Midwest Plumbing and Heating Company. In early 1954 Eslinger let a co-worker in on his plan of looking into the possibility of getting a new appointment as a Local 541 Business Agent, explaining he had been back in the union for some two years and thus eligible for the position. Several union members, said to be disgruntled with recent conditions at the local, were actively backing Eslinger's return. Local 541 at that time was under the leadership of Earnest Anderson as President, and Karl Rogers, Vice President.

On the morning of April 26, 1954 Eslinger left his residence on his way to work but never made it to the job. Alerted that her husband was missing from work Mrs Eslinger retraced his normal route. On a wooded stretch of Eighty-Seventh Street, near U.S. Highway 71, she came upon her husband's car parked on the north side of the street. Eslinger's body was inside, his head bashed in with an eight-pound window-weight, and his throat slashed. Robbery was ruled out as a motive. Although no one knew of any threats, or had Eslinger talked of any, an interesting comment was made by his son. Without providing further details the son stated, "We told him not to take too great a part in No. 541 activities since he retired as business agent."

Jackson County Sheriff Arvid Owsley, whose officers investigated the murder, was quoted as saying, "It looks now as though one of two motives was responsible for the murder of Eslinger. Either somebody was afraid that Eslinger was going to make a serious effort to get himself re-elected president of local 541, or the murder was planned to scare other union officials into co-operating with racketeers." It was clear the Sheriff laid the murder at the doorstep of the union.

Floyd Hayes Turns

In the sordid story of labor racketeering there is little question Floyd R. Hayes was a pioneer, playing a prominent role in Teamster affairs, and the fate that befell him warrants recounting. In 1963, at the age of 66, Hayes was in a jam. He decided to defy the code and attempt to help himself by cooperating with the FBI.

As evidenced by his union organizing talents, Hayes was no saint. He had a police record dating to 1917 when he was sentenced to a one-year term in the Oklahoma State Penitentiary on charges of car theft. While in San Diego in 1932 he was convicted of violating federal liquor laws, receiving a 60-day sentence. He came to Kansas City in 1933, working as a truck driver for two years before becoming business agent for Local 41 in 1935. He was a former President of Teamster Local 41, and in 1954 was elected Secretary-Treasurer of the local while under indictment by a Jackson County grand jury. Hayes also had been a member and officer of Joint Council 56.

The aforementioned Jackson County indictment was handed down in 1954 and involved charges of perjury stemming from a beating Hayes, and Local 41 business agent Stanley Clevenger, inflicted on a Teamster member at the union hall. In March 1959, Hayes was indicted federally on income tax evasion charges. He pled guilty, was sentenced to an 18 month term, and while in jail was continued on his full salary as Secretary-Treasurer of local 41.

After his release from prison in October 1960 Hayes opted not to seek another term as Secretary of Local 41, instead retaining his position with Joint Council 56 until 1961. He then became an organizer for the Joint Council and for Local 41.

Nothing in his background would lead one to suspect Hayes would ever decide to cooperate with law enforcement. So why did he? In February 1962 Roy Williams, Hayes, and 5 other Teamsters, were indicted by a federal grand jury at Kansas City, Missouri, charged with embezzling $200,000 in union funds by means of kickbacks, bill padding and payoffs. Despite government witnesses testifying that Williams accepted kickbacks pursuant to a deal arranged by Floyd Hayes, the jury found him not guilty. Not so for Hayes, who was found guilty of the very same charges.

In May 1963, Hayes received a four-year prison sentence. Subsequent events left Hayes feeling betrayed and abandoned by fellow Teamsters, and for that reason he agreed to cooperate and testify. The Government had every reason to believe Hayes' testimony would insure a conviction of Roy Lee Williams. The decision to talk would cost Hayes his life.

Hayes was nobody's fool and knew full well the implication of his decision. Nick Civella had to protect a most valuable asset, Roy Williams, who by this time was in Civella's pocket. Fearing the mob would get to him by means of a car-bomb, Hayes installed a remote control starting device on his car. What Hayes failed to do was alter his pattern of activities. Every Thursday evening Hayes and his wife bowled in a league at the King Louie East bowling alley. Thursday evening June 11, 1964 was no exception.

After the bowling session ended that evening Hayes and his wife departed the alley and he alone headed toward his car, parked off by it self, away from other patron's vehicles. His routine was a set one. First, upon reaching his car, retrieve the remote starter, back away and activate the starter. While he was doing this his wife stood back some 75 yards waiting. Just as Hayes reached his vehicle, putting his bowling bag down, a car sped into the lot a shotgun protruding out from the passenger side window. The car pulled up to Hayes and a blast from the weapon knocked him to the pavement. The passenger hopped out of the car, leaned over his fallen prey and finished Hayes off.

Screaming as she started toward her husband, Mrs. Hayes was shot by the driver of the murder car. Miraculously she suffered only a superficial wound to her midsection. In the end, as aware and cautious as he might have been, his failure to alter his routine, and his passion for bowling proved fatal.

Civella's Man

When Hayes was debriefed by FBI Agents he told them that within one year after Roy Williams was elected President of Local 41, Nick Civella controlled the Teamster Union in Kansas City. He based this conclusion on the fact Williams personally told him on any number of occasions that all major decisions and union problems were discussed with Nick Civella before a final decision was made. For instance, Williams would not fire anyone if Civella voiced an objection.

Over time a close working relationship developed between Roy William and Nick Civella, however, there were occasions in these early years when Williams was reluctant to go with the flow. One such occasion involved an arrangement put together in the mid 1950s by Orville Ring, then President of Local 541. Ring had made a deal with a local doctor whereby the doctor received a monthly fee from the Local's treasury, believed to be $1.00, for every member of Local 541. In return each member and their dependants were entitled to receive an outpatient visit.

Floyd Hayes, during his FBI debriefing, spoke of being approached on several occasions by the doctor suggesting that Local 41 also adopt the plan Local 541 had in place. At the same time Sam Ancona, President of Local 955, made repeated approaches to Hayes encouraging adoption of the plan on the grounds it would be beneficial for Local 41. Neither he nor Williams had any interest in adopting the plan for their local.

In approximately 1956, the exact date not recalled, Hayes tells of receiving an urgent telephone call from Williams asking him to come visit at Williams' home. Williams ushered Hayes out to a barn for a private talk, confiding that following a union meeting at the Hotel Phillips he was approached in the hotel lobby by "Hiway" Simone (Outfit member Thomas Simone), and another gangster type. Williams was instructed to accept the medical plan Local 541 was using, and should he refuse, both of his children, then his wife and then Williams would be killed. If he went along he would be taken care of, which Williams took to mean he would be allowed to continue as President of Local 41. Hayes described Williams as emotional and distraught as he spoke of these events.

Williams admitted to Hayes he had, under duress, agreed to go along with the plan and now needed Hayes to help him out by agreeing to sign Local 41 checks for the monthly plan fees. Williams had to have Hayes in his corner since the signature of the Secretary-Treasurer of Local 41, as co-signer, was required. Hayes felt he had no choice but to agree. If he didn't, Williams would be in grave danger of mob reprisal.

Both Williams and Hayes agreed the fees were excessive for the services rendered, and the deal smacked of extortion, something they both were very familiar with. They felt they should take the matter up with the big man, Jimmy Hoffa, then President of the International Brotherhood of Teamsters (IBT). The week after the meeting in

Williams' barn they rang Hoffa up and arranged a meeting to be held in Detroit.

The meeting did not get off to a good start. Sitting in the office with Hoffa were two men Williams and Hayes did not recognize, nor did they like the looks of. It was very apparent from the outset these two were present to see that the plan and the fees it called for were implemented. Williams argued against the plan, explaining the union local would be financially ruined if it had to fund it as it currently stood. Hoffa's decision came down in favor of the plan, authorizing its adoption, proclaiming it would benefit the members of Local 41. Hoffa agreed the local's treasury would be hard pressed to handle the fees, and as a solution he instructed Williams to raise membership dues to cover the payments.

Williams later informed Hayes the monthly fees amounted to $4000 a month, and, as he predicted, Local 41's treasury was unable to cope with it. One year after Williams was forced to accept the plan, membership dues for the local were raised. He also confided that sometime after the plan was initiated he made a run at the doctor suggesting a portion of the monthly fees be kicked backed to him, but he was turned away. Hayes believed neither Williams, nor any other Teamster, was receiving kickbacks from the doctor, as would normally be the case. He felt strongly the outfit was getting the kickbacks as they obviously had orchestrated the entire deal.

Confirmation came in late 1960 or early 1961 when Williams let Hayes in on a conversation Williams had with the doctor. The doctor wanted out from under the plan, and was going to move away from Kansas City. According to the doctor, Nick Civella was taking too big a cut of the fees paid by the union, and he could no longer afford to operate the plan. Several months passed without Hayes hearing anything more about the matter. The status quo prevailed. The doctor never moved from the city, nor was the outpatient plan discontinued.

Payments from the union, and kickbacks to the outfit, apparently continued on unabated.

Eventually the long arm of the law caught up to Roy L. Williams. Federal authorities in Chicago obtained an indictment in 1981 charging Williams with attempting to bribe then U.S. Senator Howard Cannon of Nevada. Shortly thereafter, while under indictment, he was elected to the top spot - President of the IBT. He was subsequently convicted of the charges and received a long jail sentence. Following in the footsteps of his former long time friend and associate, Floyd Hayes, he opted to cooperate with the government hoping to avoid confinement. Williams would be obligated to testify in various prosecutions undertaken by the government.

One of those prosecutions took place in Kansas City's federal district court in 1985. Prominent organized crime figures from Kansas City, Chicago, Milwaukee, Cleveland and Las Vegas were on trial charged with skimming millions of dollars from Las Vegas Hotel/ Casinos, a scheme Williams had participated in. By this time he was a broken man, in ill health, requiring an oxygen tank by his side while on the witness stand. However, his testimony was dramatic and revealing.

Ironically, it was in a political setting in the latter part of 1953 or early 1954 when he first met Nick Civella. He was a member of a political committee that included Civella, representing a north end political club. Other committee members included Bill Serman, Mayor of Independence, Missouri, Tim Moran, head of the Central Club, and two other individuals. Together they acted as referees for the various political clubs operating in Jackson County. Their job was to sort out the various candidates selecting those the committee thought had the best chance of winning, and notifying the clubs of their selection with an aim toward building a unified front.

A relationship developed, Civella and Williams becoming "very personal friends" right up until the time Civella passed away. He saw Civella as an extraordinarily deep thinker who knew what he was talking about. Civella unquestionably furthered his Teamster career, and in return he provided assistance to Civella. At Civella's request he put "a lot of younger people to work at the union." He recognized Civella as "representing a powerful group here in Kansas City", and as a person who knew many of William's Teamster superiors and associates in other parts of the country, including Jimmy Hoffa, Bill Presser, Frank Ranney, Allen Dorfman, and people in New Orleans and San Francisco.

When the infamous 1957 Apalachin gangland conclave was uncovered banner front- page headlines named Civella and Joe Filardo as attendees at the meeting. Civella later confided in Williams the meeting's agenda included a discussion of "territory and cooperation." According to Civella, he had Kansas City as his territory, and he maintained working relationships with other areas, having friends in Wisconsin, Chicago, Cleveland, and New Orleans. He offered his assistance anytime Williams had occasion to be in an area where he felt he would have difficulties. All he had to do was contact Civella who in turn would reach out for his friends. As Williams viewed it, "I took him as a friend. I didn't know what business he was in or anything else until the papers came out about the Apalachin thing."

He would soon discover anytime a disagreement arose between them, in one way or the other, his superiors would hear of it, and he would be asked to comply with Civella's requests. However, in 1958 Williams ran right up against Nick Civella's ambitions and discovered just where he stood in the scheme of things. Civella wanted in on the "money store" - the Teamster Central States Pension and Welfare Fund.

To set the stage, in 1955 Jimmy Hoffa, following the lead of other unions, capitalized on the concept of negotiating pension plans for Teamster members by means of collective bargaining. He successfully negotiated the first such benefit plan in January of that year encompassing 100,000 union members in the south and mid west. Under the plan employers were required to pay $2.00 per member each week, totaling ten million dollars for the union's pension fund in the first year. Ten years later, as the number of union members covered doubled, and employer contribution rose to $7.00 per worker per week, the fund was taking in six million dollars a month.

The enormity of the fund was irresistible for Hoffa. He coveted personal control, and to reach his goal he manipulated how the fund's board of trustees, administers of the fund, would be constituted. He handpicked the union and industry trustees, including Williams in that number. At the same time he arranged it so that he was in a position to dictate how the fund's money would be handled, rather than placing it with banks for investment purposes. Hoffa recognized the potential inherent in the millions of dollars flooding in to benefit him personally, and also his friends and associates.

The way Hoffa saw it, why shouldn't the fund be the union's own bank, lending money to people who in return would do something for Hoffa or the Teamsters. In 1956 the first such loan was made directly by the fund itself. The door was now open. From that point on, with Hoffa in control of the fund, the lion's share of loans granted involved a cash kickback, a mob connection, friendship, or all three.

Coincidental with the growth of the pension fund, in the mid to late 1950s Las Vegas was poised to assume the title of gambling mecca of the world. Financing for the construction of the lush hotel-casinos that would dominate Vegas was a problem since normal banking channels were closed when it came to the huge loans required. Banks simply were not inclined to invest in such ventures. The mob was looking to expand its interests ever since "Bugsy" Siegel built the first big time hotel/casino. Meanwhile the Nevada legislature was campaigning to keep the mob out. The answer for mob lay in their ally Jimmy Hoffa, and access to the fund, popularly referred to as the "money store."

The benefit to both sides was obvious. Only those loan applicants willing to front for gangsters would be approved, and Hoffa, along with his mob associates, controlled the approval process. In return for a loan, the applicant not only was required to kickback money, but also had to relinquish control of casino management, opening the door for the mob to steal gambling proceeds, commonly known as "skim."

Not be left out of the gold rush, and recognizing the enormity in having access to the "money store" in terms of cash and influence, Nick Civella started pushing for Williams, as a fund trustee, to follow his lead in supporting selected applicants for fund loans. Williams stiffened, refusing to go along, a course of action unacceptable to Civella. Williams described what happened next.

He had attended an evening union meeting at the Teamster Hall, then located a 116 West Linwood, and upon leaving the hall headed for his car. He was about to get in when he encountered two formidable appearing men, one standing on each side of the car. "Get in Mr. Williams and park your car over in the other lot", one of them instructed. Moving his car as directed, he was then told, "Take the keys because we intend to bring you back." Shoved into a big car and blindfolded he sat between two men. The drive took some 20 minutes. When the destination was reached he was pulled out of the car and walked into a building, his footsteps echoing in his ears. Seated on a stool, a bright overhead light blinded him temporarily. His eyes adjusted but he found himself staring out into blackness. A voice out of the darkness explained the reason he was there. Simply put, he would have to cooperate closer with Nick Civella.

It was impossible to determine how many people were present, so there was no one to recognize. They threatened his family, naming his two daughters and ticking off their ages. He would cooperate fully or his children, his wife and then himself would be killed. Asked if he understood, he replied that he did. He was then led away, driven back to his car.

Williams' situation was, to say the least, precarious, and he needed advice. Following the lead of a fellow teamster he paid a visit to Jimmy Hoffa. If anyone understood the mob certainly Hoffa did. Williams recounted how he had refused Nick Civella's request for his support on certain pension fund loans, and the threats made to him and his family. Hoffa was sympathetic and understood Williams plight telling him, "You can run but you can't hide. My advice to you is to cooperate or get your family killed. Roy, these are bad people. And they were here a long time before you and me came. And they'll be here a long time after we're gone. They've infiltrated into every big local union, every conference and pension fund - even the AFL-CIO! I'm tied tight as I can be." His final word - go along with Civella.

Still desperate, he sought a second opinion, turning to Frank Fitzsimmons, a Hoffa confidant and prominent Detroit Teamster figure. Fitzsimmons was of the same mind as Hoffa telling Williams, "I know the same people Jimmy knows, and I can't help you."

Out of options, Williams capitulated, and met with Civella to tell him so. He was now under Civella's complete and utter control. "I made no bones about it. I was controlled by Nick, and I think everybody knew it. And when he threatened me, why, that's when I became his boy."

Having Williams locked up tight all Civella needed was an opportunity to get into the game. The former Landmark Hotel/Casino in Las Vegas provided Civella with just the opportunity he was looking for.

In the early 1960s Frank Caracciolla, better known as Frank Carroll, whose wife was Joe DiGiovanni's niece, was in the process of building a new unique hotel/casino in Las Vegas, the Landmark. The plan called for the hotel/casino to be housed in a high-rise circular tower. A time came when financial distress put Carroll's plans on hold. Through Teamsters channels a meeting was arranged in July 1962 attended by Carroll, Nick Civella, Roy Williams and Tano Lococo. The location selected for the meeting was Roy Williams' Leeton, Missouri farm, some miles southeast of the Kansas City. Carroll's financial plight would be the vehicle Civella used to capitalize on the mob's ability to influence pension fund loans, and make some serious money. Civella instructed Williams to take an active part in support of Carroll's quest for a $7 million pension fund loan.

In November 1962 a second meeting was arranged, held at the Prom Hotel in Kansas City. Besides Williams, Civella and Carroll there were two new faces in attendance, Max Jaben and Morris "Snag" Klein. The purpose of the meeting was to sort out various details and loose ends to insure that Carroll's loan deal went through, and Civella's needs were secured.

It turned out to be a rough road with many set backs but eventually in August 1966 the fund granted Carroll a $5.5 million loan specifically for the construction of the Landmark. Now it was time to take care of those responsible for getting the loan approved.

Since these under the table dealings are not part of any formal contract, it is difficult to sort out who got what. According to an Oakland Tribune news account dated September 26, 1969 Carroll complained privately it cost him a half million dollars to get the loan.

A credible source of information, reported Nick Civella was to receive a hidden interest in the Landmark Hotel/Casino, and at a future time Williams would be paid $200,000 for his part in the loan deal.

Another source told of hearing talk that a kickback of $ 340,000 was paid, of which $250,000 went to Hoffa, the remaining $90,000 going into Civella's pocket. The astute Civella was said to have made the decision to give the lion's share of the kickback to Hoffa, reasoning it was a wise investment for future considerations.

Subsequently corroboration of the $90,000 kickback figure surfaced. Scrutiny of the Landmark deal revealed that one Jake Gotlieb, a Jimmy Hoffa associate, in 1964 had purchased the adjacent Landmark Apartments from Plaza Tower Inc., Frank Carroll's Vegas corporation, for $1.65 million. In September 1966, Gotlieb turned around and sold the property back to Carroll's corporation.

As part of the transaction Gotlieb wrote a check for $90,000 payable to Kansas City coin dealer Jeryy Katz who happened to have in his employ none other than Max Jaben. Gotlieb left a paper trail for investigators when he deducted the $90,000 from his federal income taxes as a finder's fee paid in the Landmark Apartment deal. Katz cashed the check receiving seventy $1000 bills, the rest in $100s. Civella, Jaben and Klein are reported to each have received $30,000.

Whatever form the kickbacks took, and how much was involved, there is no question kickbacks were made, and all those who took part, including Roy Williams and Jimmy Hoffa, were adequately compensated. This was exactly the way the system was set up to work, and in the ensuing years it would be repeated over and over to the benefit of Cosa Nostra families and Teamsters Officials and operatives.

Missing from the Landmark deal was a key ingredient common to all pension fund loans arranged by the mob. Carroll was denied a gambling license by the Nevada Gambling Control Board, and sold the property on October 28, 1968, depriving Civella the opportunity to control casino management, and "skim" money from casino proceeds. There would be other opportunities for Civella in the future

Chapter XII
The Charlie Binaggio reign

C HARLES BINAGGIO WAS the next in line to lead the outfit, taking over in the mid 1940s. He was born January 12, 1909 in Texas. While in his teens he was described as a minor police character. In 1927 he was arrested for auto theft in Denver, Colorado, receiving a sentence of two years probation. In 1930 he was arrested again in Denver this time on weapons charges. The charges were reduced to vagrancy, and he received a 90 day suspended sentence on the condition he leave the city in six hours.

After the usual stint as a street criminal, he joined the north end outfit as a young adult working for John Lazia. He was not considered an established syndicate figure compared to men like Gaetano

Lococo, Tony Gizzo and Charles Gargotta. However, by the time Lazia was gunned down in 1934 his status obviously had improved substantially, as the 25 year-old was named a pallbearer at Lazia's funeral along with Gargotta. In later years Gargotta would serve next to Binaggio as his number one man, and they would be so closely tied together that they were commonly referred to as "the two Charlies." As was the case with so many mob notables, Binaggio's background is clouded by reason of his police record having been cleaned out during a period when the department was underworld controlled.

Of what is left of his police record, it is known Binaggio was held in 1941 for investigation of manslaughter by motor vehicle, but released when a coroner's jury found no criminal liability. In 1943 he was charged with violation of federal liquor laws, however the charges were dropped due to insufficient evidence. In September 1945, along with 13 other subjects, he was arrested by the State Highway Patrol at the Green Hills gambling club in Platte County, Missouri, subsequently paying a $50 fine. At various times, upon arrest or contact with law enforcement, he gave his occupation as caddie, oil producer, and beer distributor.

What is abundantly clear, his rise to prominence was achieved through politics, as it was with his mentor John Lazia, and he was most often characterized as a political leader rather than a crime boss.

In the period from 1934 to 1944 he fought his way to the top both politically and as an underworld force. His start was as a Pendergast machine precinct captain under the sponsorship of Charlie Carrollo, the out front political and crime syndicate leader at the time. He escaped the flurry of government investigations in 1939, leading to the downfall of Carrollo and Boss Tom Pendergast, unscathed. By 1942 Binaggio had tight control of the 11 eastern precincts of the old First Ward. Binaggio's rise to power came at a time in Kansas City's history where the criminal organization rather than the politicians called the shots.

As with Lazia before him, Binaggio gathered around him young men of energy and ambition, and he consolidated his power base to the point he was recognized as the man to deal with politically. He became the best-known political boss in the State of Missouri, his influence extending from Kansas City to St. Louis.

Charlie Binaggio did not look the part. His manner was quiet, calm, masking the true danger he represented. He was dapper preferring blue suits and tinted eyeglasses. He enjoyed tending to roses in the yard at his residence on West 70th Street. One report described his sensitive hands, used for, of all things, embroidering baby clothing. He was handy, could fix things, and did so for his neighbors. He had the benevolence of a political leader as evidenced by the food bill at his political club running to $500 a month.

His move to expand his power came in 1944 when he severed his connections with the Pendergast faction, forming an alliance with Henry McKissick, the fat, jovial, second ward Democratic leader who controlled 4-6000 deliverable votes. The Binaggio-McKissick combine jumped into the 1944 Missouri gubernatorial race supporting Mayor Roger Sermon of Independence. Sermon may have lost, but Binaggio's control of the First Ward was clearly demonstrated.

Two years later Binaggio and McKissick again joined forces, and along with other political allies made a foray into the first district aiming to wrest control from the dominant Pendergast faction. They established headquarters in what had been the Jeffersonian Club, 716 East Fifteenth Street, naming it the First District Democratic Club. The first district consisted of the first, second, third and fourth wards. These wards had formerly been aligned with Jim Pendergast, heir to his uncle Boss Tom's political mantle, but never as popular as his uncle. Jim was described as a man who does not make friends easily, which seems unusual for a politician.

A story making the rounds at the time alleged Binaggio and his men had for months been demanding Jim Pendergast agree to a coalition of forces. Pendergast refused, and thereafter received numerous phone calls threatening to him and his family, prompting him to obtain a permit to carry a revolver. Subsequently Tony Gizzo, the prominent gangster, approached him making advances of friendship, and in response Pendergast wanted to know how could one expect his friendship when he had been threatened repeatedly. Gizzo displayed surprise, wanting to know who was threatening Pendergast. Upon hearing of the telephone calls, Gizzo is said to have made it clear he was the top man in the city, the one who gives the orders. Furthermore, what he says goes, and he hadn't told anyone to threaten Pendergast. Gizzo promised it would end right away, and it did.

On May 27, 1948 McKissick was elected as President of the new First District Democratic Club. Seven vice-presidents were also elected, among them Guy Givens, veteran of Cas Welch's east side faction whose former bodyguard, Ferris Anthon, was murdered by Binaggio's right hand man, Charlie Gargotta.

Binaggio's rise in the underworld rode the coattails of his political prominence. He took over the horse race wire service in Kansas City, undoubtedly an arrangement forged with the Capone mob. He was part of a beer distributorship, Duke Sales, another link to the Chicago mob. He shared in most all major gambling operations. He was hooked into mob leaders in other cities, including what was labeled at the time as the "Capone-Costello Syndicate". He worked to spread operations to Colorado, Iowa and elsewhere.

Binaggo took a seat at the table along with James Balestrere, Tano Lococo, Tony Gizzo and Charlie Gargotta, as the Kansas City outfit's "Big Five". For public consumption he was the mob's leader, however there is sufficient evidence establishing the real power, as it had always been, rested with those who worked quietly behind the scenes.

Bolstering this analysis of mob structure were the comments of powerful Chicago mob boss Tony Accardo when interviewed by two Kansas City detectives investigating Tony Gizzo's ties to Accardo. Accardo was quoted as telling the detectives, "I never even met the Binaggio or Gargotta. They were punks." But as to Tony Gizzo, Accardo's reaction was entirely different, describing Gizzo as his "very good friend".

Long time Bureau of Narcotics Agent Claude Follmer, in testimony before the Kefauver Committee, spoke of his personal experiences with Charlie Binaggio, who he talked to often. In Follmer's opinion Binaggio took orders from men higher up. "I heard he was a Mafia member, but when I used to ask him about it he would laugh and say he had never heard of the Mafia. He received only a percentage of the rackets he operated, and he told me that for what little he got out of it, it wasn't worth it, he was under so much pressure to open more games from the people above him."

The Binaggio-McKissick combine were instrumental in the infamous 1946 "ghost vote" election, leading to Federal and local vote fraud indictments. The Government's case suffered a set back when on May 27, 1947 the safe at the election board was blasted open and the evidence, fraudulent ballots, was stolen. Adding to the stink, Mary Bonomo, who it was said was ready to cooperate with the authorities regarding the vote fraud case, was murdered.

At 11:15 p.m., July 11, 1947, Bonomo, 39 years old, was shotgunned as she sat in front of her fruit market at 9th and Brooklyn. A newspaper report indicated the U.S.Attorney General's office had confirmed Bonomo was regarded as a possible government witness in the vote fraud investigation, and the FBI had been ordered to initiate an obstruction of justice investigation.

Binaggio was tabbed as the mastermind behind these events, but there was no supporting evidence and he was never charged. A close associate, and gambling major domo, Morris "Snag" Klein was charged, convicted, and sent to jail in connection with the vote fraud investigation.

Binaggio Moves To Open The City

Binaggio's aim was to open the city up to gambling, and the election of 1948 was pivotal if he was to have any chance of succeeding. He made it clear he had to have a governor, and money was the key. Money is power in politics, so Binaggio turned to his underworld allies. In return for their financial backing they would be cut in for a share once the vice doors were opened.

The New York Mirror, a daily newspaper, in April 1950, placed the figure of crime syndicate contributions to Binaggio at $2 million, identifying Chicago gangster Charles Fischetti as the person delivering the money. Well-known Chicago columnist Lee Mortimer reported monies were given to Binaggio at a meeting held at Fischetti's penthouse in Chicago attended by Frank Costello and Joe Adonis, top of the heap racket figures from New York City.

Local Kansas City law enforcement sources revealed they had received information that just prior to the 1948 election Binaggio had received $125,000 from Frank Costello. Binaggio supposedly used $100,000 for election purposes, pocketing the remainder for himself.

Still another report alleged Binaggio had accepted between $100,000 and $200,000 from gambling interests in the St. Louis, Missouri, and East St. Louis, Illinois, areas upon his assurances he would see to it that gambling prospered just as soon as the new State administration went into office.

The names Frank Costello and Charles Fischetti appear frequently in connection with Binaggio. One newspaper report had Costello in Kansas City throwing a gaudy party in a leading Kansas City Hotel, attended by Tony Gizzo, Charlie Gargotta, and Fischetti.

Fischetti, Brooklyn, N.Y. born, maintained residences in Miami Beach, Florida and Chicago where he was a major player operating gambling and bookmaking establishments throughout the city. He was a cousin and former bodyguard/chauffeur for Al Capone. He was also associated with the Manhattan Brewery Company, the Chicago firm that supplied beer to the Kansas City distributorship Binaggio and associates had an interest in.

Illustrative of Fischetti's strong ties to Kansas City, in March 1944 he found himself embroiled in a government investigation resulting in a material witness warrant being issued for his arrest by the U.S. District Court, Southern District, New York City. Fischetti fled Chicago becoming a wanted fugitive sought by authorities around the nation. FBI Agents tracked him down, and at 12:10 a.m. March 25, 1944, they arrested him in a suite at the President Hotel in Kansas City where he had registered on the afternoon of March 21. Present in his hotel room when the agents nabbed him were Anthony Ross Ferina, John B. Blando, President of Superior Wines and Liquors, and Tony Gizzo.

Whatever the sums the mob contributed or where they came from, there was general agreement Binaggio had taken in a substantial amount of money. Indicative of this was the manner in which Binaggio's precincts operated in the 1948 primary and the general election. Money was said to have flowed like water. When in the past 10 motors cars had been enough for each precinct, 20 or even 25 cars were now used. It allowed Binaggio and associate "Pat" Noonan to travel the State of Missouri in behalf of inaugural candidate Forrest Smith. The money, and the number of workers it brought in, overwhelmed the opposition.

The election of 1948 proved to be but an illusion of success for Binaggio. On the one hand Binaggio displayed the ability to deliver huge majorities for his two key candidates, Forrest Smith for Governor and Joseph T. Lenge for Jackson County Assessor. Another of his candidates, J.A. Purdome, was elected Jackson County Sheriff, and large majorities went for other Democratic office seekers, including Presidential candidate Harry Truman. Binaggio was now confident he was in the driver's seat, and in a position to dictate policy in both Kansas City and the State of Missouri. This led him declare the city open for gambling and vice. He would be proven wrong as to the extent of his influence and ability to follow through in opening the city up.

In his book "Crime in America" Senator Estes Kefauver outlines testimony his committee heard in 1950, that provided a vivid picture of Binaggio's political wheeling and dealing leading up to the election of 1948 and thereafter.

Roy McKittrick, former Missouri Attorney General, testified that gubernatorial candidate Forrest Smith urged against his opposing Smith, and if he agreed, Smith would support him in 1952 for the U.S. Senate. Smith was in need of campaign money and asked McKittrick to line up the financial and political support of Clarence "Gully" Owen, former part owner of a race wire service in St. Louis. In January 1948, McKittrick decided against the deal offered by Smith declaring himself a candidate for Governor.

Following his announcement he was paid a visit by Charlie Binaggio who came right out stating he had to have a governor, explaining he had been forced to close up gambling enterprises he owned and operated, and he did not like having to run things underground all the time. Binaggio was open about his business telling McKittrick, "It is just like that bank over there. I am in the gambling business. I don't want any chiselers, but I want to operate." McKittrick had no doubt the candidate Binaggio supported would win as Binaggio had many, many friends and supporters in St. Louis, controlled Kansas City, had good enough alliances in St. Joseph, and was well supplied with money.

McKittrick claimed he was not of a mind to allow slot machines, bookmaking and other gambling operations, and therefore unlikely to secure Binaggio's support. The next approach came from "Gully" Owen who offered him $35,000 from the "gang" if he would drop out of the race. The amount of the offer was later raised to $50,000.

If nothing else, Binaggio was persistent, recontacting McKittrick with another offer. First off Binaggio pointed out McKitrrick couldn't win the election and it was a big mistake to continue on. With that in mind, if he would withdraw and run for Attorney General, the East St. Louis gang would pay all his expenses for the Attorney General's race, up to $1000 a month, to continue throughout his term in office as Attorney General. On top of that, Binaggio promised Smith's support as the Democrat nominee for U.S. Senate in 1952, all campaign expenses paid. To show good faith, Binaggio would put $25,000 in a bank of McKittrick's choice to be held until it was time for the Senate race. Binaggio remarked, "Politics is an expensive business, and if I can't have a governor I am going to quit."

McKittrick turned all the offers down, refusing to back out of the Governor's race. Thereafter, it was evident he was losing strength among certain political elements in St. Louis and elsewhere in the State. He told the committee it was generally understood that $100,000 went to the Smith campaign chest from St. Louis' east side, labeled the "Capone crowd."

Shortly after his election as Governor, Smith appointed Jacob L. "Tuck" Milligan, and Sheridan E. Farrell, both described as "Binaggio men", to the four-member Kansas City Police Board. They joined two holdover members from the prior administration. Three votes were required to implement any policy or personnel changes in the Police Department. It was no secret Binaggio was out to oust Chief of Police Henry W. Johnson, and wanted other changes in the department. Binaggio is alleged to have informed Police Board members that when one wins an election, like we did, there ought to be changes in the police department.

R. Robert Cohn, a holdover member of the board, told the Kefauver committee he had been approached several times by Binaggio, and other emissaries, suggesting he join their team and support their program. He rejected the proposal. He took it a step further paying a visit to Governor Smith advising of the pressure being put on him by Binaggio. He came right out stating that if the Governor supported the Binaggio programs Cohn still would not go along. The Governor insisted he had no knowledge of Binaggio's activities, and he wanted Cohn to remain on the board.

Hampton S. Chambers, the other holdover member, also testified telling of a meeting in the lobby of the Hotel President at which time Binaggio laid out the changes in the police department he wanted, including the removal of Chief Johnson, and naming the police officials he wanted transferred. Binaggio's man for the Chief's job was reportedly a police captain who had been fired for running a crap game.

Following Binaggio's approach, Chambers was contacted by a Kansas City businessman who reluctantly inquired whether Chambers wanted to make $50,000 or $75,000, but would not give up where the money was coming from. Chambers declined the offer. He then received an anonymous telephone call advising him he would be sorry if he didn't take the money. He was under constant pressure to go along with those looking to shake up the police department, and he was receiving threatening phone calls once or twice a week.

Chamber's continued resistance finally prompted a Binaggio reaction. Binaggio told Chambers he could look forward to being summoned by the Governor for a talk, and he had better get it right. Sure enough Chambers was called to the State capitol to see Governor Smith. Chambers mentioned to the Governor that his "political friend" (Binaggio) in Kansas City had warned him before hand he would be summoned, and wondered if there was a leak in the Governor's office. Smith replied he didn't think there was any leak. Chambers gave the Governor a full report on the pressure being placed on him by Binaggio. The Governor's reaction was to rub his hands together, look down at the floor, and say nothing.

Former President of the Police Board J.L."Tuck" Milligan, a life long friend of Governor Smith, testified that upon hearing rumors Kansas City was to become a wide-open town, he called Charles Binaggio to his office. "I told Binaggio that if all I had heard about his gambling connections were true, he had better get out of politics because he could not build a political organization on corruption." According to Milligan, Binaggio agreed indicating he was planning to quit politics.

During another meeting with Milligan, one that included Police Commissioner Robert Cohn, Binaggio mentioned a Police Captain, John Braun, as a possible new Chief of Police. Milligan had looked into the Captain's record and found him unqualified for the job, a finding Commissioner Cohn agreed with completely. Binaggio was also interested in civilian job openings for "his people", and was told if he had capable people they should apply with the personnel director at the police department. Milligan was not in favor of applying the patronage idea to all police department jobs

The fourth member of the police board to testify before the Kefauver committee, Sheridan Farrell, admitted he had asked Governor Forrest Smith, a friend for 25 years, to name him to the police board or the election board. Asked if Binaggio had anything to do with his police board appointment, he responded, "I think he helped on it." Farrell was asked to explain his expressed opinion favoring, to some extent, an open town. Farrell believed when it came to professional gambling there ought to be some night clubs with gaming where people could have a little fun and enjoy some night life, something the city was lacking. What he had in mind was a casino type operation, and "Of course it ought to be legalized." In Farrell's opinion a 17 man vice unit was excessive when considering the shortage of personnel on the police department, and besides, there was no vice in the city.

Governor Forrest Smith made a voluntary appearance before the Kefauver Committee, and denied he asked McKittrick to stay out of the race, or asked for "Gully" Owen's support. As far as Charlie Binaggio, he didn't even know Binaggio by name until around November 1947 when Binaggio approached him in the lobby of a Kansas City hotel stating he hoped Smith would run for Governor, and if he did, he could count on Binaggio's support. He learned who Binaggio was by asking the hotel desk clerk. The only other pre election meetings he had with Binaggio were of the same casual type in hotel lobbies.

The Governor admitted that after his election Binaggio had visited him several times at the State capitol. On one occasion Binaggio, in the company of five or six others, simply wanted to see what the Governor's office looked like. On another occasion Binaggio was looking for suggestions on a good place to go fishing. He testified to a lack of knowledge regarding the two factions on the police board, or that Binaggio was pressuring the two hold over members. He denied he had received a report from R. Robert Cohn on the Binaggio situation, and described Cohn's visit to the Governor's office as purely social. Regarding the letter summoning board member Chambers for a meeting, Smith had done so as a "good fellow" upon hearing that Chambers was looking for an excuse to visit Jefferson City.

Later Senator Kefauver would describe Smith as either a much lied about person, or a man of exceeding bad memory. This appears to be an exceptionally gracious characterization of Smith's testimony. In the Kefauver Committee report to the U.S. Senate of its findings, the following conclusion was proffered:

"It is abundantly clear that Binaggio did support Forrest Smith, and that his organization was active in the governor's campaign... but whatever Binaggio's expectations may have been, there is not substantial evidence that Governor Smith made any kind of commitment to Binaggio, or that Binaggio was successful in opening up the town. On the other hand, it is inconceivable that Governor Smith, being an experienced politician, could have failed to know of Binaggio's background, or that Binaggio expected a quid pro quo for his support. Smith's assertions under oath that he did not discuss politics with Binaggio, or discuss Binaggio's expectations, are simply not credible."

From where Binaggio stood he had every reason to believe with the election of his supposed good friend Forrest Smith as Governor he would be repaid for his efforts in Smith's behalf, and allowed to name new members to the Kansas City police board. In turn, he could then signal the green light for gambling and vice activities. Furthermore, his influence in local, county and state councils would discourage interference with these activities. Beyond that, a grateful Democratic administration in Washington D.C. would keep the Feds at bay. Unfortunately for Binaggio none of his expectations became reality.

The failure to influence the police board was followed by further disappointments. Binaggio's man, Vic Glennon, was given the post of Chief Clerk of the Kansas City Election Board, on top of which Governor Smith appointed two of the four members of the board who were in Binaggio's camp. It appeared to be a patronage coup, however it was not enough for his ward workers, hungry for political jobs. They felt that all of the election board employees should be fired and replaced with the Binaggio faithful. This was not to be, and only a few of the employees were replaced.

Binaggio's next move was an effort to influence the Missouri Legislature to support a cigarette tax bill, along with a companion bill that would have increased the number of jobs in political offices controlled by Binaggio men. The estimated impact of an increase of one million jobs to Binaggio's political payrolls was enormous. The bills passed the house, but were stopped in the State Senate, another severe blow reflecting negatively on the level of Binaggio's influence. Now even his closest allies recognized he had failed in almost every political move attempted.

Efforts to gain an audience with President Truman were rebuffed. Governor Smith remained friendly, but refused to allow open gambling and vice, or grant Binaggio control of the police board he so desperately needed. Binaggio was faced with the ominous prospect that he would fail to deliver on his promises to the syndicate. In an act of desperation he attempted to bribe Police Commissioner R. Robert Cohn.

As described by Cohn to the Kefauver Committee, it was a night in June 1949 when Binaggio appeared at the Cohn's residence, and the two men talked outside in Binaggio's car. Binaggio appeared very distressed admitting he was on the spot, and the "boys" were after him as "we" are behind schedule and nothing had opened up. "They" were making it hot for him and Binaggio sure wished Cohn would change his mind regarding the police department situation. According to Cohn, Binaggio appeared like a man who was drowning. It had been six months since Governor Smith had been elected and not only had Binaggio made no progress in opening the city up, but it looked like nothing would happen unless they could get a Binaggio man to replace board member Chambers when his term expired.

Without warning Binaggio pulled a roll of bills from his pocket and tossed it to Cohn. Taken completely by surprise, Cohn just tossed the roll back at Binaggio like it was a "hot rivit". Binaggio sat there a few seconds speechless, and then said, "Are you mad at me?" Cohn replied, "No, but I am disappointed".

Binaggio was guilty of another miscalculation when he agreed to let William Hoizhausen, a lumber dealer, become president of the St. Louis police board. Hoizhausen had been recommended to Binaggio as the "right guy" for the job. Binaggio had never met the man, and if he had been led to believe he could control Hoizhausen, the he had been misled. Hoizhausen showed himself to be a sternly upright man who would not bend to any outside pressure. This was not good news for the "boys" in St Louis, and worse news for Binaggio.

Although under Binaggio the outfit had muscled into policy operations, gained control of the race wire service, and opened a handful of gambling houses, it was viewed as penny-ante, when compared to Kansas City of the 1930s. Furthermore, the expectations of the national syndicate had not been met.

Under Fire From A Federal Grand Jury

Adding to Binaggio's mounting troubles and setbacks, he was linked to the 1949 murder of Wolf C. Rimann, the former golf pro and coin machine kingpin, with extensive liquor establishment interests. Adding insult to injury, even more heat was generated when Governor Smith ordered an "all out probe" of the murder by Federal, State & Local authorities, causing a further clamp down on what little gambling there was.

Binaggio was now in the sights of the federal grand jury called into session on September 28, 1949, along with top outfit figures,

Tony Gizzo, Tano Lococo, and Charles Gargotta. Events transpiring in Kansas City were picked up and reported on by national magazines focusing even more attention on the city and Charlie Binaggio. Binaggio's supporters cried foul, blaming Jim Pendergast for prompting his good friend, President Harry Truman, to push for the grand jury investigation in order to bury Binaggio. None of this could have sat well with the shadowy power brokers in the Kansas City crime "family."

The St. Louis Globe-Democrat, in an article appearing in its May 23, 1954 edition, alleged that Charlie Gargotta " revealed gang secrets to the Federal Grand Jury in Kansas City, including hidden race wire partners and cuts, owners and the take in the numbers racket, and partners in gambling casinos". Further, that Charles Binaggio also talked freely to the grand jury. If these allegations were indeed true, it represented a breach of the oath of secrecy, and would not be ignored by syndicate bosses anywhere.

The Grand Jury had a full plate with Internal Revenue Service agents hard at work beating the bushes putting together tax cases against the two Charlies. Binaggio, of course, had many sources of revenue the agents could scrutinize, some more or less open, others concealed.

A main source of his income was his interests in the race wire service, and other gambling operations, including a dice and card game at 9th & Woodland, overseen by Tano Lococo, closed down by police in March 1950, a victim of the unfavorable climate; The Last Chance Saloon where dice, card games and a horse race book operated; a dice game at 3111 Holmes, a companion to another operation at the Missouri Electric Construction Co. 3107 Holmes, another victim of the times, closed in 1950; and a gambling operation Binaggio had high hopes for located at 1800A E, 32nd Street, opening in late March 1950.

Binaggio had an interest in the Stork Club in Council Bluffs, Iowa, taken over by the Kansas City mob in 1947. Binaggio, Tony Gizzo and others were partners in the Coates House sports book formed in February 1947. There was information floating around of an interest he obtained in a gambling operation in Colorado Springs in 1949. He and Charlie Gargotta, were cut in at the Green Hills Club in Platte County, an off and on casino operation, finally closing down and sold in 1949. Binaggio was also reported to have a piece of the policy wheels the mob took over in 1949.

Binaggio's wife, Cecelia, along with Mrs. Irene Sarno, operated a fur concession at Chasnoff's Inc., and it was strongly believed he had invested in the company. He had recently given up his one- third interest in Ace Sales & Equipment Company, a firm dealing in construction equipment. He had an interest in Duke Sales, the beer distributorship handling Canadian Ace Beer, known as "Capone beer".

Time To Get Out

According to Kansas City law enforcement sources it was common knowledge that major Kansas City mob figures Tano Lococo, Tony Gizzo, Joe DiGiovanni and John B.Blando suggested to Binaggio the time was ripe, if it were ever going to happen, to throw the town wide open. Binaggio allegedly resisted on the grounds the time was not right as long as the grand jury was in session.

Another story circulated that Binaggio sent Henry McKissick to see these rackets figures in an attempt to settle the dispute between them and Binaggio. The response to the peace offering was to take McKissick down to the Missouri River wrapped in a blanket, with a weight around his neck giving McKissick every reason to believe he was about to be dumped him in the river. The threat had the desired effect as McKissick thereafter dropped out of sight and was not heard from. Whether fact, fiction or embellishment, it made for a good story.

For Binaggio enough was enough. Placed in a negative limelight by national magazines embarrassing him and his family, hounded by a Federal Grand Jury probe, and under pressure from national and local syndicate figures, he sought to get out. Until he could make a clean break he attempted to placate the syndicate by keeping up his efforts to open the city up. Later reports tracing Binaggio's activities disclosed he had made more than 50 out-of-town trips in 1949 and 1950, supposedly in an attempt to generate funds to repay the mob's investments made on his promises of open gambling.

When the Kefauver Committee moved on from Kansas City, opening hearings in San Francisco, they continued to uncover information concerning Binaggio's activities. Testimony was heard documenting attempts by Binaggio to get involved in gambling enterprises in the State of California. There was speculation this was a further attempt on his part to generate a substitute source of income for himself and mob leaders he represented. He was said to have been in contact with former Kansas Citizen Sam Termini, aka, Sam Murray, the gambling boss of San Mateo County, California. The two were close friends in Kansas City, Termini having been one of those indicted in the vote fraud case of 1946 - the charges subsequently dismissed.

Binaggio and his wife traveled to California in the summer of 1949 to visit Termini who at the time held an interest in the Tahoe Biltmore casino located on the Nevada side of Lake Tahoe. A California Crime Commission report speaks of Binaggio advising Nevada gaming officials his trip was to look over the pacific coast with a view to bankrolling Termini in what would be the largest gambling location west of the Rockies, featuring no limit gambling games. The deal never came to fruition, and the Tahoe Biltmore ended up in bankruptcy. Nothing was working for Binaggio.

According to a story carried in the St. Louis Star-Times, a meeting was held in January 1950 on the tenth floor of the Jefferson Hotel in St. Louis attended by Charlie Binaggio, accompanied by his driver/bodyguard, Nick Penna, and politico Pat Noonan. He attempted to work things out with syndicate big wigs having a vested interest in open gambling. The newspaper claims Binaggio asked those in attendance for more time, indicating that things would start moving soon. One group wanted Binaggio to step down from power, while another wanted him to either make good on his promises or return their money. Either way nothing good came out of the meeting.

With nothing panning out, Binaggio moved forward with plans for retirement, something he is said to have been considering as early as August 1949. In March 1950, he made application for a transfer of address to 1024 W. 70th, his true address, from 1208 Admiral Blvd., his first residence in Kansas City maintained only for voting purposes and to legitimize his association to his first ward power base. We can't know to what extent, if any, Binaggio made known his intentions, but it was rumored the powers to be in the syndicate were aware of his plans.

The unrest among syndicate interests mounted. A March 1950 report had "Buster" Wortman, part of the East St. Louis Shelton Gang, meeting in Venice, Illinois, with Eagan gang members, and harsh words were directed at Binaggio. If Binaggio had made an enemy of Wortman then he indeed faced a formidable threat.

Frank "Buster" Wortman, reputed by many as king of the rackets in St. Louis, Missouri, East St. Louis, and downstate Illinois, was as strong as, if not stronger, than the St Louis Cosa Nostra "family." For 25 years prior to his death in 1968 he was the representative of Chicago's Capone syndicate, reportedly traveling twice a month to confer with ranking members of the organization. His varied interests included a string of racehorses, vending and amusements firms, and drinking establishments. Policy gambling generated $2000 to $3000 a month, with a portion of these proceeds passed on to the Chicago Capone mob, and he also controlled any number of dice games. After hours liquor joints, bingo, and other vice operations, had to make payoffs to Wortman similar to Kansas City gambling operators paying the "lug." In the late 1940s, assisted by hoodlums from Chicago, Wortman moved in on Clarnece "Gully" Owens' race wire service, just as the outfit had moved in on the wire service in Kansas City.

Still another St. Louis newspaper story reported on a gathering in St. Louis for the funeral of a relative of Cleveland racket leader Pete Licavoli. The local St. Louis outfit boss made the arrangements for syndicate big wigs traveling in from cities around the country. Representatives from Cleveland's Mayfield Road outfit, the Capone mob in Chicago, the Smaldone "family" of Denver, and representing Kansas City was a group the newspaper labeled, the "Binaggio-Balestrere mob."

The out of town visitors were guests at up scale west end hotels, but no names appeared on hotel registers. Was Binaggio part of the Kansas City contingent? If not, did these heavy hitters in the mob use the occasion to discuss the Binaggio situation? Questions to which there are no answers, only speculation.

It is believed Binaggio, as a last gasp, made an offer to syndicate forces to step down and turn over everything he had. His offer was rejected. Investigators, and knowledgeable sources, agree Binaggio was instructed to stay out front and keep trying. In reality Binaggio was approaching the end of the road.

A confidential source described Binaggio's demeanor in the last weeks of March 1950 as nervous, easily agitated, and generally not himself. Did he fear what the future had in store for him, or was it the pressure of the grand jury, or just an accumulation of all that had gone wrong in his world. Whatever his feelings were, he hid them well. He continued to walk the streets with his small daughter, without bodyguards, formulating his plans.

In March 1950 he bought a quarry business in New Mexico, and was telling friends he was making a deal to become a top figure in gambling operations in that State. He openly discussed his retirement date, the week of April 3, 1950, stating things were too hot in Kansas City for him.

Relying on political connections in making his New Mexico plans, he reached out for Dennis Chavez Jr., son of U.S. Senator Chavez of New Mexico, a relationship that was to be kept quiet. Al S. Marshall, a Washington D.C. lobbyist, arranged for Binaggio and Chevez Jr. to meet. Marshall, in the past, had handled the acquisition of war surplus construction materials for Ace Sales & Equipment Company, a firm set up by Binaggio, Eddie "Spitz" Oschadey, Morris "Snag' Klein, and a cousin of Spitz, in 1945. Marshall was known to have traveled to Kansas City in March 1950, accompanied by Chavez Jr., and met with Eddie Oschadey and other Binaggio inner circle associates. The two men registered in at the Phillips Hotel on April 5, 1950. In light of the events occurring overnight, they checked out the next day.

End Of The Trail

On the morning of April 5, 1950, Charlie Binaggio visited the First District Democratic Club, 716-18 Truman Road, remaining till the middle of the afternoon. From the club he went home and worked in his yard. Driver and bodyguard Nick Penna stopped by around 3:00 p.m., as was the routine, staying for supper. Binaggio was his normal, calm, self, showing no signs of stress or worry. He had called his close associate and top lieutenant, Charlie Gargotta, and arranged to meet at the Last Chance Saloon. Before he left he gave his wife her allowance of $1000. He had $2000 earmarked for the wife of an associate who was in the penitentiary. In addition he had some $8-10,000 in his pocket, but needing more had his wife get him an additional $3000. He left the house with something between $14-16,000 in cash money.

That afternoon at the Last Chance, Charlie Gargotta received several calls, and during one of the calls he supposedly was heard to say, "Well, what in the hell do they want, a cut?"

Penna drove Binaggio to the Last Chance on Southwest Boulevard and Binaggio immediately went over to Gargotta engaging in a short whispered conversation. Still talking, they went over to Homer Cooper, night manager, and Gargotta asked for the loan of Cooper's new yellow Oldsmobile, not an unusual request, as they had borrowed it on other occasions. It was 8:15 p.m. when the two Charlie's instructed Nick Penna to wait there as they expected to be back in 20 minutes. Gargotta had a date and when the woman called he told her something had come up, he would be delayed 30 or 40 minutes, and should be back no later than 9:00 p.m.

Binaggio had not carried a gun for years, and Gargotta, under Federal indictment at the time, had not carried a gun for some months. By 4:00 a.m., when they had not returned, Penna left to go home figuring someone had taken Binaggio to his residence. While waiting at the Last Chance Penna had not displayed any concern for his boss' welfare.

Cab driver Walter Gambil, 43 years old, had a shift starting at 3:00 am, and whenever possible he liked to have breakfast around 4:00 am at a small café at 712 Truman Road. On the morning of April 6 he pulled his cab to the front of 720 Truman Road, and his walk to the café took him past the Democratic Club. He heard the noise of water running inside, but didn't see anything when he looked through the window. Gambil called the police from the café to report the possible water line break and went outside to await their arrival. He waited only a short time before two officers arrived. Upon inspection they found the east side door, of the two doors to the Democratic Club, ajar some 6-8 inches. The venetian blinds were askew, and peering over the shoulder of one of the officers Gambil saw the body of a man lying on the floor just inside the door. The officers went to their car to call it in while Gambil went for his breakfast.

Lying on his back, just inside the door, was the body of Charlie Gargotta, his head in a pool of blood. He was attired in a dark blue, double-breasted suit his hat lying next to his head. Pouring from the ceiling was a steady stream of water from a faulty toilet on the floor above. The slats of the blinds were bent down as if someone had grabbed them as he fell, and on the windowsill was a broken chain of car keys.

Gargotta had been struck in the back of the head by one bullet fired from a distance, followed by three more bullets pumped into his head forming a semi circle around his left eye. There was evidence of powder burns indicating the three shots were fired at very close range. Gargotta was carrying $2000 in cash.

Inside an office, set off from the remainder of the room by a small railing, slumped back in a chair, hands serenely at his lap, was the body of Charlie Binaggio. He was dressed in a light grey suit, his size 7 Knox hat lay on the floor, a half smoked cigarette underneath him in the chair. His dead eyes seemingly focused up at the framed photos of President Truman and Governor Smith that dominated the main wall of the club.

Binaggio had been shot 4 times at close range, the wounds neatly spaced, two in front of the left ear, one behind the left ear, and one in the forehead over the left eye. Powder burns indicated the gun was held almost against Binaggio's head. The large sum of money he was carrying when he left home was gone. If the killers had taken the money they saw fit to leave Binaggio with $25.

The police discovered a tape recorder installed beneath Binaggio's desk in his private office, a microphone in the desk draw, and a hidden button beneath the desk to activate it. But he had not met his killers in that office, located just behind where he was found murdered.

It appeared Binaggio had been taken completely by surprise, while Gargotta appeared to have bolted for the door before being shot down. No doubt a professional hit, the assassins leaving behind no evidence for the police to work with. The shell casings had been picked up, the front door knobs wiped clean. There were at least two of them, as two different guns had been fired. The coroner fixed the time of death between 11 p.m. and 1 am. If accurate, it meant the meeting must have been a lengthy one before the deed was done, or else the assassins were late in arriving.

The crime scene was pretty much all there was to go on and it gave rise to a number of theories. Had the two Charlies been grilled during an extended meeting, and was what they had to say enough to seal their fate? Was it Binaggio's insistence on stepping down and getting out that resulted in a decision to eliminate him?

Viewing the crime scene one could picture Gargotta, a skilled killer in his own right, in those last seconds sniffing out danger, sensing these friends he and Binaggio had willingly met, were in fact not friends at all. Did he then put his hat on, take out his car keys and make for the door? Might he have figured Binaggio was the main target, and he would be allowed to simply walk out? Or, could it be that Gargotta had set Binaggio up, arranging for Binaggio to leave his driver and bodyguard, Nick Penna, behind? Then when the time was right, his mission accomplished, he went to leave believing he was immune?

One thing is clear, the two Charlies had to have known who they were meeting, and felt comfortable being in their presence. These were inherently cautious, suspicious men who would never meet strangers, or persons suspected of having evil intent, without some form of protection, especially in light of the mounting set backs of the preceding months.

Mob bigwig Tony Gizzo got the news at around 5:45 a.m., awakened by the screams of his wife who was on the phone with Binaggio's wife. Within the hour a moving truck was at the Last Chance gambling location, and all gambling paraphernalia was cleaned out. Other gambling locations were stripped and closed.

Of course the murders were high on the agenda of the Kefauver Committee. Gizzo provided the committee with a version of the outfit's party line put out immediately following the murders some four months previous. Upon hearing the news he took command of the inquiry, calling a number of fellows who hung around his cigar store at the Coates House, including John Mangiaracina, Tom "Hiway" Simone, Joe Guerra and Nick Penna, instructing them to meet him there. They all met in an effort to learn what they could about the murders.

According to Gizzo, "We done everything. We talked to everybody about it. We couldn't find out anything. We are still trying to find out what is behind it." Did Gizzo think the killing was the result of the Mafia? He responded, "I couldn't say. I couldn't get on the limb and say anything like that unless I was sure."

Far different from the aftermath of the Lazia murder, the crime "family" quickly lapsed into silence, and inactivity, despite Gizzo's transparent fairy-tale of great concern. Few theories, and no names, emerged from any source as to the triggermen's identities. Not even the tried and true pronouncement that it was "out of town imported killers" was leaked out for public consumption. The law enforcement effort met with a blank wall of assumed ignorance by friends, associates and even enemies of the two. No reprisals to the killings followed, no suspects being stalked, no meaningful activity. Added all up, it seems clear the outfit not only wasn't taken aback by the double murder, but had in fact orchestrated it.

In underworld terms it was logical that Binaggio had to be killed. He had miscalculated as to the candidates he supported and reneged on his promises, therefore was seen as having misappropriated the money invested with him. Control of his political machine was slipping away, he was the focal point of a federal investigation, and he was generating the glare of national publicity. His desire to get out could be viewed as a sign of weakness, pushing him into the arms of the Feds if faced with a long jail term.

Still, theories abounded as to the source of the decision to kill the two Charlies. One had the orders coming from high places, based on the supposition that events had escalated to a point where the Kansas City "family" was not able to act alone in the decision, needing the support of the Chicago and New York crime "families." Since Binaggio's actions had consequences outside Kansas City, it is certainly plausible the decision to kill him was mutually agreed upon. However, it seems clear, the execution was planned and carried out by the Kansas City outfit, willing to accept the closing down of the town as the price for Binaggio's life. If, as reported by a source close to Binaggio, he had been holding out on his mob superiors, this alone would have been sufficient to justify his murder.

Binaggio and Gargotta lay in state at the Lapentina Funeral Home. A continuous stream of people came to pay their respects to Binaggio, more than 1500 in all. Funeral services were held at the Holy Rosary Church in the North End on April 10, 1950. Binaggio's pallbearers, both active and honorary, included judges, legislators, state senators, and others in high places. More than 500 floral pieces were on display, many from far away places like Miami, Reno, Chicago, Los

Angeles, and New York, all devoid of names. Both Charlies were buried in St. Mary's Cemetery.

There was a controversy as to whether or not Binaggio should be accorded a Christian service and burial, and the decision was in the affirmative. Reverend Raymond C. Jackson, Vice Chancellor of the Catholic Diocese of Kansas, addressed the huge throng attending the funeral, and as part of his remarks stated:

"As Catholics, we abominate and we condemn syndicated crime and vice. It is as despicable as it is evil. We condemn the underworld and all its barbarous and cowardly ways. But we condemn also the over world, liquor executives, public officials in high and low places, and the like, who though able to retain an aura of respectability, sacrifice every decent principle for their own contemptible and selfish ends. The same blood is on their hands as upon the hands of the villainous characters whom they both use and protect."

In the opinion of a knowledgeable law enforcement source, Binaggio, in the early 1940s, was appointed by mob leaders as their political front man. They overestimated their power to control him, and underestimated his ability as a politician. Within a short period of years he no longer needed their support to win elections, and in fact could win with the candidates the bosses opposed. This, together with the fact he was strong willed and not easily coerced by his bosses, brought about his downfall.

The fallout from the double homicide was widespread. The Kansas City Star reported that on April 6, 1950, a record was set at Western Union offices for the largest press files ever dispatched from Kansas City to other newspapers around the country for a single story. At total of 37,824 words were sent over the wire. At the Kansas City Star branch office more than 10,000 words over the normal daily file were dispatched.

Aftermath

President Harry S. Truman's reaction to the furor in his hometown was to side step the murders, his spokesman proclaiming Truman had no association of any kind with Binaggio, and thus had no concern in the case. On the other hand his political advisors had other thoughts, fearing the killings could become a red-hot political issue, and do great harm to the Democrats unless the administration employed every means available to solve the case. The murders received front-page coverage in the nation's capitol, and throughout the East. The news accounts pointed out the Binaggio faction was not allied with the Truman-Pendergast forces. Missouri interests in Washington D.C. were aware of Truman's contempt for Binaggio, and his support of Jim Pendergast in resisting Binaggo's political aspirations. The President's door was always open to Pendergast, but shut tight when Binaggio was in town.

The political upheaval stemming from the murders contributed greatly to the formation of the Special Senate Investigating Committee headed by Senator Estes Kefauver, cited extensively throughout this story. The concept had not been to the liking of Truman and the Democrats prior to the double murders in Kansas City, and their opposition to the idea was even stronger after the murders. Their concern was the investigative committee would focus on them, plus revisit the 1946 theft of ballots scandal, all of which meant embarrassment for Truman Democrats. The administration favored a rival initiative by the Senate Interstate Commerce Committee, anticipated to be far less intrusive, as its inquiry was limited to two interstate gambling bills sent to Congress by the Justice Department.

When news stories focused on the Truman administration's desire to impede the Kefauver initiative, the tide turned. In what the Kansas City Times newspaper described as a "surprise move", Democrat leadership called for an all-out investigation of interstate crime and gambling syndicates. A five-man committee was recommended, three Democrats and two Republicans, drawn from the Interstate Commerce and Judiciary Committees, backed by a $150,000 appropriation to carry out the probe. The Times also described the decision as a "move seen as recognition of the implications of the Binaggio slaying." Out of political turmoil and gangland murder the Kefauver Committee was born.

The Binaggio-Gargotta murders did nothing to impede the federal and state grand jury investigations that were in progress, and since it would be a key area of inquiry for the Kefauver Committee, scheduled to begin its inquiries in Kansas City, the outfit was hit with a triple whammy.

The federal grand jury completed an 18-month term in September 1950 during which it heard testimony from hundreds of gamblers, enforcers, law enforcement personnel, bookkeepers, lawyers, and other individuals. They found links between Kansas City racket operations and those in, among others, Colorado, Nebraska, Iowa, and Kansas.

The federal grand jury reported it had indictments prepared for Charlie Binaggio and Charlie Gargotta, but they had answered to a different authority. It was this grand jury that indicted Tano Lococo and former outfit Boss, Charles Carollo, plus 11 other individuals. Both Lococo and Carollo were convicted and sentenced to jail.

This was also the same grand jury that disclosed, in an interim report, they had uncovered gambling operations in Kansas City amounting to approximately thirty-four and half million dollars. Further, since the activities avoided interstate commerce, the grand jury was relegated to bringing charges on tax violations and levying tax liens.

Tax liens and claims amounting to more than $500,000 were levied. Liens were assessed on the estate of Charles Binaggio, amounting to $70,672.73; $38,158.49 on the estate of Charles

Gargotta; $28,057.84 against Gaetano Lococo; $6,589.20 against Walter Rainey; $14,401.24 against George R. Clark; and $240,000 against the estate of Wolf Rimann.

It was this Jackson County grand jury that chipped in indicting twenty-six men on gambling charges including prominent rackets figures Tony Gizzo, John Mangiaracina, Max Jaben and Walter Rainey, plus exposing payments to Jackson County deputy sheriffs by tavern owners and others to facilitate vice operations

The federal grand jury exposed a tax-fixing scheme described as "undoubtedly the most sordid and vicious uncovered in Jackson County." The scheme was up and running during the period George R. Clark was the Jackson County Assessor. Clark was one of those indicted by the grand jury for tax evasion for the years 1944-1948.

Clark held the position of County Assessor from 1940 to August 31, 1949, when he left office. Prior to that, for seven years, Clark was a field deputy in the office of the collector of the Internal Revenue Service, and prior to his IRS service spent three years as a golf pro at the Hillcrest County Club. This would have been at a time when the murdered Wolf Rimann was an integral part of the country club.

Clark certainly started out on the right foot, campaigning for the Assessor's position on the promise of cleaning up the mess created by rampant political favoritism and inefficiency. He, in fact, did reorganize the assessor's office, resulting in county tax assessments increasing by more than one hundred million dollars. His performance in office earned him re election in 1944 for another term. Then things went south for Clark.

He aligned himself politically with Charles Binaggio and Henry McKissick becoming embroiled in the 1946 ghost vote primary election. Along with McKissick and eight others he was indicted federally in December 1947 on charges of conspiring to deprive voters of their civil rights. All ten defendants, after standing trial, were acquitted by a jury. In 1948, rather than run again for Assessor, he opted to join the newly formed democrat faction popularly known as the Binaggio-Clark-McKissick faction.

The tax scheme brought to light by the grand jury involved Claude Lewis, a deputy assessor responsible for real estate assessments. Lewis arranged for properties to be kept off the tax rolls, and in collusion with professional real estate adjusters "adjusted" the assessment on those properties, doubling, and at time tripling, the normal rate. The only way the property owner could get the inflated assessment lowered was by payment of a "fee" (bribe) through the crooked adjuster. Of course, neither the tax assessments collected for off the rolls properties, or the "fees" ever made it to county coffers. A second deputy assessor, Edward D. Collins, in charge of the personal property, and merchants and manufactures tax assessments, ran a similar scam.

It is a given the crime family would have its fingers in the pie, and take advantage of the tax scheme. With access to the scam, the outfit could utilize it to bring pressure to bear in furthering their illicit enterprises, and/or stifling resistance by individuals and legitimate businessmen. Even one foolishly displaying a lack of respect to a crime family figure might find himself facing increased tax assessments. Such was the case for the credit manager, and son of the owner, of a Kansas City department store when he refused to allow the wife of Morris "Snag" Klein to open a charge account, and was accused of being discourteous in doing so. The next thing he knew his real estate taxes had been jacked up. Upon protesting the tax hike he was informed he would have to make things right by Mrs. Klein and apologize for his conduct. Only after complying by offering an apology was his tax assessment returned to its original level.

When informed the grand jury had exposed the tax scam, Clark professed to be in the dark concerning the whole sordid affair. "This is all news to me. It has been revealed to me by the grand jury since I left office. But I had no idea anything like that was happening when I was in office. I thought I had a pretty good record as assessor." Two days after the grand jury report was made public deputy assessors Lewis and Collins failed to appear for work at the assessor's office. The current County Assessor, another Binaggio man, Joseph Lenge, stated no immediate action would be taken against Lewis and Collins while a complete investigation of their activities was underway. Further, should any irregularities be uncovered then immediate action would be undertaken against them.

Clark was not the only public official caught up in the grand jury's net. Samuel C. Hayden a former Missouri state representative, long time justice of the peace, and an assistant county district attorney, was named by the federal grand jury in its May 1950 interim report as a partner in Town Recreation, a large scale gambling operation. Among his partners in the operation were Charles Gargotta, Tano Lococo and Walter Rainey. After publication of the grand jury report Hayden was fired from his position in the county district attorney's office.

Another partner in the Town Recreation gambling operation was Robert S. Greene, Superintendent of Jackson County buildings. Greene tendered his resignation on May 8, 1950, several days after being named in the grand jury report.

The Kefauver Committee continued to uncover information concerning Binaggio's activities just prior to his death, while holding hearings in San Francisco. The St. Louis Post Dispatch publicized the fact witnesses told the committee Sicilian and American gangsters had set up quarters in a tourist court in Tijuana, Mexico. The individuals residing there or visiting included the infamous international drug trafficker Frank Coppola; Tano Lococo from Kansas City, who had purchased a motel in Nogales, Mexico; Tony Lopiparo a St. Louis mob leader; Sylvester "Kansas City Sam" Carrolla, formerly New Orleans crime Boss, deported to Italy; Frank "Bomp" Bompseiaro, San Diego rackets figure and committee witness; Sebastian Gallo, formerly of Detroit; and Giacomo Bartlino, Carlo Sciortino and four others from Palermo, Sicily.

In the summer of 1949 Charlie Binaggio, accompanied by his wife, Nick Penna, and Morris "Snag" Klein, traveled to the western United States and then to Mexico where they visited with Coppola in Tijuana. Coppola had landed in Tijuana after being deported, and was in possession of a Mexican visa obtained in Kansas City, but one the Mexican consul denied having any record of.

Mexican authorities happened upon the group when Tony Lopiparo was arrested near the Tijuana motel where the group was staying, riding in a new Cadillac he had no ownership papers for. Lopiparo identified himself to the police as being in the slot machine business. Inquiries revealed the Caddy was owned by then St. Louis mob Boss Tony Giardano, partners with Lopiparo in the Anthony Novelty Co. of St. Louis. Tony Lopiparo's ties to Kansas City were well established, for one, having been part of the Kansas City Narcotics Syndicate case broken up in 1942. Frank Coppola interceded with the Mexican authorities attempting to secure Lopiparo's release but to no avail.

Their curiosity piqued, and the smell of narcotics trafficking in the air, the Mexican authorities raided the motel arresting some of the 12 men they found there including Coppola, Sylvester Carrollo, and some of the newly arrived Sicilians.

Coppola's ties to Binaggio were substantial. Considered an international Mafia figure, and like Nicolo Gentile, active in the rackets everywhere he went, including New York, St. Louis, Los Angeles,

Chicago, Detroit, Peoria, New Orleans, and Sicily. During the period 1944-45 Coppola was active in New Orleans teamed up with the infamous Frank Costello, known as the "Prime Minister" of organized crime. Binaggio was said to have been a frequent visitor to the "Big Easy", and Coppola had accompanied Binaggio on frequent visits to St. Louis.

Coppola entered the United States illegally in 1926 from Cuba. He was first deported in 1947, and again in May 1949. Prior to this last deportation, hoping to return to America, he greased the skids contributing $2000 to assist Democrat candidates in the 1948 election, money he sent directly to Charlie Binaggio. Thereafter, with Binaggio posting a $2000 bond, Coppolla was able to return to the states on a temporary visa in 1949. He came to Kansas City, checking in at the Pickwick Hotel, spending several months in the city while Binaggio made strenuous efforts to stave off deportation. The efforts failed, and Coppola was deported in May 1949.

Upon word of the murder of Binaggio the entire group of gangsters holed up in Tiajuana made a rapid departure. Testimony taken by the Kefauver committee led to a theory the murder of the two Charlies was ordered at the Tijuana meeting by an international cartel of gangsters, and carried out by an assassin committed to them. There is little to support this proposition.

Chapter XIII

Gizzo Steps In

WITH THE MURDERS of Binaggio and Gargotta, and the intense fallout that followed, Tony Gizzo stepped in as the out front leader of the Kansas City crime "family." With an ill wind blowing through the city Gizzo and his associates made every effort to maintain a low profile and stay out of sight.

Big Jim Balestrere, still the power behind the scenes, made an outward show for anyone interested of his lack of involvement in out-fit matters. He played this card in front of the highest profile public forum of the day, the Kefauver Committee:

Q: When did you last have a business?
A: It has been quite a while back. I don't remem-
ber how far it has been back. I had a lot of busi-
nesses in Kansas City
Q: What do you live on?
A: What do I live on? Didn't I just get through tell-
ing you about $250 a month I get from Rainey
(Walt Rainey had rented the White House
Tavern, however at this time Rainey was in
prison) and then I stay with my son and my son
buys the groceries. I don't need nothing else.
Just me and my wife.
Q: You are a poor man?
A: I am not poor and I am not rich.

Balestrere also wanted the committee to know that he did not have a bank account or cash.

Joe DiGiovanni, another behind the scenes power, portrayed himself as just another businessman running Midwest Distributors along with his brother. Furthermore, he had his hands full defending his firm against a threat by City and State authorities to take his liquor license away. Knowledgeable sources claimed it was as the result of the Kefauver Committee throwing the spotlight on DiGiovanni, causing him and his liquor distributorship embarrassment, and leading to various other difficulties, that he opted to move aside, becoming far less involved in outfit matters.

A man who definitely would have been a leading candidate to assume outfit leadership, Gaetano Lococo, was under the cloud of an Internal Revenue Service investigation, eventually leading to his indictment on May 11, 1950 on tax charges. He pled guilty, and in September 1950 went away to prison.

So it was left to Anthony Robert Gizzo, known to everyone as Tony. He was born in 1901 claiming New York City as his birthplace. He lived in New York City for 9 years before coming to Kansas City. At age 22 he was arrested and charged with possession of cocaine. It was on this occasion, hoping to make his troubles go away, that he offered arresting officers a bribe that was refused. He was convicted on drug charges and sentenced to a jail term. He was incarcerated on January 24, 1924 and released on November 13, 1924. It would be last time he saw the inside of a prison.

Gizzo's complete criminal history is unknown, his records having been removed from the police files in the 1930s. It is known that Gizzo followed the well-worn path, starting out as an ordinary every day street criminal, often paired with non-Italian associates, before recruitment into the criminal outfit. What follows is that which can be pieced together regarding those instances he ran afoul of the law.

After his narcotics arrest and short jail stay, he and his pal, William Clifford, were again arrested in February 1925 in connection with a shooting incident, but were released for lack of identification and evidence. They were again arrested in August 1925, with two other subjects, in connection with the $900 robbery of a Pullman Company cashier. Records indicate all five subjects were "tried" on vagrancy charges and released.

Gizzo suffered another arrest in April 1926, along with Charles Gargotta, after a police chase. Police officers had spotted the two in what turned out to be a stolen car, and the chase was on. Gizzo and Gargotta abandoned the car, attempted to flee and were arrested. The disposition of this matter is unknown. In May 1926 Gizzo and James Duardi were arrested for investigation in the murder of former police officer Jack Farrell, and both were subsequently released.

Gizzo's rise in the underworld began when he was recruited by the outfit as an enforcer working for John Lazia in the 1920s, joining

Tano Lococo, Charlie Binaggio and Charlie Gargotta as "Lazia men." Over many years in the rackets Gizzo developed a long list of liaisons with top racket figures in Chicago, Detroit, New Orleans, Los Angeles, New York City, and St. Louis. He counted among his friends any number of individuals at the very top echelons of the underworld. People such as crime bosses Tony Accardo in Chicago, Frank Costello in New York City, and Jack Dragna in Los Angeles. Frank Erickson, another associate, was recognized as the most influential bookmaker in the nation. When Frank Scalise, another prominent New York City Cosa Nostra Boss, was shot down in a mob hit in 1957 his personal notebook was recovered. The list of names included major syndicate figures throughout the country, and Kansas City's own Tony Gizzo was one of them.

Senator Kefauver described Gizzo as having "more contacts with more people of this type over the United States than almost anyone else we have come across." Gizzo had a ready explanation. He met many of these people on a social basis between 1935 and 1938 when he owned a string of racehorses and traveled the country racing them at various tracks.

It made sense the flamboyant Gizzo would include among his friends the era's most notorious "girlfriend to the mob", Virginia Hill. She was probably best known as Benjamin "Bugsy" Siegal's paramour. In fact, when time ran out for Siegal the mob had him killed as he sat on a couch in Hill's Los Angeles home. However, Siegal was but one of many racket figures to have had the pleasure of Hill's company, and on the occasion of her appearing before a U.S. Senate committee she ticked off an impressive list of mob notables who were admitted "acquaintances" including the name of Tony Gizzo.

Another prominent Chicago racket figure with established ties to the Kansas City crime "family" was Charles "Cherry Nose" Gioe. He was at one time described as a runner for the Chicago mob on trips to Kansas City where his contact was Tony Gizzo. The two men were responsible for an arrangement whereby "lay off" betting action (Bets between bookmakers) was placed with Chicago outfit bookies. On the occasion of the Chicago outfit and Gioe needing a favor they, of course, knew they could count on their good friend Tony Gizzo.

In 1947 Chicago racket figures Paul "The Waiter" Ricca, Louis "Little New York" Champagne, Phil D"Andrea, a former Capone bodyguard, and "Cherry Nose" Gioe, were incarcerated at the Federal Penitentiary, Leavenworth, Kansas, having been convicted of extorting more than $1 million from the Hollywood movie industry. Eugene Bernstein was a Chicago income tax attorney representing Ricca and D'Andrea, and appearing as a witness before the Kefauver Committee in Chicago told of his travels to visit his clients at the penitentiary. On each of ten or twelve trips to Leavenworth, Kansas, accompanied by Chicago mob Boss Tony Accardo, they were met upon their arrival in Kansas City by Tony Gizzo who furnished them with a car and driver for the trip to Leavenworth. Bernstein presumed these arrangements had been made in advance by Accardo. Accardo was able to gain admission to the penitentiary by posing as a Chicago attorney.

The four Chicago racketeers had each received a 10-year sentence, but to the surprise of everyone, normal parole procedures having been by-passed, they were granted paroles after serving only three years. Bernstein traveled to Kansas City in August 1947, the day before the four were to be released, and met Gizzo in a suite at the Hotel Muehlbach. Gizzo, as in the past, arranged for transportation to Leavenworth. The quick parole raised a storm, resulting in what one newspaper labeled a "scandal reaching into Washington", and precipitating a federal investigation. Despite the furor the Federal District Court in Chicago refused to interfere with the parole board ruling.

Gizzo's pal "Cherry Nose" Gioe's good fortune ran out on the night August 18, 1954. Just as he got into a borrowed car, parked on Chicago's near north side, he was accosted by gunmen who fired some 12 shots at him, five finding their mark. The Sicilian born Gioe was 53 years of age when he died.

Gizzo made no bones about being, off and on, in the bookmaking business for 25 years. He admitted to the committee having done business with any gambler in the country he could call. He laid off bets in Omaha, Chicago, Minneapolis and Reno. Of course, as one the 'Big Five" he shared in most of the major gambling enterprises owned by the crime "family." He had varied interests including a piece of the Green Hills Club, interests in Wichita, Kansas, gambling operations, and a piece of Glendale Beverage and Duke Sales, beer distributors handling "Capone beer."

Probably his greatest source of power stemmed from his close relationship with Big Jim Balestrere. He was considered Balestrere's personal representative while Big Jim quietly worked behind the scenes. Gizzo looked after Balestrere's interests, and in return was said to get a small cut from each. The relationship allowed Gizzo to wield extraordinary power. During the Charlie Binaggio reign it was not uncommon for him to countermand Binaggio's orders.

Along with Charlie Binaggio, Gizzo had been active in the First Ward Democratic Club and inherited, upon Binaggio's murder, the political leadership. Unlike Binaggio he was not a political animal, more inclined to leave the political work to others. The everyday chores of running the political club were handled in his behalf by Joe Galucci, and a rising political star by the name of Alex Presta.

On September 1, 1951, Gizzo suffered a heart attack and was hospitalized at St. Mary's Hospital. He was forced out of circulation for several months thereafter.

His son Robert, a narcotics addict, was a constant source of worry for the Gizzo family. In August 1952, Robert was in trouble again having been charged federally with forging prescriptions in order to obtain narcotics. On August 8th he appeared in Federal District Court where he was given a suspended sentence following a guilty plea, and the Judge recommended he be sent to the Ft. Worth Texas Federal Medical Center for treatment of his drug addiction. He was released from the medical center in December 1952 and returned to Kansas City.

Within a week of his release from custody, Robert was found to have used heroin and morphine resulting in his parole being revoked. In February 1953 he received a three-year sentence and was sent back to the Medical Center in Ft.Worth. Young Gizzo escaped from the Medical Center on March 11, 1953, and was declared a federal fugitive, hunted by the FBI. The same month he escaped he robbed a Dallas, Texas drug store at knife point. He was tracked down and arrested in Lewisville, Texas.

Tony Gizzo was out of Kansas City on an extended trip when he learned of his son's arrest. He made his way to Dallas checking into the Baker Hotel on April 1, 1953 under the name J.D. Ritter. Gizzo suffered a heart attack and died at a local Dallas hospital.

Working backwards, and relying on various sources, Gizzo's activities just prior to his death were pieced together. It was learned he had attended the Sugar Bowl football game in New Orleans on New Years Day, 1953. From there he traveled to Hot Springs, Arkansas. One report had him meeting up with Chicago racketeers Tony Accardo, Murray "The Camel" Humphreys, and possibly Jake "Greasy Thumb" Guzik while in Hot Springs. What is established fact, he and his wife checked into the Arlington Hotel, Hot Springs, Arkansas, at a time prominent New Jesery rackets boss Abner "Longie" Zwillman, a close associate of Frank Costello of New York City, was staying at the hotel. Zwillman and Costello had shared interests in gambling operations on a national scale. After Zwillman checked out on February 26, Gizzo moved to the room Zwillman had occupied. That Gizzo and Zwillman would not have got together to talk a little business is highly unlikely.

Two Kansas City gambling figures, George Beskas and Paul Kastle, checked into the Arlington on February 27, and left March 18, 1953. Beskas subsequently showed up in Dallas joining Gizzo at the Baker Hotel.

Upon learning of the arrest of their son, Gizzo and his wife checked out of the Arlington Hotel on March 29, 1953, traveling on to Dallas. The Chicago Illinois Crime Commission reported it had developed information that while in Dallas Gizzo had made contact with Joseph F. Civello, Dallas rackets Boss, convicted drug dealer and attendee at the infamous 1957 Apalachin gangland convention, and Ross Musso, a member of the Dallas criminal organization.

Chapter XIV

The Future

G IZZO, IN THE tradition of those who preceded him, brought along men he trusted as aides, bodyguards, and enforcers. Nick Civella became his driver and companion, and others such as John Mangiaracina, Thomas "Hiway" Simone, Louis "Black Louie" Cangelose, Max Jaben and Morris "Snag" Klein, were men who would, in the future, play a large role in outfit affairs.

In June 1953, the Kansas City Crime Commission provided an analysis of the state of affairs following Gizzo's demise. "The best information developed indicates there is a good possibility Nick Civella is in line to take over the reins of the criminal organization."

Civella was characterized as having been "an active hoodlum here for years."

The question remaining unresolved, according to the Crime Commission, was whether Civella could overcome reports that he did not have the united support of the "North Side mob." A prior attempt on his life, laid at the doorstep of the crime "family", was said to support those reports. Another prominent candidate for the job was identified as John "Johnny Mag" Mangiaracina, but at the time he was incarcerated, scheduled to be released in the fall of 1953.

Confirmation that the word on the street had Nick Civella tabbed to take Gizzo's role came from a law enforcement source, adding that, like Gizzo before him, he would be responsible to those powers behind the scenes, Jim Balestrere, Joe DiGiovanni, Joe Cusumano, Joe Filardo, and Tano Lococo

A federal law enforcement official, extremely knowledgeable concerning the Kansas City outfit of that era, offered his analysis of the leadership situation. He stated it was a fact Nick Civella had been elevated to the out front leadership position. The question to be considered was how did a person of Civella's caliber, a former tire thief, rise to such heights? The answer was provided to him some years back by an individual he considered one of the best-informed persons concerning the Mafia outside the organization itself.

The principal way a member can advance rapidly within the organization is by performing some act of "special merit". What was the special act Civella had performed leading to his promotion? In this source's opinion, there was one main matter of grave import to the mob in the decade of the 1950s, the elimination of Charles Binaggio and Charlie Gargotta. It took fortitude only in that it was not 100% popular to kill them. The mob's board of directors agreed it had to be done, but many looked on Binaggio as a friendly benefactor. In this source's opinion, the authority for the killing came down from Chicago Boss Tony Accardo

All things considered, a good case could be made for the unlikelihood that Nick Civella would ever make it to the top. Born in Kansas City's "Little Italy" on March 19, 1912, he was first arrested at the age of ten as an incorrigible. During prohibition he dabbled in bootlegging, earning a three-month county jail stay on an alcohol conviction. Like those before him he was a common criminal involved in tire thefts, auto theft, robbery and the like

Unlike so many of his peers, he resisted recruitment into the outfit, apparently displaying his lack of respect for the "Mustache Petes" by word and deed. Joined by his brother Carl and some other young associates, they operated on their own, outside of the outfit. They way they saw it, by remaining independent they were big fish in a small pond, rather than little fish in a very big lake. Despite their actions they continued to be pressured to join the organization, and most of their band did. The Civellas and Joe "Buggy" Anch were among a few that refused.

In the early to mid 1940s there were a rash of holdups of protected gambling operations laid at the doorstep of Civella and his running mates James Maroon and Anch. They had crossed the line and efforts to recruit them turned to efforts to kill them. Civella had forged strong bonds with a number of his peers who had given in and joined the outfit. These bonds endured and friends were tipping Civella off as to Big Jim Balestrere's efforts to kill them.

What was the reason for the Civella brothers disdain for the entrenched outfit, and their outward defiance of it? One story attributes their rogue behavior to having witnessed their father fall victim to the Black Hand in the form of a extortion letter demanding payment of $2.00 a week. This would have been particularly infuriating considering their parents were described as poverty ridden, their father walking to and from his menial jobs to save the nickel carfare. It fomented into a hatred for the old line Sicilian extortionists who exploited the decent people of the north end and ran the outfit. The Civellas defiance emerged early on. Forming a band of like-minded associates they carried out hit and run forays directed against the old-line racket bosses, stealing their whiskey. It was a risky path to follow, and Nick Civella came very close to paying the ultimate price.

When Civella associate James Marron was shot to death on December 2, 1940, found in his car left in an alley behind the 500 block of Troost Avenue, Civella left the city traveling to Chicago. On the evening of December 26, 1940, Civella was observed leaving the Merry Gardens dance hall after he had held it up, grabbing the cash box. A police officer happened to be on the scene, and witnessing the robbery ordered Civella to halt. Failing to heed the officer's command Civella was shot twice. Despite the circumstances of his arrest, Civella beat the case and returned to Kansas City.

"Bugey" Anch's time ran out on January 22, 1946 when he was found lying under the Lydia Avenue viaduct shot five times, and beaten about the face and head. The police tied Anch to numerous hold ups of gambling games.

Eight days later, while sitting in the passenger seat of his own car, parked outside Truckers Liquor Store, 1801 E. 15th Street, Civella visited with Jackson County Deputy Sheriff Louis Cuccia, who was seated in the driver's seat. Sometime after 1:00 a.m., January 30, 1946, a car rolled up next to them and from inside the car shotgun and pistol fire was directed at Civella's car. Cuccia was hit in head and died several hours later at General Hospital. Civella escaped unharmed. He had no explanation to offer the police for the shooting, however, the police had no doubt Civella was the intended target. They were well aware Civella and Anch were partners in crime, tied to the gambling game holdups, and there was a price on their heads.

Once again Civella sought refuge in Chicago. There he remained until he was called back at the behest of Boss man Tony Gizzo. Gizzo was one outfit big shot that had always held a soft spot for the Civella boys. In earlier times Gizzo had an interest in a tire shop and the Civellas sold stolen tires to him. Whether the request came from Chicago or locally, Gizzo was urged to clear the way for Civella to return. He agreed and took Civella under his wing, making him his driver. As the story is told, Civella proved himself an astute and competent operator, displaying organizational and planning skills far beyond Gizzo's. He was now a member of the outfit, and became not only Gizzo's driver but also his confidant and idea man. In some quarters it is strongly suspicious it was Civella who orchestrated the murder of Binaggio and Gargotta, that act of "special merit" previously refered to.

Upon Gizzo's death, Civella was well positioned, and driven by great ambition he pushed hard to be named the boss. He may not have had the full support of Jim Balestrere, but other influential voices supported him, especially Joe Filardo, who by this time was high up in the outfit leadership structure, one of the quiet men in the shadows. Reportedly, Balestrere eventually went along when assured the matter had been approved back east by Cosa Nostra's ruling Commission.

Civella had come a long way, and in terms of longevity as outfit Boss he would outdo all those who preceded him.

Sources

Abadinsky, Howard. *Organized Crime (2nd Edition)*.

Chandler, David Leon. *Brothers In Blood*, E.P. Dutton & Co.

Cook, Fred J., *Mafia*, A Fawcett Publications Inc.

Dorsett, Lyle W., *The Pendergast Machine*.

Fox, Stephen. *Blood & Power*, William Morrow & Co.

Gosch, Martin & Richard Hammer. *The Last Testament of Lucky Luciano*, Little Brown & Com.

Hammer, Richard. *Gangland USA*, Playboy Press.

Kansas City Times & Star.

Kansas City Journal Post.

Larson, Lawrence H. & Hulston, Nancy J., *Pendergast*, University of Missouri Press.

Maxwell, H. James & Bob Sullivan Jr. *Hometown Beer, A History of Kansas City Breweries*, Omega Innovation Marketing.

Messick, Hank, Lansky, Berkley Publishing Corp., *The Silent Syndicate*, The McMillan Co., New York.

Nelli, Humbert S., *The Business of Crime*, Oxford.

O'Neil, Pat. *From the Bottom Up—The Story of The Irish in Kansas City*, Seat O'Pants Publishing.

Pitkim, Thomas Monroe & Francesco Cordasco. *The Black Hand—A Chapter in Ethnic Crime*.

Reddig, William M., *Tom's Town*, J.P. Lippincott Co.

Reid, Ed, *Mafia*, A Signet Book.

Servadio, Gaia. *Mafioso—A History of the Mafia from Its Origins to the Present*, Stein & Day.

Sterling Claire. *Octapus*.

Turkus, Burton & Feder, Sid. *Murder Inc.*, Manor Books Inc.

Index